AMERICAN EMPIRE

AMERICAN EMPIRE

The Political Ethics of
Twentieth-Century Conquest

John M. Swomley, Jr.

THE MACMILLAN COMPANY
COLLIER-MACMILLAN LTD., LONDON

to my wife,
Marjie

Grateful acknowledgment is made for permission to reprint from:
The Origins of the Second World War by A. J. P. Taylor. Copyright © 1961 by A. J. P. Taylor. Reprinted by permission of Atheneum Publishers, New York and Hamish Hamilton, Ltd., London.

The Cold War and Its Origins, 1917–1960 by D. F. Fleming. Reprinted by permission of Doubleday & Company, Inc., New York and Allen & Unwin, Ltd., London.

The Macmillan Company
866 Third Avenue, New York, N.Y. 10022
Collier-Macmillan Canada Ltd., Toronto, Ontario

Library of Congress Catalog Card Number: 76-119147

First Printing

Printed in the United States of America

Contents

INTRODUCTION

MOST AMERICANS ASSUME that, on the whole, United States foreign policy is concerned with the prevention of war, or when war comes, with the resistance of aggression. They believe American aims have always included the extension of freedom and a better standard of living to other peoples. President Lyndon B. Johnson put these assumptions into words when he cloaked the U.S. invasion of the Dominican Republic with moral purpose. He said:

> Over the years of our history our forces have gone forth into many lands, but always they returned when they were no longer needed. For the purpose of America is never to suppress liberty, but always to save it. The purpose of America is never to take freedom, but always to return it; never to break peace but to bolster it, and never to seize land but always to save lives.
>
> One month ago it became my duty to send our marines into the Dominican Republic, and I sent them for these same ends.[1]

In similar fashion the Second World War was identified with moral purpose. Millions of Americans were led by Franklin Roosevelt, Winston Churchill, and other political leaders to believe that we entered that war to defend ourselves and our allies from unprovoked aggression. Instead of war to make the world safe for democracy, Roosevelt proclaimed the Four Freedoms. Theological and lay spokesmen of the Church, such as Reinhold Niebuhr and John Foster Dulles, joined in the propaganda chorus in an effort to per-

[1] Statement of June 3, 1965. Quoted in U.S. Department of State Publication 7971 (Washington, D.C., 1965), Inter-American Series No. 92.

suade the churches that the United States was fighting to end tyranny and establish freedom in the world. To this day the overwhelming majority of the American people believe that American participation in the Second World War was both necessary and just. Many believe that the Second World War, the cold war, and the Korean War were begun by aggressor nations and that the United States reluctantly entered these conflicts as the champion of both freedom and international morality.

The actualities of foreign policy are not always as moral as the popular assumptions or the official explanations. The evidence for this will be seen in the causes and consequences of the major crises of foreign policy from 1939 to 1969. It is one purpose of this work to examine the actual and ostensible motives of American policy during those years within the light of an ethical overview or judgment of these actions. Another purpose of the book is to examine critically the position of "political realism" which is, in effect, an intellectual defense of U.S. military foreign policy. A third purpose is to suggest that a creative foreign policy cannot be built on traditional balance-of-power or realpolitik concepts, but must be based on the dynamics of social change. These dynamics arise out of human need or out of the resentments caused by efforts to maintain power and privilege at the expense of justice.

This is not either a history book or a record of all the events that contributed to the beginning or ending of a given war or period in foreign policy. Rather, it is a critical analysis of the popular assumptions about foreign policy which have been widely promoted by establishment spokesmen within the military, the government, the Church, the university, the labor movement, and the business community from the beginning of the Second World War. The reason for being concerned about the myths and slogans which many people accept is that these are vehicles by which the makers of foreign policy continue to gain public acceptance for military and business expansion at public expense. If we recognize the importance of ideas for shaping reality, then it is essential to examine critically both the official statements and the myths believed by millions of people.

The attempt to get all the facts about any war or foreign policy is difficult enough. Even when the historians agree on the facts, they do not all agree on their interpretations. But something is gained for public understanding of foreign policy when different interpretations are made available. Citizens can evaluate the official propaganda better if they are aware that it is simply one interpretation of international relations derived from the interests of a military–industrial complex rather than the only logical interpretation which an intelligent person might make.

It is equally important to subject foreign policy to ethical scrutiny. Leading professors of ethics whose political position has often been identical with that of the State Department or Pentagon have popularized slogans such as "war is the lesser of two evils" or have stressed the relative justice of the American position or insisted that positions other than support of American global power are irrelevant or utopian or naive. Invariably they assert that ethical critiques of foreign policy must be such that statesmen could reasonably be expected to accept them, which is another way of saying that modest rather than major changes of foreign policy are the only ethically proper ones.

Ethics is relevant to foreign policy because it is concerned with matters of human need, human relationships, and justice in more than simply the expedient way usually implied in the word *politics*. In this sense it is indispensable to politics, for it tells the policymaker he must be concerned with more than immediate power and with humanity instead of simply national interests.

Most discussions of ethics and foreign policy assume that the purpose of ethics is to give guidance or advice to the statesman on how to conduct foreign policy in the national interest. Such guidance, it is thought, must not be so moral as to be impractical or impossible in terms of the courses open to him.

Yet it must have enough claim to morality that it cannot be said to be simply a rationale for selfish interest or a drive for power. Since it is assumed that no statesman will act contrary to the military–economic–political bases that sustain his government, such ethicists traditionally talk about the "lesser of two evils" or "politics as the art of the possible." There is seldom an attempt to suggest that the military or economic or political context in which the statesman operates might be too narrow or so corrupt or unjust as to require its drastic change.

Those who function within the limits of what is immediately possible think of themselves as "realists." They accept the political context as narrowly defined by their own nation's leaders and attempt to introduce moderate, as opposed to fundamental, ethical demands upon those in positions of power. In general, they accept Machiavelli's position that ethics is a function of politics or a product of power rather than the other way around. Realism demands the acceptance of the immediate facts and the adapting of oneself to them.

A second and quite different purpose of ethics is to provide guidance for the individual citizen who has no immediate responsibility for the conduct of government, but who has ultimate responsibility because he has to bear the consequences of political decisions. The assumption here is that all persons have the responsibility to participate in the foreign policy debate and that many of them ought to hold positions that differ from those of the statesmen who finally determine policy. It is assumed also that these critics of government will give more priority to justice and other values than to the power realities that are primary to the leaders of government. Those who are primarily concerned about human freedom or justice or peace may find these concepts incompatible with the policies of their government. They have a choice then of working within the system to try to humanize it or of opposing the system in an effort to supplant it with something better.

In adopting the second rather than the first purpose of ethics as his orientation, the writer believes that ethics should not be confined to choices statesmen are ready to make. Instead, statesmen can be influenced or compelled by an ethically sensitized public opinion to consider additional possibilities. Instead of permitting national political leaders to set the stage on which citizens watch the issues of foreign policy played out, the people can become sensitized enough to the demands of justice that they move onto the stage and play a leading role. If a substantial number of citizens give a priority to justice instead of to nationalism, they can induce statesmen to accommodate.

The citizen then becomes the focus of discussions of ethics and foreign policy rather than only the statesman. Statesmen, however, are not neglected. Their policies are subject to modification because they must to some degree be guided by what articulate public opinion will tolerate. Moreover, future statesmen are often drawn from those trained by contemporary critics.

Those who refuse to be guided chiefly by the power realities that statesmen feel they confront are not necessarily idealists who have utopian answers to the problems of international power. They may have a different set of ethical or political assumptions that guides their analysis of international events. Or they may place a given political problem in a larger context than those committed to a particular economic or military outlook are prepared to do. For example, a governmental leader whose economic and military viewpoint is that of the military–industrial complex may believe that a Communist-led revolutionary group in Vietnam must, at all points, be opposed, because, if victorious, it will indefinitely oppose American business expansions or military bases. Another group may believe that the military–industrial complex does not represent the total national interest and ought not to be the basis for American hostility to other movements. Or it might also believe that Communism is capable of change and that nations with a common industrial system have to operate as industrial nations have to operate instead of like Genghis Khan. There may be still other analyses of the problem such

as the ability of nationalism coupled with economic cooperation by the West to modify the foreign policy of a Communist
state. Other analyses would lead to still other conclusions that
radically or drastically would change a traditional foreign
policy.

It is the function of ethics to propose values that inform and
guide political or social analysis and action. At the outset, we
must acknowledge that ethics is a matter of orientation or
commitment. An orientation towards or devotion to nationalism or to government-sponsored free enterprise as the national interest will produce a discussion of ethics and foreign
policy different from an orientation towards world community,
some other supranationalist loyalty, or a genuine *laissez-faire*
approach wherein American-controlled international corporations or businesses run the risks they claim justify their substantial profits. Similarly, an orientation towards the use of
military power as the decisive factor in world politics would
result in a different ethical analysis from one relying primarily on other forms of power.

If one holds, as does this writer, that all value is personal
and that priority should be given to the preservation and en-
hancement of human life in a context of freedom and justice,
his analysis of international relations will be different from
that of a person whose values are primarily nationalist or
materialist or racist. The "personalist" believes that persons
are the primary values. All ideals, all property, all power have
meaning only in relation to persons. Justice, for example, is an
abstraction unless it is a description of right relations between
persons. The personalist agrees with Kant that persons should
be treated as ends and not as means to achieve wealth or status
or power. Love for persons means willing for them the best
possible life and striving to achieve it.

A primary concern for persons is not necessarily the result of any law or commandment, but the result of one's
orientation. An orientation towards self or the extensions of
oneself, such as nation, race, class, or property, is what the
Bible calls idolatry. The idol in Old Testament terms was in-

animate, made of wood, metal, or stone. As such, it was possible to attribute to it the personal or group interests already held and to worship it as if it were God. Idolatry is the repudiation of a larger love and justice in the interests of parochial loyalty identified with self. An orientation towards love, on the other hand, is an acknowledgment that man cannot live by and for himself alone. His destiny is bound up with all his fellow human beings and the way he treats them. An orientation towards love may seem to make sense in the abstract, but when the immediate crisis or evidence of hostility seems to belie it, then it is only by an act of faith that we continue to assume that love is the process by which human beings must relate to each other. Jesus' concept of God as love implies that love is so much a part of the structure of life that it, rather than hate or fear or competition, is the key to community at every level of existence.

On the surface it seems contradictory to talk of foreign policy and having an orientation towards love because it is assumed that one nation's foreign policy is necessarily antagonistic to another's. While this is to some degree true, it is also accurate to say that we live in a highly interdependent world which is sustained by cooperation and threatened by outbreaks of antagonism. The destiny of the people of each nation is bound up with the welfare of all people.

Foreign policy is not necessarily antagonistic; it refers to the efforts by a nation–state to influence the people or governments of other nations. It includes questions of trade, travel, communication, conflicts of interest, and cooperative efforts to reach a desired goal. In general, there are five ways of implementing national policy: diplomacy, economic power, military power, the power of attractive example, and propaganda. Diplomacy, economic aid, and propaganda may be used to induce or persuade others, just as more freedom or a better standard of living in a given nation may influence others to follow that nation's example. It is chiefly the threat or use of military power or the attempt to achieve exclusive or dominant economic control that produces conflict between nations.

It is these conflicts of interest that present the chief ethical problems in the field of foreign policy. Since the international situation includes the present context of war, armaments, economic imperialism, military alliances, totalitarian allies and adversaries, it is assumed that foreign policy is always a choice among evils. A discussion of ethics, however, need not be confined to evil choices or to a given context which seems to dictate such choices. It should be concerned about larger contexts, structural and other changes in economic and political systems, the power groups which determine the national interest, and for what end.

It is possible, for example, to approach foreign policy from one or more of a number of positions. One approach is to recognize that conflict is inevitable given the tendency of man to seek his own or his group's welfare, often without regard to the well-being of others. Therefore, the only solution to conflict is to institutionalize it so that there are lawful or acceptable ways of engaging in it. Just as violence has been institutionalized in cities and states so that only government has a legal right to use violence, so violence must be institutionalized on the world level through the disarmament of nation–states and the establishment of some form of world government. If, on the local and national level, economic, political, and social conflicts take place without mass violence, it is assumed that this can be done on a world level as well. Those who hold this position tend to view the present system of nation–states as the reason for the continued use of mass violence in the form of war. Therefore they want to change the international structure. The application of ethics to foreign policy in this position is to view the present structure as the reason for mass violence to persons and, therefore, to devote all possible energy to changing the structure.

A second approach to the problem of foreign policy is to assume that the chief reason for conflict between nations is not the divergence of national interest, but the control of nations by hostile economic, political, or military elites. If in nation X there is a controlling business elite that wants to dominate the raw materials, markets, or industrial facilities of nation Z; conflict is inevitable. According to this theory, it is not necessarily in the national interest of X to invade or dominate Z, but the business elite that controls the government is able to make its interest seem to be the national interest. The way to end violent conflict is, according to this view, to eliminate such elitist or class domination within each nation so that the cause of war disappears.

A third approach to foreign policy is that of military deterrence. A nation that has military power may either alone or in alliance with others try to prevent war by the threat of defeating or destroying the "aggressor." There are numerous variations of this approach, such as the building of a mighty empire and the use of garrisons around the world or the conquest of buffer states or the creation for collective security of an organization of nations that have mutual interests, such as the League of Nations.

A position held by some nations historically is that of neutrality. The nation avoids alliances with other nations and seeks recognition by others of this special status, using diplomacy, economic power, or other means for gaining its will.

Some also believe that conflict between nations can be channeled into nonmilitary activity, such as economic competition, the space race, etc.

Still another approach to foreign policy is that of influencing the peoples under foreign governments to bring pressure on these governments to adopt a friendly foreign policy toward the nation in question. The newly formed Soviet Union was successful in creating support among intellectuals and the labor movements throughout the Western world so that, in the middle and late twenties, many groups in other countries had a policy of nonsupport of their own government if it should go to war with the USSR. This power of attraction which a nation may cultivate has been employed not only by the Soviet Union but by others. Gandhi's policy of nonviolence in India had a tremendous power of attraction for Englishmen affiliated with the Labour party. It was the postwar ascendancy of the Labour party that led to Indian independence.

This brief survey of various approaches to the question of foreign affairs is not intended to be comprehensive, but to indicate that foreign policy is either determined or modified by the political or ethical presuppositions held. It must not be assumed without further exploration that every foreign policy is necessarily a military or war policy or that the people of a nation must necessarily support the policy chosen by those who determine the national interest.

It is not even necessary to propose an approach to foreign policy that governments could actually pursue. Criticizing policies without proposing alternatives may serve as a stimulus to others who are more able to advance alternate courses or put them into practice; or the existing policies may be so thoroughly inhumane that modification or correction is inadequate. Criticism, then, contributes to more fundamental change via the building of revolutionary movements.

The people of any nation, especially those in Christian, Jewish, and humanist groups who claim a commitment to ethics, need not assume that they must subordinate their concern for other persons to the aims of those who conduct their nation's foreign policy. Ethical judgments about foreign policy, especially if they are prophetic and articulate, may in fact influence the conduct of foreign affairs. They may also produce or encourage the formation of revolutionary movements dedicated to altering or eliminating existing policies that are inflexibly maintained.

In the chapters that follow we shall examine critically the political ethics that have been used to build the present American empire and shall propose an ethics of liberation or dynamic social change instead of one based on the national interest or on the selfish aims of those who determine that interest. Other chapters will examine the popular myths about various wars or enemies of the United States as well as the methods by which the American empire has been built.

1

THE RISKS OF REALISM

ETHICS IN INTERNATIONAL relations necessarily concerns itself with the management of power. In general, there have been two approaches to such management.

One approach assumes that war is a result of a particular organization of society and therefore can be eliminated by a restructuring of society. Those who hold to this view have been characterized as "idealists," or utopians, because they have postulated ideal goals as political possibilities in the fore-seeable future.

Another approach assumes that war is a result of a struggle for power and that this struggle is a result of man's nature, or his tendency to selfishness and violence. War is therefore an inevitable aspect of the struggle for power. Wars, according to this approach, are either just or unjust. They can be prevented by the threat of countervailing power, by armed deterrence, by military alliances, by collective security, or by other similar strategems of military power.

Those who hold to this view characterize themselves as "realists" because they believe that self-interest, national interest, the struggle for power, and the long-existent armaments system are the realities of international politics and cannot be structured out of existence.

There are Christian realists who try to bring into their discussion of power politics certain Christian norms or values. Reinhold Niebuhr indicated that "an ultimate norm or value is set in judgment over the historically relative and ambiguous achievements of man's existence."[1] This ultimate norm of Christian love is to the Christian realist always a contrasting standard or judgment, an impossible ideal rather than a redemptive force or living presence that alters political conduct.

Niebuhr emphasized recognition of the sinful nature of man as the real root of his realism and his criticism of idealism. His position has been summarized as follows:

> The idealist may thus be defined as the person who seeks to bring self-interest under the discipline of a more universal law and in harmony with a more universal good. In the opinion of its critics, however, idealism is characterized by a disposition to ignore or be indifferent to the forces in human life which offer resistance to universally valid ideals and norms.[2]

The idealist position that war can be eliminated by a restructuring of society has led to various analyses of what it is that causes and sustains war. The Marxist, for example, believes that it is the capitalist organization of society that is the root of the struggle for power as, for example, in the competition that arises over markets and raw materials.

Those who believe that nationalism is the basic structural reason for war tend to think in terms of some form of world government as the solution to the power problem.

Those who believe that armaments or armed forces are the one thing that makes war possible or without which war could not be waged favor complete disarmament as the answer.

Each of these analyses contains essential truth: that economic rivalry is a source of war, that nationalism sustains it because nation–states are the ones who wage war, and that armed forces are essential to the waging of war. It is possible to recognize these truths without at the same time believing that any particular proposal for eliminating war is feasible either immediately or in the foreseeable future.

If, for the sake of argument, we concede that the elimina-

---

[1] Reinhold Niebuhr, *The Structure of Nations and Empires* (New York: Charles Scribner's Sons, 1959), p. 291.

[2] Harry R. Davis and Robert C. Good, *Reinhold Niebuhr on Politics* (New York: Charles Scribner's Sons, 1960), pp. 64–5.

tion of capitalism is desirable, there is no reason to believe that it can be eliminated in the near future. Nor is it clear that the adoption of socialism or communism will end either nationalism or war. The existence of China and Russia, each ruled by a Communist party, has eliminated neither disputes over their boundaries nor the armed forces to guard their mutual frontier.

The proposal of world government is similarly not feasible in the immediate future, for at least three reasons. The first is that world government presupposes the demise of nationalism or the decision by sovereign nations to give up their sovereignty. No method for persuading states to give up their sovereignty has yet been devised, although it is possible that in the future, economic necessity and a long experience of working together in regional economic units may result in political units larger than some of the present nations. Regional units, however, do not necessarily lead to a world unit.

A second problem in the achievement of world government is how to get such a government elected by the people of the world so that the central government is not simply the creature of nations that could withhold real power to govern or that could withdraw and nullify the world organization. For national governments to arrange for their citizens to vote in such an election would be tantamount to the yielding of sovereignty.

A third problem is that legal structures are not created simply by the conviction of people that they are desirable. Law reflects rather than causes social and political changes. If government is to be based on consent rather than on police power, it presupposes a confidence that stems from acceptable economic, political, and social arrangements, which we speak of as being the development of community. Such arrangements are not the product of constitutional conventions or propaganda, but of actual cooperative or working relationships. World organization has to be based on consent or something approaching unanimous acceptance. Otherwise, attempts to force decisions on sovereign states simply mean war.

The third proposal for ending war, disarmament, raises similar questions. Armaments have for centuries been such an integral part of the nation–state and the system of nation–states that the acceptance of genuine disarmament is, in effect, the yielding of national sovereignty and the abolition of the state system. The simple advocacy of universal disarmament assumes that there are only technical problems to be negotiated, whereas the real problem appears to lie at a deeper level. That deeper level includes the whole question of nationalism and its relation to the military spirit; it includes the orthodoxy of violence which involves the idea that without weapons one is at the mercy of unscrupulous foes who will use clandestine methods and surprise attacks to destroy your nation; it includes also the question of how to divest powerful economic groups of the weapons and the military threat system by which they maintain and expand their power over people and resources around the world.

The term *utopian* has therefore been applied to such proposals as a classless society, world government, and world disarmament because there seems to be no connection between them and present reality, no practical step-by-step method of moving from the present to the desirable goal. Of the three proposals considered, disarmament seems to have more chance of ultimate acceptance because a number of great powers have already given lip service to it and have entered negotiations for it. The negotiations, however, never deal with the underlying assumptions of the state system; nor do they include the smaller powers that are involved in serious conflict. There is an assumption, which has no basis in research or fact, that if the Soviet Union and the United States agree, the rest of the nations will accept their conclusions. Neither France nor China, for example, has accepted the nuclear test ban agreement worked out between the United States and the Soviet Union.

Political idealism and utopian proposals cannot be dismissed out of hand, however. They focus attention on the real problems, and their advocates are effective critics of existing foreign policy. Moreover, by keeping a desired goal constantly in the forefront of public discussion, it may someday be possible to take the practical steps that lead to the goal.

The dominant approach to international relations in the United States, however, is that of maintaining the status quo, or a nonwar situation, by means of superior military force, military alliances, and other power arrangements, which are summed up under the term *realism*. The term *realism* which has become a name for a school of thought in international relations does not, in this writer's view, imply that it is the wisest or best approach to foreign policy. Just as those who call themselves liberals may be most illiberal or intolerant of ideologies of the far right or left, so realists often advocate action which is quite unrealistic.

Those who claim to be realists or practical men because they think of themselves as dealing with the realities of power have no greater claim to wisdom or success in international politics than do the idealists. If anything, they create more problems than the idealists because they concentrate too much on military power as the answer to difficult or complex situations.

Realists could be described by Benjamin Disraeli's remark, "A practical man is one who persistently repeats the mistakes of his ancestors."

Certainly the traditional or characteristic approach to international politics is that of realism. This is the way most leaders of the large status-quo nations have looked at the international scene. They have assumed that armed might is the decisive factor in international politics.

Books on foreign policy are also, for the most part, written from the standpoint of those who identify with their own nation–state, or at least with a Western civilization that is already privileged and powerful. Those who identify with the privileged and powerful prefer to keep things relatively stable, at least in their national vicinity. Most such realist writers in the United States are political liberals. They tend to believe that by maintaining a peace based on what they consider to be enlightened deployment of power, evolution in the less enlightened nations will, in the long run, make them more like us. They also tend to assume that nations which do not fit this liberal analysis or are captives of an alien ideology may simply have to be contained by our armed might so as to provide an opportunity for the continuing development of the rest of the world.

As was suggested earlier, realists believe that the nature of man and the state require the use of military power to counterbalance or to hold in check other nations. In practice, they believe other nations are less just or enlightened than their own, so they always think in terms of the use of power by their relatively enlightened nation to checkmate the selfish power of other nations. Reinhold Niebuhr, for example, refers to the United States and the other "open societies of the West" as having "achieved a tolerable answer to the problems of the community (chiefly the one problem of making freedom compatible with justice and stability)."[3] Many Negroes and even some white intellectuals would not agree with Niebuhr's estimate of the United States. Nevertheless, he and other American realists do put the United States in a special position. American realists, for example, do not advocate the building up of military power by rival nations to hold their own nation in check, even though the United States is by far the world's greatest military power. While they insist that man, as such, is egoistic or aggressive, they tend to believe that it is the Communist or certain other nations which are the chief problem.

In a general theological sense, the realists are right in believing that man tends to be self-centered rather than God-centered, that he tends to put the interest of self or his group ahead of that of others. But the fact of individual sin does not necessarily mean that rival nations are always more sinful. Nor does it mean that sin always or generally expresses itself in power terms which threaten the existence of other individuals. It may, for example, express itself in the pride of unique

[3] Niebuhr, *Structure of Nations and Empires*, p. 294.

achievement, in bragging, in economic competition, envy, or innumerable other forms on a personal level.

It is possible to refer to human beings as power-seeking only if the word *power* includes much more than the political realists generally mean by the term. The power to persuade or induce is quite different from the power to compel. Likewise, the kind of power or influence a "weighty" Friend exercises in a Quaker meeting is a far cry from the kind of military power used by the United States in Vietnam.

If it is argued that it is man's nature that is aggressive or that makes national military power necessary, then why is it that nations have to conscript, propagandize, and in other ways create a militant or aggressive spirit in their citizens in order to permit foreign military adventures?

If it is necessary for nations to create an aggressive spirit in their citizens, it becomes apparent that the structuring of society is more responsible for war than any mass pressures of individual citizens giving vent to their nature.

Actually it is a mistake to think of a nation–state as a unit with a common purpose or a national interest. The machinery of the state is in the hands of one or more groups that use propaganda appeals to patriotism, financial awards or contracts, conscription, military training in schools, and various other devices to mold as much of a unit consciousness as possible. It may be that some men in positions of leadership are aggressive or greedy or attribute to their own nation a messianic character to save the world from some evil ideology, but this does not mean that every citizen or even a majority would approve external aggression without the stimulus from and the rationale of the few.

The political realist is also in error in assuming that nation–states are by nature aggressive and can be curbed only by equal or superior power on the part of other states. Such an assumption overlooks the fact that some nation–states are not aggressive and are even consciously nonaligned so as to avoid entanglement in military alliances or other power arrangements. Realism fails, for example, to distinguish between states whose policy is to concentrate on internal development and those whose policy is the control and development of resources in other countries.

If we acknowledge the fact that individuals and states are at times aggressive and at other times nonaggressive, then it is difficult to escape the conclusion that there are causes of aggression. Aggression in men is frequently a product of frustration or of something that seriously threatens the life or happiness of individuals. It is also the result of ambition or greed.

If aggression is the result of external threats or frustrations or can be attributed to a state of mind that imagines danger or is the result of the ambitions or greed of a dominant group, then it is not the nation–state as such which is aggressive, but the existence of rival states or ideologies or internal forces seeking power which lead to aggressive action. If aggression is caused or arises out of the interaction of nations, then there is no validity to the idea that war is inherent in the nature of man or the state. Some states, for example, have not been involved in war for a century or more.

A more serious criticism of both political and Christian realism lies in the assumption that power is to be used in the interest of stability. The balance-of-power concept and the whole system of military alliances are intended to prevent open war. Realism therefore presupposes that certain states will have long-term predominance of economic and military power, that others will be deterred thereby, and that questions of justice, social change, industrial development of underdeveloped nations, etc., are secondary or minor issues. In other words, a nonwar state of affairs is dependent on the power to enforce the kind of "peace" desired by those possessing the power.

Actually, the terms *realism* and *Christian realism* are in no way ethical in the usual meaning of this word. The realist is primarily interested, not in preventing war, but in making use of power for the national interest. *National interest* in turn is a cover term for the economic interests of the dominant business groups and the strategic interests of the armed forces, which in contemporary America and most other industrial countries are so allied as to be included in the designation *military–industrial complex*. Occasionally some realist will identify the national interest with a more idealistic purpose, such as the spread of democracy. There is little evidence to support such a hypothesis. In practice our political and military leaders make no serious or sustained effort to establish democracy in other countries. They are prepared to and, in many cases, prefer to work with autocratic or dictatorial regimes that they believe maintain a stable atmosphere in which American business can freely operate and that will work easily in alliance with our armed forces.

Realism is thus a kind of extension of the laissez-faire idea into international politics. It presupposes that the successful operators who have already accumulated their power will determine the outcome of world politics by the exercise of their power, if necessary alone but preferably by some system of alliances.

In a revolutionary world the realist tends to be nonrevolutionary and even anti- or counterrevolutionary. When open war occurs in spite of the power arrangements of the realists, those starting the violence are dubbed the aggressors because they disrupt the status quo. Actually, those maintaining the status quo by the deployment of their military power are also involved in violence and aggression. By their armed power they prevent necessary social change, maintain corrupt rulers, and exploit other countries for the benefit of their nation's foreign business interests. The mere fact of a military alliance or military presence in another country gives to the external power an interest in preventing any governmental change that would disrupt or end the alliance or the business relationships it makes possible. This is one of the basic reasons the United States supports corrupt and dictatorial governments. The working relationship with such rulers is satisfactory to their American military and political counterparts. The groups who desire political change within those countries necessarily have to oppose the rulers approved by American officials and hence also oppose the American military presence.

Under such circumstances the political realist position of support for military power around the world is counterrevolutionary. From the standpoint of the groups seeking social change within their own nations, the American military presence is the aggressor and the realist provides the intellectual rationale for such aggression.

When overt war occurs between the nations that use armed power or alliances to maintain the status quo, there is no way of determining objectively who is the aggressor. Everything depends on the interpreter's loyalty. Similarly, there is no such thing as a just war in the present world scene. The states who use their armed power to prevent change assert that any use of armed violence to achieve change is unjust, whereas those who want change see their armed violence as just and their opponents as unwarranted aggressors. The nation seeking to change the status quo is not more of an aggressor than the state seeking to preserve the status quo by armed violence instead of consent.

This means that the realist conception of power is static rather than dynamic. Realists think of military alliances or other power arrangements, not as the power to produce change, but as the power to maintain equilibrium. If they thought of using power to produce change, they would have to become revolutionaries, using armed power to oppose the power of their own government.

In other words, military power to the realist is not primarily or even occasionally in the service of any ethical end, unless he identifies ethics with the status quo or the alleged national interest of his own country.

If the realist saw ethics as related either to love or to justice and therefore requiring social change, he would have to stop thinking of power in terms of military alliances or balance-of-power arrangements and think instead in terms of power as a means to achieve change.

The political realist is naive if he assumes that the possession and use of massive military power is decisive or that the deployment of power via military missions or alliances is decisive. Since the advent of nuclear weapons, it may be the nonuse of power that is truly realistic. If it is the refusal to negotiate that precipitates a nuclear showdown, wisdom may demand negotiations or other methods of dealing with adversaries. Or, it should be noted, if the stationing of American military power in Asian or other lands creates a nationalist reaction against the local government or the United States as its ally, the use of such alliances is self-defeating.

The whole power analysis of the realist needs to be called into question. Power to the realist, as we have suggested, is not the ability to induce change, but the ability to impose one's will on others. A good illustration of the realist position is his oft-repeated slogan that if you must negotiate, you should "negotiate from strength." However, if the agreement that flows from such negotiations is to be lasting, it should be mutually satisfactory. It should be negotiated so as to be in the national interest of all parties to the agreement rather than in the interest only of the stronger power.

Armed power as a method of dealing with others is a useful concept only if there is no other way of accomplishing purpose. It is the peculiar error of the realist that he narrows his ethical choices to the lesser of two evils and his political choices to armed power alternatives. The reason he does so is that he makes no effort to think objectively about national conduct or international affairs. He is primarily concerned with the national interest and with any means to preserve or achieve it.

It would be possible for idealists from every country in the world to arrive at some common understanding about ethical and political issues involving disarmament, for example. It would not be possible for realists from every country in the world to arrive at a common understanding about their own stock in trade, armed power arrangements, because they are primarily nationalist in orientation and primarily loyal to the economic orientation of the dominant group or groups in their country. This means that ethics to the realist is always relative to the national interest of his own state. He does not think primarily in terms of what is best for humanity or for the poor and downtrodden in nations victimized by his own nation's power.

The chief, if not the only, occasion when realists have been divided in their support of American foreign policy is the war in Vietnam. Those who have opposed it have done so for a number of reasons, the major one being that they do not believe the national interest of the United States will suffer if Vietnam is not in the American sphere of influence. Some, like Hans J. Morgenthau and Walter Lippmann, think of the war in Vietnam as being in the tradition of colonial wars with the United States fighting a tide of nationalism and antiimperialism that cannot be overcome. Morgenthau also believes that "an ideologically oriented military policy is not only ineffective but counter-productive. For since it treats all Communist governments alike, it forces them to act alike. Thus it is our own policy that transforms China from a threat to the national independence of the nations of Southeast Asia into the protector of those nations from white imperialism."[4]

The war in Vietnam can be considered such an obvious mistake of a military-oriented foreign policy that it is clearly an exception which does not validate or invalidate realism. It has united realists who feared it would interfere with more important interests or who saw it as an overextension of America's limited power; idealists who saw it as morally wrong because of its imperialism, brutality, and disregard of the international community; and those devoted to drastic or revolutionary action because they wanted to see Vietnam transformed by its own people without outside interference.

The chief challenge to the existing realist approach to foreign policy and international politics arises, not from a typical idealist point of view, but from the necessities and the dynamics of social change. The alternative to realism is not idealism, but a more dynamic, or in some cases revolutionary, policy of social change.

[4] Hans J. Morgenthau, *Vietnam and the United States* (Washington, D.C.: Public Affairs Press), p. 48.

There is a widespread recognition on the domestic scene that if labor or black Americans or any other group begins to upset the status quo, there are causes or situations that give rise to the unrest. On the international scene concessions offered or made in the course of negotiation or other planning are often termed *appeasement* by realists. On the domestic scene, on the other hand, such attempts to understand the point of view of the other group and to adjust to it are a recognized part of political life.

Any foreign or domestic policy that claims any relationship to ethics must therefore begin with a concern to understand the grievance, or feeling of injustice, that exists within another or other nations. It cannot be concerned only with one's own national interest. Yet, it need not be contrary to the national interest unless that interest continues to be interpreted narrowly as being identical with business or military imperialism. It is in the total national interest to prevent war and to promote world-wide economic health. World economic health is dependent, not on American monopoly, but on the development of underdeveloped countries and mutual trade, in both of which private capital may share if it is prepared to run risks and accept the regulations of the various nations or regional groups. As we shall see in succeeding chapters, war is frequently the result of efforts to dominate other nations or to maintain a status quo at the expense of other nations. It is difficult for nations to gain the support of their own and other peoples for a war to upset the status quo unless there is a plausible case to be made for a serious injustice. In each of the cases to be examined—Japan, Germany, Korea, Central America, and Vietnam—the use of armed power to preserve the status quo precipitated war or intensified the preparations for an eventual showdown. It is a falsification of history to assert that armaments or military alliances or balance-of-power arrangements keep the peace unless peace is defined as the temporary absence of war. Peace is the by-product of justice that is never static. Justice involves the meeting of human needs, and those needs are constantly changing.

2

ETHICS AND FOREIGN POLICY

A CREATIVE FOREIGN policy is dynamic; it recognizes the necessity of constant social change instead of maintaining outmoded institutions. Social change is both necessary and inevitable. It is necessary in a world where millions of men who want freedom have not attained it. It is inevitable in a world that has had a foretaste of plenty and needs no longer to be tied to primitive labor and living conditions.

When a nation's foreign policy is that of political, economic, or military domination of others, it does not demonstrate a concern for their freedom or well-being. Because it denies the worth or dignity of those it seeks to dominate, it provokes resistance, division, and enmity. Nations that do not measure up to the standards of God or to their own professed ideals of freedom and justice are judged by God and by men and are found wanting. The more apparent their shortcomings, the more they are likely to create or stimulate human hostility.

The key to a dynamic foreign policy in our day is liberation because people who live in poverty or as vassals of an economic or military elite are not free to use their full potential. Liberation in origin is a biblical concept. In biblical terminology, it is called *redemption*, which really means setting men free from whatever it is that enslaves them. *Redemption* in the Hebrew scriptures means deliverance from captivity or slavery or from oppression and violence. The central or key event in those scriptures is the liberation of the people of Israel from slavery in Egypt. The commemoration of this event in the Passover meal is still central to Judaism.

24

Redemption is also central to Christian thought. Jesus is called the Redeemer, the one who sets men free. All too often this has been interpreted by Christians as meaning to free men from sin, which is narrowly interpreted in terms of certain vices. But Jesus was described in the New Testament as one who came to "preach good news to the poor . . . to proclaim release to the captives, recovery of sight to the blind and to set at liberty those who are oppressed." (Luke 4:18). Evil should be understood as anything that keeps men from becoming genuinely free, whether that thing is a social structure, egotism, drug addiction, or an obsession with power. Sin is the acceptance or willing of such unfreedom as an alternative to commitment to the redeeming God.

The biblical preoccupation with redemption suggests the importance of liberation to ethics. It suggests that individuals and nations are to be judged by the degree to which they are liberating or enslaving influences. In this respect modern political judgments and ethical judgments coincide. Just as world attention was at one time focused on the demand by colonial peoples for freedom to determine their own destiny and in eastern Europe, for freedom from Stalinist terror, so today the cry is primarily for freedom from the economic and military power of the United States. The indictment by millions in Latin America, Asia, and elsewhere is that a rich, powerful, industrialized nation employs its armed forces and its ability to control banking, shipping, and other resources necessary for trade in order to prevent smaller nations from using their own land or mines or oil for the benefit of their own people.

Liberation, however, is not to be identified merely with technical independence of one nation from another. It must include genuine freedom from indirect control by a great power. The word *freedom* as it is used in foreign policy discussions today is not very precise. It can refer to freedom of one nation from the control of another while being dominated by the economic or military power of a third power. The term *free world* refers, not to nations that are genuinely free, for many are dictatorships, but rather to nations that are open to or controlled by American business penetration and that are not in the Soviet or Chinese sphere of influence. The achievement of independence from one major power is not to be identified with liberation if the net result is dependence on a rival power. Gaining independence from the United States while becoming dependent on the Soviet Union or China is not liberation. Yet the foreign policy of the United States is such that smaller nations, such as Cuba or Vietnam, are driven to dependence on others in order to become free from U.S. control.

Nor is liberation simply political self-determination, for a nation's standard of living may be so low as to make it dependent economically or its people subject to the control of a domestic or foreign power elite. Liberation implies a quality of life that asserts the importance and worth of persons in such a way that they are free from poverty, from control by more powerful interests, from superstition, fear, hostility, or from anything else that enslaves them. The United States, for example, is wealthy enough that it could launch a major program of modernizing and improving agricultural methods in underdeveloped nations where many peasants are virtually bound to the land as toiling serfs. This would be an illustration of an important step in the direction of full liberation.

Closely associated with the biblical idea of liberation is the idea that setting men free is costly. Liberation, or redemption, is not dependent upon ransom in the sense that a kidnapped child is set free by the payment of a specific sum of money. Rather there is the implication that the powers that do the enslaving are so strong that it is costly to oppose them. The cross must be understood, not as a ransom, but as the costly result of seeking the liberation of men. The truth in this insight has implications for those in any part of the world whose purpose is the liberation of men from the powerful political, economic, or military forces that dominate them. This truth is understood by those who risk their lives in planning or organizing for revolution.

Redemption in the New Testament is costly in a very special way. It is understood as requiring the paying of a price oneself, rather than exacting a price from others. Liberation is not the the freeing of one group of people by enslaving another. A revolution whose aim is to free one group of people by enslaving or destroying another is not a genuine act of liberation in New Testament terms. It is simply replacing one power group with another.

In the New Testament, liberation of your enemy is an integral part of achieving genuine freedom for yourself. It is the system that enslaves both. If an enemy is subjugated and the process of superiority and inferiority continues, oppression is not ended. Violence simply produces a new ruling group and therefore another subject people. But if the accent is placed on transforming systems or, as Paul put it, on a struggle "against principalities and powers" instead of "against flesh and blood," then the circle of conquest and subjection can be broken. Marx came close to this idea when he defined revolution as the transformation of a system but did not insist on violence as a requisite of revolution. But Gandhi and Martin Luther King more clearly understood the difference between genuine liberation and the limited independence which one group of people can gain by destroying or subjugating their former oppressors.

Man is liberated insofar as he is no longer alienated from God. Man is at enmity with God because of his enmity with his fellow men. His enmity or hostility, which is manifest in fear, hatred, anger, guilt, and many other enslaving emotions, must be eliminated if he is to be genuinely free. The New Testament term for the process by which men cease to be enemies and are truly liberated from hostility is *reconciliation*. This can be defined as the process of changing enemies into friends.

Liberation then is not achieved if persons or nations live in independence maintained by hostility to others, by arming against them, or by exploiting them. Liberation is impossible without peace because there can be no freedom from fear or enmity or military rivalry. But peace is not simply the absence of war; it requires the affirmation of the existence and worth of our fellow men or, in other words, justice for all.

In the Hebrew scriptures, the word for peace, *shalom*, means harmony, the perfect unity of righteousness, mercy, and truth. Peace means that the goal of God for men—community —has been realized. In the New Testament, peace (*eirene*) has been revealed in Jesus Christ who represented in himself community with God and man.

The biblical message sounds utopian if it is interpreted as a blueprint for foreign policy. Even the churches have not realized within their own membership the kind of mutual respect and freedom that the Bible proclaims as the goal of God for his people. The biblical approach, however, is to be understood as a direction or orientation, and not as an impossible ideal that provides an excuse for its avoidance. If statesmen are not guided by the biblical orientation, there is no reason for committed Jews or Christians to neglect their own ethical commitments. Foreign policy, if it is to fit broadly within the biblical approach, must therefore include practical steps towards the liberation of men from poverty through the ending of imperialism and the cooperative development of agriculture, industry, and education; it must include practical steps toward the reduction or elimination of all those elements, including armaments, monopolies of raw materials and strategic waterways, etc., that breed hostility; it must include functional and other approaches to world unity.

Liberation at the very least means that American policies of military intervention in other countries must be ended. It means no more wars to maintain or extend the hegemony of the United States. Reconciliation at the very least requires an ending of hostility with both Russia and China. It demands recognition that a highly interdependent world depends for its survival on the well-being of our adversaries and their inclusion in all efforts to sustain life and improve its quality. Reconciliation with both Russia and China also involves liberation of our former enemies, Germany and Japan, instead of continuing to make them into our own military and economic image and using them as buffer states.

The liberation of people in other lands is, of course, impossible as long as the American people suffer from two related popular illusions: moralism and the invincibility of national power. The idea that the United States has never lost a war has been combined with the belief that all its wars have been fought for freedom, justice, or other ideal values. Moralism is the tendency to assume that our action is ethically good or valid without subjecting it to the scrutiny or judgment of any objective criticism or values. It is not only the tremendous physical and economic power of the United States but also this assumption that the American way is morally right that has created the notion of invincibility. Some Christian moralists have contributed to the idea that America has been morally right or more moral than her enemies in certain ways. They have accepted the political propaganda of war being fought for freedom or justice or to oppose tyranny, in spite of their own doctrine of man which implies that groups act only or chiefly from their own group interest.

The biblical analysis of man directly contradicts the idea that American wars or any wars have been fought for ideal values. The biblical view is that man is not by nature capable of the kind of impartial love of his fellows that we attribute to God. Man puts his own interests first and seeks power and privilege for his own group or nation instead of serving the welfare of all. Then he rationalizes or justifies his action so as to convince himself and others that he acted virtuously. The political leader, for example, instead of admitting that his country is an aggressor or seeks power over another nation, claims that the nation under his leadership acted for freedom or in self-defense or at the request of some other government that needed help in preserving its independence. This identification of evil with good, of identifying one's nation with God, is not only self-righteousness but idolatry.

Such a view of man raises immediately the question whether nations and their leaders can serve a larger interest than that of their own economic or political group. It can be argued that political leaders have to act from other than ethical motives if they are to remain in politics, for those who put them in office will not tolerate action that jeopardizes their economic position or the military security or superiority of the nation. According to this position it is an illusion that high government officials represent the total national interest. The biblical analysis of sin tends to support this position and helps expose the illusion that those in power represent and protect all essential interests. Theoretically, each citizen and his welfare should be the concern of government. But in practice governments respond more to those who are economically powerful than to the unemployed, to the professional military officers than to draft-age youth. It is this fact of life that has led Marxists to state that government operates in the interest of the dominant class. The much earlier Christian analysis of man as being a creature functioning in his own self-interest indicates that this problem is not unique in societies dominated by a military–industrial complex. In the Soviet Union, no less than in the United States, there are party leaders, industrial managers, and military figures whose voices and interests are more influential than those of ordinary workers.

Because government is largely guided by economic elites, sometimes in alliance with churchmen, labor leaders, and the military, the only checks upon such otherwise unbridled power are counterinterests reflected in the organization of minority groups who have a different approach to foreign and domestic policy. These minorities must rely, not on the good intentions of those in government, but on alerting the people to other points of view and on aiming action at changing the basic direction of domestic and foreign policy. Such minorities might be built by organizing those people who realize that their own interest is more like that of the common people in other countries than like that of the power elite of their own nation. Or such a minority might exist among people who are committed to a God of love and therefore to the welfare of others.

The fact that man has an inclination to put his own group's

interest above the welfare of all does not mean that he must necessarily be bound by self- or group-interest. It is possible to be freed from this captivity of sin through an encounter with God in which man acknowledges his finiteness, yields his pride, sacrifices his self-interest, and commits himself to a larger loyalty. In other words, all men are not by nature doomed to support a foreign policy of military or economic dominion over others just because the molders of foreign policy find it in their interest to do so.

In practice, however, there are few citizens' groups who question the basic assumptions of foreign policy or of those interests that determine it. There are, in general, three reasons for this. Many citizens tend to identify with the power structure in the hope of benefiting from it. Others know from experience that any basic opposition to the assumptions of those in power will be crushed or discredited by propaganda labels without being given any adequate opportunity to present their real views in the public-opinion-forming media. A third reason is the sheer difficulty of getting a hearing for a policy based on different assumptions. This has led some citizens to accept another illusion: that it is better to go along with existing policy in order to be able slightly to modify it than it is to oppose it and be written off as unrealistic.

The biblical response to all such compromises with evil is such a complete orientation or commitment to love of God and neighbor that one is willing to run risks, be ostracized and ridiculed for the sake of that love. The whole biblical thrust also rejects the idea of cooperation with evil in order to modify it slightly. If the assumptions that underlie a given foreign policy are wrong or intended to perpetuate injustice, a slight modification will not avoid the ultimate danger inherent in the course taken.

Another proposal for compromise with evil which has resulted in confused thinking about foreign policy is that of the "lesser evil" which Christian realists advanced during World War II. The assertion that there are only two evil choices in a complex international situation is basically an effort to direct attention to the evil course already predetermined as the one to be chosen. In most complex foreign policy problems, there are a number of possible choices. To reduce them to two is to deny their complexity and to indulge in oversimplifications. When Reinhold Niebuhr asserted that Christians had the choice, prior to World War II, of submission to Nazi tyranny or of support of the war, he neglected certain other choices, such as collective security with Russia, Britain, France, and others; negotiation to avoid war and prevent tyranny, including economic assistance under certain conditions or embargo under others; nonviolent resistance; neutrality while the Russians and Germans fought over Eastern Europe (Harry Truman's proposal); and perhaps still others. The fact that none of these was acceptable to Niebuhr was no reason for stating the case as being either submission to tyranny or engagement in war. Of course submission to tyranny was also unacceptable to him. Instead of stacking the cards by a lesser-of-two-evils approach, it is always preferable in political and ethical analysis to explore every conceivable choice before deciding on the least evil or, stated positively, the best possible choice. Someone has quipped: "A relativist is one who when confronted with two evil choices takes both of them." The realists' choice of war over tyranny resulted in both tyranny and war. Hitler's tyranny was succeeded by Stalin's sway over Eastern Europe; Tojo's, by that of Chiang Kai-shek, Mao Tse-tung, and Syngman Rhee in Asia.

In actuality there is a connection between war and tyranny. It was World War I, the postwar military alliances against Germany and the heavy war reparations that, it is now agreed, brought Hitler into power. This clearly indicated that there is a connection between the evil in our political actions and the evil in our adversary's; that more war on our part will not stop the tyranny in the world that was created by earlier wars and sustained by continued military containment. To assert that one evil can overcome another instead of bolstering it is to deny Jesus' statement that one overcomes evil only with good and to brand this important Christian insight as irrelevant.

The lesser-of-two-evils argument implies that there never were relatively good choices. But the ability of propagandists to make only two evil choices credible is indicative of the mood of crisis that has come from an earlier refusal to consider other choices that might have forestalled the crisis.

The biblical insight that one does not overcome evil by evil has further application to foreign policy. American foreign policy after 1947 was based on the theory that evil in the form of political or military expansion by the Soviet Union should be "contained" by the political, economic, and military expansion of the United States. The attempt to contain evil is based on the false assumption that evil can be confined to a given land, people, or system. As such, it is based on a false doctrine of man. Instead of recognizing that all men are sinners, it assumes that a whole people or the system under which they live is so much more evil that a less evil or relatively good nation has the responsibility of containment. In fact, there are neither devil nor angel nations. It is precisely when a nation begins to think it is good enough to represent God in chastising other nations that it is in greatest trouble. Its self-righteousness or arrogance of power, as well as its effort to contain others, breeds antagonism, increases rivalry, and leads to war. A nation that believes it has a messianic role in history, with responsibilities thrust upon it to save civilization by using its power against rival nations, is itself a serious threat to civilization. There are also pragmatic reasons for rejecting the theory of containment, such as the fact that systems of ethics or politics cannot be confined geographically if the conditions are ripe elsewhere for their acceptance. So while NATO was at the peak of its power in Europe and the U.S. Navy controlled the Atlantic Ocean, Cuba passed under Marxist leadership.

The biblical method of overcoming evil is rooted in the concept of repentance, on the assumption of mutual guilt. Those people who claim a commitment to God or to love and justice always have the responsibility to acknowledge and forswear their own share in the evil. The clear implication of the biblical message is that the evil in our adversary is somehow related to the evil in us. This is another way of saying that there is no devil theory of international relations, that we must analyze and acknowledge our own motives and actions that have precipitated the crisis now confronting the world. It is, of course, impossible at one and the same time to believe that the United States has been the champion of peace and freedom in the world and also is in need of repentance for having extended its dominance throughout the world by making war.

At the present time there are many in the United States who have opposed the war in Vietnam and are willing for the United States to repent of that war, or to repent for the power of the military–industrial complex or the actions of the CIA. Unfortunately millions of these same Americans are not yet ready to recognize that American policy in Southeast Asia is simply a continuance of the policies of global intervention pursued in Latin America for almost a century and in Europe and Asia since our involvement in World War II.

In succeeding chapters there is an analysis of the myths about recent wars which tend to encourage the popular idea that the responsibility for these wars lies with other nations. That analysis suggests that those who have determined the American national interest have not been interested in the liberation of men around the world or in the reconciliation of man with man or in repentance for our share in causing the world crises of recent years. They have preferred to place the accent of foreign policy on containment of some nations and intervention in others instead of on social change or on meeting the needs of the people around the world.

It is not sufficient, however, to indicate that those in the economic, political, and military seats of power have guided the United States into a position of world hegemony or the formation of a new American empire. Churchmen led by Reinhold Niebuhr, John Bennett, and others in the field of Christian ethics provided the religious rationale for the military foreign policy that created the contemporary American empire and the policy of global intervention culminating in the war in Vietnam. Niebuhr, for example, wrote:

Our anti-imperialistic tradition . . . does make for a certain hesitancy in exercising the responsibilities of our imperial power, since we fear that we may violate the cardinal principle of liberalism, the "self determination of nations." We cannot afford such hesitancy, even in a world in which the weak nations are as preoccupied with anti-imperialistic slogans as we are.[1]

The political support of World War II, military containment, the cold war, the Korean War, and the development of regional military alliances and of the domestic military power base for global intervention were justified and encouraged by the ethical theory of Christian realism. That theory included attacks on minority religious groups who on Christian grounds opposed the government's military foreign policy. Such groups were called "perfectionists" or accused of "ascetic withdrawal" because they did not join the trend toward support of global intervention. Such attacks were less important, however, than the well-developed theory that man is a sinner who functions from self-interest rather than from the motive of Christian love; that collective groups, especially the nation, are similarly motivated by their group interest or have a tendency toward the selfish use of power and therefore the power of other nations must be used to contain or balance their military might.

Such theory raises at least two important questions. (1) If nations are incapable of acting from principle or with "generosity," as Niebuhr asserts, do individuals or groups within a nation have an obligation to support or oppose the "national interest"? (2) If the power of nations must be curbed by the power of other nations, are Christians, Jews, and others concerned with ethics limited to a balance-of-power approach to international relations?

Those realists who write about ethics and foreign policy differ in their analyses of norms or about the relation of morality to foreign affairs. George Kennan indicates that the concepts of right and wrong should not be carried over into national affairs, and Hans Morgenthau considers the national interest as the one standard for political ethics.[2]

[1] Reinhold Niebuhr, *Faith and Politics* (New York: George Braziller, Inc., Publishers, 1968), p. 218.
[2] Robert C. Good, "National Interest and Moral Theory," in *Foreign Policy*

Niebuhr speaks of norms or values that are different from the national interest,[3] but these norms are to keep us humble or aware that we can't measure up to them while we continue to pursue the national interest. It is, of course, impossible in any meaningful way to assert that the nation must follow its interest and also to talk about religious norms that transcend that interest if in fact realism demands a complete priority for what is considered the national interest.

Robert Good indicates that relations between states are not moral but political.[4] But this does not absolve individuals and collective groups within states from a concern for morality in foreign affairs. It might be argued that citizens of a state should not be concerned about morality because the state after all is representing their real interest. There are those who think of the national interest as being determined by responsible statesmen who, in effect, serve as trustees for all the people in the nation. Over against this is the fact that those who make the decisions about foreign affairs are largely or entirely drawn from certain economic and military elites who find it difficult to separate their own class or group interests from what they call the national interest. What is good for General Motors is necessarily good for the United States is one recent expression of this. The overwhelming majority of the people are not involved in discussions of foreign policy, but are manipulated by propaganda to accept the fiction that there is a national interest identical with the interest of those in power.

The important question for ethics to decide is whether individuals or groups within nations should willy-nilly accept the national interest as decisive for their conduct or whether they should evaluate foreign policy by norms other than the national interest. At this point it ought to be clear that a church that claims to be supranational cannot act as if it

---

in the Sixties, eds. Roger Hilsman and Robert C. Good (Baltimore: The Johns Hopkins Press, 1965), p. 277–8.

[3] Reinhold Niebuhr, *The Structure of Nations and Empires* (New York: Charles Scribner's Sons, 1959), p. 291.

[4] Good, "National Interest and Moral Theory," p. 279.

were simply a part of a nation whose international conduct is determined by the interest of its ruling elites. Christian ethics becomes meaningless if in each country it is simply adapted to what seems to be in that nation's interest. Christian realists who insist that biblical ethics or other morality should not be used to help determine the behavior of states are asking that the churches, populist movements, and other groups simply endorse the class interest of those who determine national policy. It is necessary for many people to understand that they have more in common with their fellow human beings, their fellow Christians, Jews, and others in other countries, than they have with those in their own nation's power elites. It is the power elites in each country who conscript young men to fight their battles and who tax the middle and lower income groups to pay for the various military and governmental services that protect their overseas investments and bases. The ecumenical movement in the churches will be as meaningless as the Marxist shibboleth about the solidarity of the working class if Christians continue, as workers have done, to let national interests determine their conduct towards their fellow Christians in other lands. Likewise the concern for justice, about which many Christians and Jews speak so easily, must motivate them to oppose those national actions that perpetuate privilege rather than assist in the liberation of other peoples.

The facts of human sin and of national power in the service of selfish interest are a justification, not for acceptance of the national interest, but for resisting it. Two theologians who have no quarrel with Niebuhr's doctrine of sin have issued a call to a different and revolutionary course of action, wherein the national interest is subordinate to other claims:

> The revolutionary claims made by the modern world are these: men's lives are more important than anything else; natural resources, power, and wealth should be used for the benefit of everybody; the incentive of all organizations of society, political and economic, should be to further the growth of men and women to find their highest good in true fellowship with one

another; and all men should, therefore, have real equality in opportunities for self-development.[5]

The second question posed by Christian-realist theory relates to the balance-of-power idea. The idea that power is contained by concentrations of power is not a biblical insight. Instead the New Testament emphasis is on the superiority and effectiveness of unarmed love or of suffering servanthood. It can be argued that Niebuhr's view of man as sinner, which is biblical in origin, leads logically to the idea that sinners must be restrained or deterred from sin by other sinners. Yet even this is not the biblical way of dealing with sin. Nor is there any such thing as a disinterested effort to restrain or check the power of other states. Yet Niebuhr, among others, seems to understand the balance of power as implying in the words of another writer, "the existence of powers sufficiently unconcerned by the merits of whatever [caused the crises] to be willing to add their weight to whichever side was the weaker and thus prevent the possible victory—and implied hegemony of the stronger."[6]

The idea of a disinterested, or objective, nation or nations maintaining the balance of power contradicts realist theory about the self-interest of nations. Nations may act to preserve their own hegemony or their own security position, but they are not interested in a balance in the sense of an equality of power. Rather they prefer an imbalance of power in their own favor. Instead of thinking of a balance of power as the Christian realists' way of restraining the political or military sin of great powers, it is possible to suggest a quite different analysis. This analysis suggests that Christian realism is not biblically derived, but is instead the result of an American ideology which is based on the Western heritage of political liberalism.

This idea, which was first suggested by A. J. Muste, has

[5] M. M. Thomas and P. Devanandan, eds. *Communism and the Social Revolution in India* (Calcutta, 1953), p. 7, quoted in Charles West, *Communism and the Theologians* (Philadelphia: Westminster Press, 1958), p. 171.

[6] Ernest B. Haas, "The Balance of Power," *World Politics*, 5, No. 4 (July 1953), 458.

also been set forth by W. C. McWilliams in the December 1962 *American Political Science Review.* McWilliams wrote:

> . . . of far more significance is the fact that Niebuhr accepts the liberal goal as the valid goal of social policy. Religion, in a rather unusual role, has very little to say about ends of life and policy which liberalism does not say. . . . The Heavenly City of Reinhold Niebuhr retains a distinctly modern form in which to cast its eternal perfections.
>
> In fact the best state in this world—as opposed to the heavenly ultimate—seems strikingly to resemble the United States. Niebuhr's best state must be an "open" and a "pluralist" society which, at the same time, must have an "organ of dominion and authority." Democracy, a perennial necessity, is also desirable in that it "obscures" the element of domination in the central organ by making it public rather than the presence of a ruling class.[7]

The political liberalism at the root of Christian realism idealizes evolution instead of revolution as the method for social change. It therefore tends to think in terms of legal, economic, and political reforms for dealing with the present world scene, even though the world situation is becoming more and more revolutionary. Having rejected in advance a revolutionary program, the political liberal finds himself in a position of support of war in behalf of the status quo rather than in one of civil disobedience or revolution, however creative or nonviolent it might be.

Liberalism emphasizes as its goal the greatest happiness of the greatest number. Freedom, which is an important emphasis of liberalism, is impossible without a reasonable degree of security. Social security and stability are, therefore, as much an object of political policy as freedom. This emphasis is the basis for the liberal's advocacy of the welfare state.

It is, in a real sense, the culmination of the whole Western political tradition of political democracy and social and economic security for the whole population. It tends, therefore, to identify itself with Western culture. The liberal, to all practical purposes, tends also to support and promote the war-

[7] References to Reinhold Niebuhr are from his *Structure of Nations and Empires,* pp. 28, 34, 35, 59–65, 234–8, 291–4.

fare state as the protector of Western culture. Or as Professor McWilliams puts it:

> Niebuhr [is] in the camp of the liberals; beginning with John Locke, who regarded the state of war as merely an annoyance as compared with the loss of "freedom" that would be entailed by accepting the iron peace of Hobbes' *Leviathan*. . . . If conflict is the price of freedom then Niebuhr will accept conflict; and not only accept it, but sanctify it in the name of a higher morality.[8]

Liberalism is based on the assumption that government exists to protect all essential interests. It does not think of government as functioning in the interests of one class. A primary function of government in the liberal view is to maintain the conditions or the agencies by which conflicts of interest can be adjusted with as little coercion as possible. This seems to be an unrealistic appraisal of modern governments as they operate either domestically or on the world scene. Minorities in the United States, especially Negroes and Mexican–Americans, have for years been repressed; and in most countries the poor, the unemployed, and the workers are largely disregarded by governments. In similar fashion, poor or developing nations are economically and politically manipulated in the interest of strong nations under cover of the United Nations.

The significant thing in this analysis is that Christian realists, when seen from a more revolutionary perspective, are theological apologists for American foreign policy and the domestic phenomenon we call the American way of life. Christian realism is necessarily pessimistic in today's world because it is an ethic for defending a political order that is threatened both by nuclear war and by revolutionary trends in Africa, Asia, and South America. Hope, therefore, is centered on the idea that fear of mutual annihilation will prevent war and that revolutionary tendencies will in time die down if standards of living can be raised by Western technology and economic-aid programs. To give these time to

---

[8] W. C. McWilliams, "Reinhold Niebuhr: New Orthodoxy For Old Liberalism," *American Political Science Review*, December 1962, pp. 878, 880.

operate, it is necessary to stabilize the world scene with American military leadership in much the same way as Britain was supposed to have given the world a Pax Britannica. But it is also significant that the religious rationale for World War II and subsequent U.S. foreign policies has contributed greatly to the world-wide dominance of the United States and the revolutionary reaction to the American empire. It is impossible then for the revolutionaries to view the religious rationale for U.S. military and political ascendancy as an effort to be theologically objective. They understand it as ideology in the service of the United States in much the same way as Americans understand Leninism as ideology in the service of the Soviet Union or Maoism as Chinese ideology.

Charles West also sees Christian realism as a type of American ideology:

> It is hard for all believers in Niebuhr's types of Christian action of a pragmatic sort, to understand that their "realism" transported out of an Anglo–Saxon environment sounds to others like ideology. It presupposes so much in the way of stable self-conscious individuals and groups that a chaotic or tyrannical society's members have no point of contact with it. It justifies so much of the Anglo–Saxon way of life that it builds up the the authority of the white man. In relation to Communism it tends to presuppose a community of "free" nations against a tyranny, whereas the perspective of another country sees the danger of two great power colossi—one hard and direct, the other softer and more diffuse to be sure, but neither welcome as dominating power.[9]

Christian realism when understood as ideology is a profound disservice to those churches and other movements that have been misled by it. Rather than use theology or ethics as an instrument of nationalism or Western culture, Christians should see the biblical goal as one of liberation from all such narrow loyalties and from all efforts to subject some men to the will of others. In Christian thought, the nation is not the bearer of meaning in human history. It does not give men a perspective from which to evaluate history with any degree

[9] Charles West, *Communism and the Theologians* (Philadelphia: Westminster Press, 1958), pp. 168–9.

of objectivity, for nations are armed communities which see other similar groups as obstacles to their success.

The Church, on the other hand, was intended to be supranational with obedience only to a God of all men. The Church is to take a God's-eye view of history and culture. Unfortunately, the Church, by and large, has been so tied to the state since Constantine that it has not been able to transcend nationalist loyalties. Yet here and there individual churches and small sects have been able to do so. Similarly it is not the nation which is the great liberating force in history. The Church, which has its commission from the Redeemer—the one who sets men free—is to be the liberating force in history. Those who are familiar with the riches, pomp, and worldly authority of the Roman Catholic church or with the middle-class Protestant churches, equally tied to nationalism and economic wealth, may seriously ask, what do these institutions mean by liberation? Is it only liberation from personal sins? Or is it also liberation from poverty, injustice, war? Fortunately there are black churches, Asian and African churches, underground churches, Quaker meetings, and groups within the Catholic and Protestant churches whose work is liberating. In each instance these churches are minorities, conscious of their identification with those who suffer and therefore understanding of their mission as one of liberation. Any group which stands in this liberating tradition must of necessity be critical of its own nation's empire-building and of any institutional activity, including its own, which would set some men free at the expense of others. This means that within the nation there must be committed groups who will by their prophetic criticism refuse to accept any foreign policy that is based on war, preparation for war, imperialism, military occupation of other countries, economic exploitation, or the like. If a nation is to have a dynamic foreign policy, it must be compelled by its creative minorities to encourage the liberation of men everywhere from whatever it is that enslaves them. Instead of realism which accepts the national interest as normative for foreign policy, liberation must become normative for both ethics and politics.

3

POWER AND AGGRESSION

THERE IS A POPULAR ASSUMPTION that aggression begins and wars occur because "peace-loving" nations have not taken seriously the whole problem of armed power. This assumption has been stated in such slogans as "If you want peace, prepare for war." It has been stated in other ways. General George Marshall, in his report to the nation as Chief of Staff in 1945, wrote: "We must enforce our will for peace with strength. . . ." He also asserted that if we had had universal military training, the Korean War would not have occurred.[1]

A more dramatic statement of this position appeared in an editorial in the *Army and Navy Journal* of September 1, 1945:

> The censure [for the Pearl Harbor disaster] will not be upon General Marshall or even upon Admiral Stark, but rather, as President Truman subsequently observed, upon the American people, then rotted with pacifism, unwilling to allow Congress to adopt the urgent recommendations of the High Command for appropriations to enable adequate defense. . . .
> The lesson is clear . . . for every one of our 140 million people to realize that in this war-torn world preparedness alone will avert another Pearl Harbor. . . .

A civilian source, *Collier's* magazine for February 22, 1947, in equally strong language asserted, "After World War I the United States led off the disarmament parade," but added that "one big reason why World War II happened at all was that the Axis nations thought we were too weak and lazy and enamoured of peace at any price to deliver ever again any such fighting effort as we put forth in World War I."

[1] *New York Times*, January 24, 1951.

Hanson Baldwin, the Annapolis-trained writer on military affairs for the *New York Times*, in referring to this idea, said:

> The assertion that "We were unprepared" has been applied, with almost monotonous repetition, to the state of American armed forces before World War I, before World War II, and in fact before all our wars. But the statement is sophistry. For what were we unprepared? Preparedness is relative, not absolute; there are degrees of preparedness. Before the Second World War this nation had a navy equal to any and the best long-range bomber in the world; the National Guard had been federalized, conscription had started, and the factories of the country had already commenced the manufacture of war orders. Nevertheless, we were, of course, "unprepared" for the war that developed. We shall always be similarly unprepared, for there is no such thing as absolute preparedness and it is futile to strive for it. Germany, for instance, was prepared for the Polish campaign, but not for the war she got. Not even totalitarian states—much less democracies—can indulge in the luxury of absolute preparedness in time of peace. Complete preparedness is a will-o'-the-wisp, it has led any country which has attempted to achieve it to destruction.[2]

W. T. Stone wrote in February 1941:

> The "fleet in being" was powerful, well-trained and efficient. It was at least the equal of the great British Navy and was definitely superior to the Japanese fleet. The actual tonnage ratio in the Pacific was about 5 for the United States to 3.4 for Japan. And the American Navy was stronger than the combined navies of the two European Axis powers, Germany and Italy.[3]

Between 1938 and Pearl Harbor, the U.S. Navy had steadily expanded until, by December 1941, this country could easily boast the largest navy in the world. In terms of industrial and weapon preparedness, Donald Nelson, wartime chairman of the War Production Board, wrote in his book *Arsenal of Democracy*:

[2] Hanson Baldwin, "The Myth of Security," *Foreign Affairs*, January 1948, p. 254.

[3] W. T. Stone, *America Rearms*, Foreign Policy Association Headline Book Series (New York, February 1941), p. 38.

In 1941 we were spending about $15,000,000,000, or 16 percent of the national income on a war in which we were not officially engaged. . . . Between 1940 and 1941 the revival of our armament industries and the effect of the attendant expenditure upon other industries boosted the national income from about 76 billion dollars to more than 90 billion.[4]

Nelson also wrote, "We had [in 1940] about 5,000 military planes. . . . At or near the beginning of 1940 we had nearly 31,000 certified pilots and 2,280 landing fields of all types."[5] He added:

As early as 1935 we were making fighter planes with a speed of more than 300 miles an hour, and one fighter is said to have registered 375 miles an hour in 1937. In the middle '30's the American plane industry was turning out bombers capable of doing more than 225 miles an hour.[6]

Donald Nelson also reported that Max Werner, the military analyst, had asserted that "there is no doubt the American naval air arm is the finest in the world in both quality and quantity."[7] And the Russian critic A. Algasin had reported, "Soviet, German, British, and Japanese aero industries were turning to the United States for instruction."[8]

The much-publicized story that the American army in 1940 and 1941 was training with wooden rifles and simulated tanks because of disarmament is a half-truth. Nelson revealed the real reason for any deficiency in army equipment. Although he spoke of American reserves as inadequate and puny, he wrote:

After Dunkirk President Roosevelt . . . directed that every spare rifle, every spare bit of ammunition, every spare field piece that we could find in our warehouses be sent to Britain as fast as ships could be obtained to transport them. . . . He was willing to . . . pump our armament reserves dry if by so

[4] Donald M. Nelson, *Arsenal of Democracy* (New York: Harcourt Brace Jovanovich, Inc., 1946), pp. 153–4.
[5] Ibid., p. 47.
[6] Ibid., p. 48.
[7] Ibid.
[8] Ibid.

doing he could hold the last line of defense between the Nazi power and our own shores. . . . General Marshall entered into the agreement wholeheartedly and without any reservation. So did Admiral Stark. . . . And all this occurred a long spell before the passage of Lend Lease—long before the nation would probably have stood for anything like Lend Lease.[9]

In support of this is the following excerpt from the Army's *Pearl Harbor Report*: "Much of our available military resources were being utilized to assist the United Nations."[10]

In any event, any shortage of equipment was due neither to a decision to disarm nor to any failure of Congress to appropriate money. The War Department in the fiscal year that ended June 30, 1941 had unobligated for that year the sum of $1.317 billion that Congress had appropriated.[11]

If we examine the military and naval appropriations prior to the war in Europe, we discover that they jumped from a total of $924,105,181 in 1936 in the Seventy-fourth Congress (second session) to $8,402,324,975 in 1940 during the Seventy-sixth Congress (second and third sessions). In 1941 the first session of the Seventy-seventh Congress appropriated $32,960,503,444.

In three of the eight years prior to American entry into World War II, Congress appropriated more money for armaments than was asked by the executive branch in its estimated needs. And in those same eight years, "Congress exceeded Executive estimates by $1,874,513,033," in spite of the fact that Roosevelt was a "preparedness" President who generally agreed with his military commanders.[12]

Specifically, when the attack on Pearl Harbor took place, there were 2.025 million men in the armed forces, 1.424 million of whom were in the Army ground forces, two hundred

[9] Ibid., pp. 77–8.
[10] U.S. Department of War, *Report of Army Pearl Harbor Board* (Washington, D.C., 1945). Neither this nor the Navy report is available in printed form in government documents. Typewritten excerpts are available at Library of Congress. Therefore, page numbers are omitted.
[11] Senator Henry C. Dworshak, *Congressional Record*, 80th Congress, 1st Session, February 24, 1947, Vol. 93, Part I, p. 1341.
[12] Charles A. Beard, *American Foreign Policy in the Making, 1932–1940* (New Haven: Yale University Press, 1946), p. 37.

twenty-five thousand in the Air Force, three hundred ten thousand in the Navy, and sixty-five thousand in the Marines. The Army was organized into thirty-five divisions, while the Navy had three hundred forty-five combat ships on active duty after President Roosevelt had given to the British fifty destroyers. There were an additional three hundred forty-six combat ships under construction. The annual rate of production of new tanks was eighty-five hundred and of military aircraft was twenty-five thousand.[13] Furthermore, a considerable part of the industrial might of the United States was already geared to war production.

In the light of these facts, it is certainly not accurate to say that the United States was attacked because it was unprepared. On the contrary, the United States was attacked in part because our preparedness had reached such a point that Japan considered it a menace to her position in Asia. She decided to attack at once, before our armed forces become still more formidable. The Navy's *Pearl Harbor Report* stresses this fact.

> Aware of this existing weakness in relative fighting strength [of the Pacific fleet after units had been withdrawn to the Atlantic] and of the vigorous steps to overcome deficiencies, Japan early sensed the advantage of striking before these steps could become effective.[14]

The reason for the concentration of the Navy in the Atlantic was, of course, the secret battle the United States was fighting there, at a time when the American people were led to believe we were not at war. The Army's *Pearl Harbor Report* stated: "The battle of the Atlantic was the predominant factor in the public mind and dominated the policy of the War Department as evidenced by the transfer of a considerable part of the Pacific Fleet to the Atlantic."[15]

American naval strength was so great that Japan seized the moment when much of it had been transferred to the At-

---

[13] *U.S. News and World Report*, August 18, 1950, p. 22.
[14] U.S. Department of Navy, *Pearl Harbor Court of Inquiry* (Washington, D.C., 1945).
[15] *Report of Army Pearl Harbor Board*.

lantic to deal a crippling blow to the Pacific Fleet and thus reduce American naval superiority. Since it is obvious that the entire American navy cannot be every place at the same time, such an attack as that which took place at Pearl Harbor is more likely to happen to a heavily armed nation that must be overcome in a surprise attack than to a nation whose armaments constitute no apparent threat.

Pearl Harbor itself was not the weakest but the strongest point in the American defense system. The Army's *Pearl Harbor Report* said:

> Oahu [where Pearl Harbor is situated] was also the location of one of the largest troop concentrations in the national defense system of the United States. . . . This outpost was implemented with the major portion of the fleet and very substantial Army installations in order that the mainland might rest securely and be protected.

General Marshall himself said in a letter to General Short, commander of the Army's Hawaiian department, on February 7, 1941: "Hawaii is on a far better basis than any other command in the Army." He also wrote: "Frankly, I do not see any landing threat in the Hawaiian Islands so long as *we have air superiority*."[16]

At Wheeler, Hickham, and Ewa airfields, the Army and Marine planes "were tied down wing to wing in precise, tidy rows on the aprons, Air reconnaisance at dawn was confined to three Navy Catalinas covering a narrow sector extending only 200 miles northwesterly."[17]

The Navy had tied up at their berths, two by two, "ninety-four combat and auxiliary ships of the Pacific Fleet, including eight battleships, twenty-nine destroyers and five submarines. Many of their crews were on week-end shore leave. . . ."[18] The planes and the ships were a convenient target for the Japanese air force.

Later, when Admiral H. E. Kimmel was testifying before

---

[16] General George C. Marshall to General Short, February 7, 1941. Italics mine.
[17] *New York Times Magazine*, December 21, 1951, p. 67.
[18] Ibid.

the joint congressional committee investigating the Pearl Harbor attack, he explained, in the words of the news report, "why so many battleships were in harbor at the time the Japs dropped their torpedoes. They were there, he said, because their protecting carriers were away on missions to Midway and Wake."[19]

The battleships were useless against air power. The Navy and the companies making engines, steel, valves, and all the rest that went into the huge ships were a part of the "Navy lobby," or preparedness group, that insisted on continuing to build battleships.

On May 4, 1940, Admiral William D. Leahy, according to a report of that date in the *New York Sun*, "told the House Naval Affairs Committee that battleships were the best modern defense weapons."

There was also rivalry between the Army and Navy that prevented effective liaison or cooperation prior to the outbreak of war. The December 4, 1945 *New York Times*, for example, reported: "A joint Army–Navy intelligence committee, approved by the Secretaries of War and Navy by October 1, 1941, did not begin to function until after the attack on Pearl Harbor of December 7 because of interservice disagreements and difficulties, running from high policy controversy to the Navy Department's apparent inability to furnish office space, Maj. Gen. Sherman Miles declared today."

This had a bearing on the Pearl Harbor attack. Information given to the congressional Pearl Harbor Investigating Committee indicated "that the chief Army intelligence officer in Hawaii at the time of the Japanese attack had no effective contact with Navy combat intelligence and no knowledge that his own subordinate was apparently obtaining some 'top secret' information from the Navy. . . ."[20]

Another illustration of the rivalry was the Army's insistence that "any bombardment plane which operated off the land would have to be under Army command." The Navy in turn restricted the Army's right to send patrol planes beyond a

[19] *Washington Post*, January 16, 1946.
[20] *New York Times*, February 14, 1946.

distance of three hundred miles off coast. Then, "by restricting the range of its bombardment aircraft, the Navy emphasized the dependence of these planes upon carrier bases and precluded the possibility of such planes ever falling under Army command."[21]

There are morals or lessons to be derived from the Pearl Harbor attack, but they do not support the thesis of the realists or of the military–industrial complex that lack of preparedness caused or facilitated the attack.

One lesson is that concentration of military power may encourage surprise attack. Another is that military power does not necessarily provide real security. It may result in being such a threat to an adversary or in such overconfidence on the part of one's own national leadership that it may make war more likely.

Still another lesson to be learned from great military production and huge armed forces is that vested interests are developed which tend to prevent adequate change or cooperation or efforts at peaceful diplomacy or other nonmilitary methods. The military and civilian leaders of the United States were not opposed to war with Japan, as we shall note in Chapter 4. They used diplomacy, not to prevent war, but to bring it about. Because of American military and industrial might, the only question was one of timing. The Army and Navy chiefs on November 5, 1941 "submitted a joint memorandum to the President recommending that no ultimatum be delivered to Japan *at that time* [italics mine], and giving as one of the basic reasons the existing numerical superiority of the Japanese fleet over the U.S. Pacific fleet," many of whose ships had been sent to convoy duty in the Atlantic.[22]

The United States was not the only heavily armed nation among the great powers opposing Germany and Japan. Nor should we assume that the need of Britain and France for

---

[21] William Bradford Huie, *The Case Against the Admirals* (New York: E. P. Dutton & Co., Inc., 1946), p. 118.

[22] *The Navy Pearl Harbor Report*, as published in the *Philadelphia Inquirer*, August 30, 1945.

American assistance after the war had started meant that these nations were disarmed or unprepared prior to the war. Donald Nelson wrote: "The French Army was universally supposed to be the strongest in the world, and for almost a decade it had the finest air force."[23]

M. Daladier testified at the Pétain trial that "France was not disarmed" when Germany attacked. He said: "France had 3,600 tanks against Germany's 3,200 and Germany's production was not greater than ours. After the armistice on June 24, 1940, there were 4,200 planes [still available for use] in the free zone."[24]

When Britain went to war in 1939, she had the largest navy in the world. The British output of aircraft prior to the outbreak of war was in excess of Germany's.[25] By April 1939, she had doubled her territorial army so as to be able to place twenty-six territorial and six regular divisions in France ready for duty in the event of war.[26] These troops had all the small arms they needed but were deficient in larger weapons.[27] In April 1939, Britain began a program of military conscription. Although she was in no sense a match for Germany on the Continent, she had not counted on waging a war in Europe without allies whose arms and troops would supplement hers. On the other hand, in the months prior to the war she had no definite way of knowing how much, if any, assistance she would receive from the various members of the Commonwealth, nor could she know that France and Poland would be so quickly eliminated from the war.

Britain began her rearmament program in 1936, "two years after the first official warning that the national government intended to meet the challenge of German rearmament. For the five years from 1930 to 1935, British armament expenditures ranged from 88.2 million to 93.5. . . . Once the program was fully launched, however, expenditure jumped from 122.2

[23] Nelson, *op. cit.*, p. 44.
[24] *New York Times*, July 26, 1945.
[25] *Economist*, July 15, 1939, pp. 101–2.
[26] *Newsweek*, April 10, 1939, pp. 22–3.
[27] Ibid.

million in 1935–37 to 319.6 for the year 1938–39, an increase of approximately 160% in the space of three years."[28]

The argument presented by military and civilian leaders that weakness induces aggression is most often placed in the context of a military request for more weapons or more manpower via conscription. Or, after a war, initial reverses or defeat are explained as being the result of inadequate preparations. When it is demonstrated that their weapons and numbers of men under arms were not inferior to those of an adversary, sometimes other issues are raised. Since the quantity of weapons and men cannot be blamed, qualitative questions are often raised about the weapons or those who fight or command. The chief qualitative questions that arose about Allied armies in World War II relate to the surprise of U.S. forces at Pearl Harbor, which is discussed in Chapter 4, and the defeat of the French armies.

It is generally acknowledged that France was defeated because the quality of German mechanized warfare surpassed the French ability to resist it. It is not, however, possible to generalize from this that any particular rearmament program will solve a qualitative problem arising from errors in human analysis. The French decision to build the Maginot line and rely on defensive warfare such as was used in World War I was a strategic error. But just as there is no way to guarantee victory in every undertaking, so there is no way to ensure against the use of poor strategy. It is likewise impossible to guarantee that those who fight will always have high morale or fight from a conviction that the war is essential for justice. The nature of armies makes it impossible to predict in advance of a specific war whether those in charge will command well or not, whether the morale of one side will be superior to another, or other similar intangibles. Heavy militarization in itself, on the other hand, may over a period of time lower the quality of leadership or manpower, in much the same way

[28] William T. Stone, "Economic Consequences of Rearmament," *Foreign Policy Reports* 14, Vol. xiv, No. 14 (New York: Foreign Policy Association, October 1, 1938), pp. 157–72.

that great power corrupts or creates the illusion of omnipotence in those who have long held such power.

If the argument is invalid that the United States and her allies were unprepared or disarmed prior to World War II, it is even more absurd to claim that the Korean War or the war in Vietnam occurred because the United States was unprepared. North Korea or North Vietnam and the National Liberation Front were so inferior in arms and industrial capacity to the United States as to make any comparison unnecessary.

At the outbreak of the Korean War, the United States was the only nation in the world with a significant stockpile of nuclear weapons. It had established peacetime military conscription two years earlier. It had an air force of four hundred four thousand, a navy of three hundred seventy-nine thousand, an army of five hundred ninety-six thousand and a marine corps of seventy-four thousand, or a total of 1.450 million men.

When the United States invaded Vietnam, it fought against an enemy with no air force or navy of its own, using chemical weapons, including napalm and gas, against a people that had no chemical industry of its own.

The plain fact or lesson to be learned from modern war is that it is not caused by a lack of military power. Nor is war prevented by superior military power. If anything, the arms rivalry that results from attempts by one or more nations to be superior in armaments or to gain overwhelming power through military alliances is a contributing, if not a major, cause of war.

The assumption that superior military power prevents war is mistaken because it implies that men will always prefer certain injustice to possible death or prefer foreign domination and relative order to the anarchy of war with its hope of possible independence. It is mistaken also because great military powers may be unwilling to pay the economic or human costs involved in maintaining the status quo.

Superior military power short of war assumes an ability to

thwart the dynamics of history through fear. It is a delusion to believe that the status quo plus the ability to create fear can always or generally triumph over a dynamic desire to change. When both sides are prepared to go to war for their own reasons, superior power can be nullified by superior strategy or other factors. If one side is determined to achieve social change without war or by some nonviolent strategy, the adversary's superior power is even less able to maintain the status quo through fear.

4

PEARL HARBOR AND
THE WAR WITH JAPAN

AMONG THE MYTHS created and perpetuated by the realists and by those dedicated to the world-wide military supremacy of the United States is the idea that the United States was dragged into World War II by a treacherous surprise attack at Pearl Harbor. One writer suggests that "we had to choose between a peace of capitulation or a war to defend our national security." He adds: "We went to war because we were attacked and because our security and independence as a nation were gravely imperiled."[1]

President Franklin D. Roosevelt set forth this point of view. On December 8, 1941, the day after the Japanese attack on Pearl Harbor, he declared it "an unprovoked and dastardly attack." He said, "They treacherously violated the long-standing peace between us."

It was only after the war that Secretary of War Henry L. Stimson revealed the decision made by the president and his war cabinet prior to Pearl Harbor to try to get Japan to attack. "The question was how we should maneuver them into the position of firing the first shot without allowing too much danger to ourselves. It was a difficult proposition. Hull laid out his general broad propositions on which the thing should be rested. . . ."[2]

[1] Ernest Lefever, *Ethics and United States Foreign Policy* (New York: Meridian Books, Inc., 1957), pp. 27–8.
[2] Diary of Henry L. Stimson, November 25, 1941, as quoted in Charles A.

The attack was not a surprise because official Washington had cracked the Japanese code more than one year prior to the attack and was fully informed of the timing and preparation by Japan for war. The banner headline on the front page of the *Honolulu Sunday Advertiser* on November 30, 1941 was "Japanese May Strike Over Weekend."

The American people were surprised because few of the administration's plans had been publicly shared. But official Washington expected an attack at any time.

Nor was the attack unprovoked. The Army's *Pearl Harbor Report* revealed that more than a year before the Japanese attack, the Roosevelt administration had begun to wage economic war on Japan. In September 1940, the United States prohibited the export of "many strategic commodities" including "aviation gasoline and many other petroleum products, machine tools, scrap iron, pig iron and steel manufactures, copper, lead, zinc, aluminum and a variety of other commodities. . . ."[3]

On July 25, 1941, "the United States froze Japanese assets, causing bitter Japanese resentment." The American ambassador to Japan, Joseph C. Grew, on August 18, 1941, "reported the Japanese protest on United States economic pressures. On August 29 the United States applied the oil embargo. . . ." Then, on October 9, 1941, Grew "significantly reported that the frozen credit policy of the United States was driving Japan into national bankruptcy and she would be forced to act. His prediction was correct because Tojo, the only Japanese Premier to stay on the active army list in that position, was made Premier on October 16."[4]

These were not the only economic pressures put on Japan. The United States notified Japan in 1939 that the American–Japanese commercial treaty was abrogated. It lapsed six

Beard, *President Roosevelt and the Coming of the War* (New Haven: Yale University Press, 1948), p. 517.
[3] *New York Times*, August 30, 1945.
[4] Ibid.

months later, on January 26, 1940. In October 1940, subsidies on wheat shipped to Japan were discontinued. Certain raw materials exported from the Philippines to Japan were stopped in May 1941, and on July 25, 1941, "in answer to Japan's seizure of French Indo-China, the United States, Great Britain and the Netherlands, acting in concert, froze Japanese assets and stopped all trade" with Japan.[5]

The Roosevelt administration knew that the economic sanctions against Japan would lead to war. The Army's *Pearl Harbor Report* acknowledged this by stating: "It was in the fall of 1940 that we cast the die and adopted economic sanctions." Then, significantly, the *Report* adds that just before the sanctions were to be applied, "the Commanding General of the Hawaiian Department, upon Washington orders, went into an all-out alert into battle position with live ammunition. . . ."[6]

The background of the war and the events immediately preceding it are complex. The origin of the war is in the respective attitudes of Japan and the United States to China. The traditional American approach to China was commercial. Secretary of State John Hay, with the approval of President McKinley, at the time when other great powers were seeking special spheres of influence in China, sent notes to the great powers asking for an Open Door policy or equal business or commercial opportunities within those spheres. The Japanese also wanted a sphere of influence. After winning a war with China (1894–5) and receiving a sphere of influence, Japan was forced by Russia, Germany, and France to give it up. Russia took over the territory from which Japan was ousted.

After the Russian penetration of Manchuria, the Japanese–Russian war occurred. The end of that war in the Treaty of Portsmouth (New Hampshire) in September 1905, resulting from negotiations initiated by President Theodore Roosevelt, led to a Japanese sphere of influence in South Manchuria as

---

[5] Rear Admiral Robert A. Theobald, *The Final Secret of Pearl Harbor,* serialized in *U.S. News and World Report,* April 2, 1954, p. 53.
[6] *New York Times,* August 30, 1945.

well as to control of Korea. The Treaty of Portsmouth provided that Japanese rights in South Manchuria were to be conditioned on Chinese consent. By the Treaty of Peking, December 22, 1905, China gave her consent and also certain other concessions to the Japanese in Manchuria.

Theodore Roosevelt, in a statement to his successor, William Howard Taft, said:

> As regards Manchuria, if the Japanese choose to follow a course of conduct to which we are adverse, we cannot stop it unless we are prepared to go to war. . . . The Open Door policy in China was an excellent thing and I hope it will be a good thing in the future, so far as it can be maintained by general diplomatic agreement, but as has been proved by the whole history of Manchuria, alike under Russia and under Japan, the "Open Door" policy, as a matter of fact, completely disappears as soon as a powerful nation determines to disregard it, and is willing to run the risk of war rather than forego its intention.[7]

Roosevelt's Secretary of State Root and Takahira, the Japanese ambassador in Washington, in an exchange of notes[8] agreed "to respect the territorial possessions belonging to each other [in Asia and] the region of the Pacific Ocean [and to support the] existing status quo." One historian of the Far East said of this agreement:

> A legalistic view would hold that Japan had again pledged herself to the Open Door and the integrity of China; but the narrative of events leading to the exchange would support the view that Japan had given a renewed pledge on the Philippines, and in return "the United States had given Japan a free hand in Manchuria."[9]

During the First World War, Japan made a series of "Twenty-One Demands" on China at a time when the great powers other than the United States were heavily involved in fighting in Europe. The Wilson administration through Secre-

[7] Roosevelt to Taft, December 22, 1910, quoted by A. W. Griswold, *The Far Eastern Policy of the United States* (New York: Harcourt Brace Jovanovich, Inc., 1938), p. 132.

[8] Taft to Takahira, November 1908.

[9] Paul H. Clyde, *The Far East* (Englewood Cliffs, N.J.: Prentice-Hall, Inc., 1948), p. 351.

tary of State Bryan in a friendly note protested some of these as "clearly derogatory to the political independence and administrative entity" of China. These objections led to Japanese withdrawal or modifications of the points in question. Bryan, however, acknowledged that "while on principle . . . the United States has ground on which to base objections to the Japanese 'demands' relative to Shantung, South Manchuria and East Mongolia, nevertheless the United States frankly recognizes that territorial contiguity creates special relations between Japan and these districts."[10]

Japanese military operations in Manchuria in 1931 and the establishment of a puppet state, Manchukuo, led to protests by the League of Nations and the United States, but neither the league nor the United States imposed sanctions. Secretary of State Henry Stimson, in a statement to Charles Powers, the U.S. representative in Paris, said: "We do not ourselves believe in the enforcement of any embargo by our own government. . . . We believe an embargo is a step to war and if an embargo is decided upon by the League, it would be very likely for that embargo to lead to war." Stimson, however, told China and Japan that the United States would not recognize any agreement between Japan or its agents which would "impair the treaty rights of the United States or its citizens in China [including] the open door policy."[11]

The Japanese position throughout was that Manchuria was not a part of China and hence not subject to the nine-power treaty.

Japan's adventure in Manchuria was prompted in large part by hope of easing a worsening economic situation at home. Following the 1929 depression, the United States adopted the Smoot–Hawley tariff to keep out competitive foreign goods. Other nations raised their tariffs.[12]

In turn the Japanese invasion of Manchuria intensified a Chinese economic boycott against Japan. Efforts to get markets

[10] *Foreign Relations of the United States*, Dept. of State, Washington, D.C., 1915, pp. 105–11.

[11] Quoted in Clyde, *The Far East*, pp. 589–90.

[12] John H. Latane and David W. Wainhouse, *A History of American Foreign Policy* (New York: The Odyssey Press, Inc., 1940), p. 818.

in other Asian and African countries led to increased tariffs by the British within her empire and in regions where she was influential. Latane and Wainhouse in their *History of American Foreign Policy* wrote: "The more Japan was thwarted in her efforts to seek markets in the rest of the world the more she was forced back upon the policy of turning East Asia into an exclusive Japanese preserve as an essential element in the solution of her economic problem."[13]

In April 1934, Japan announced that she had special responsibilities in East Asia and that exploitation of China by foreign powers must cease. The United States, for example, was actively involved in China. Among other things, Americans held 45 percent of the stock of the China National Aviation Corporation which had "developed an extensive air service in China." The United States was also establishing training schools for Chinese pilots and in other ways becoming influential in China.[14] Japan saw such activity as a bid for American control of China.

Finally, in 1937, Japan went to war with China. President Roosevelt could have found that a state of war existed in the Far East and invoked the Neutrality Act of 1937, thus applying an arms embargo, but he did not. It was estimated that 54 percent of Japanese imports of war materials came from the United States, as well as half of the gasoline and oil used by Japanese bombers.[15]

After the Japanese began to put restrictions on Americans, Ambassador Grew complained that "equality of opportunity or the Open Door has virtually ceased to exist in Manchuria. . . ." The Japanese government confirmed the ending of the Open Door policy, but indicated that so long as this was understood, Japan "has not the slightest inclination to oppose the participation of the United States and other powers in the great work of reconstructing East Asia, along all lines of industry and trade. . . ."[16]

[13] Ibid., p. 879.
[14] Ibid., pp. 881–3.
[15] Ibid., pp. 891, 899.
[16] Thomas A. Bailey, *A Diplomatic History of the American People* (New York: F. S. Crofts & Co., 1941), p. 746.

This all-to-brief survey reveals that the United States' interest in China was that of keeping the door open for American business and that restriction of such business activity was the first factor leading to a crisis in relationships. In Manchuria, for example, the large American, British, and Dutch oil companies were being forced out of their markets.[17]

It is also obvious that Japan was confronted with serious economic problems which neither the United States nor any international group tried to understand or help solve. Neither in personal nor in international relations is it possible to be concerned only with self-aggrandizement without having a crisis in relationships.

The second factor in the crisis between the United States and Japan was the war that began in 1939 in Europe. Germany had altered the balance of power there and was engaged in the conquest of much of Europe. President Roosevelt had taken every step to help Britain and her allies in the war against Germany short of asking Congress for a declaration of war. He knew that public opinion in the country and in Congress was strongly opposed to U.S. entry into the war.

Numerous books have been written, including an authoritative study by the eminent historian Charles A. Beard, *President Roosevelt and the Coming of the War,* which indicate that Roosevelt's strategy was to take the United States into the war in Europe, if necessary by provoking Japan into attacking the United States. Rear Admiral Robert A. Theobald, who was on active duty during the war and prewar years, summarized Franklin Roosevelt's aim in these words: "There is every reason to believe that when France was overcome President Roosevelt became convinced the United States must fight beside Great Britain, while the latter was still an active belligerent, or later sustain the fight alone. . . ."

Theobald refers to the treaty between Germany, Italy, and Japan wherein each agreed to support the others if a nation not then involved in the war in Europe or in Asia attacked one of the three. "Thereafter," wrote Theobald, "the fact that war with Japan meant war with Germany and Italy played an im-

[17] Clyde, *The Far East,* p. 645.

portant part in President Roosevelt's diplomatic strategy. Throughout the approach to war and during the fighting, the primary U.S. objective was the defeat of Germany."[18]

Winston Churchill confirmed this estimate that Roosevelt's strategy was that of using Japan to get the United States involved in war in Europe. In a statement on January 27, 1942, to the House of Commons, he said:

> The probability, since the Atlantic conference at which I discussed these matters with Mr. Roosevelt, that the United States, even if not herself attacked, would come into the war in the Far East, and thus make final victory sure, seemed to allay some of the anxieties. The expectation has not been falsified by the events.

The third factor that led the United States into the war in the Far East was the old balance-of-power principle. The Roosevelt administration did not object to the various European empires in Asia nor even to Japanese control over Korea or a Japanese sphere of influence in Manchuria. It was primarily concerned about Japanese efforts to enforce a "Monroe Doctrine" in eastern Asia. In April 1934, Japan announced her claim to "paramount interest" in China, and in 1940, Japan began a limited occupation of the northern part of French Indochina. The Vichy government in France, which was collaborating with the Germans, made possible a relatively peaceful occupation. In July 1941, Japan occupied the southern part of Indochina. This occupation led the Roosevelt administration to decide that if Japan moved against British Malaya or the Dutch East Indies or Thailand, and if the British went to their defense, the United States would provide armed support.[19]

From this brief description of the power changes in the Pacific, it is obvious that Japan, like each of the great Western powers before her, was trying to establish an empire in Asia. Just as the United States asserted, via the Monroe Doctrine, hegemony over North and South America, so Japan was trying to do the same over Asia. The United States, how-

[18] Theobald, *The Final Secret of Pearl Harbor*, p. 51.
[19] Beard, *President Roosevelt and the Coming of the War*, pp. 54, 520, 553.

ever, did not intend to accept a subordinate role to Japan in Asia. Political realism thus demanded curbing Japanese power in order to grant American business a free hand and to permit in the postwar period an enlarged American political and economic influence in the Far East.

This, of course, is not the whole story, for the Japanese government, following the freezing of Japanese assets in the United States and other economic pressure, made an approach to Washington that could have averted war. On August 17, Ambassador Nomura called at the White House to receive from President Roosevelt a warning that if Japan undertook any further steps in the direction of military domination in Asia, the United States would be forced to act, even though this might result in conflict.

During the meeting at the White House, Nomura presented the President with a personal message from Prince Konoye, the Japanese premier, which indicated that he wanted to maintain peaceful relations with the United States and would meet him somewhere in the Pacific to talk over the way to do this. Roosevelt and Secretary of State Cordell Hull pursued an interesting strategy in avoiding a meeting with Konoye. They indicated they looked with favor on such a conference in the Pacific, but asked advance agreement on certain principles to assure a successful conference.[20]

On August 18, the Japanese foreign minister, Admiral Toyodo, met with Ambassador Grew to ask American cooperation "for the settlement of the China affair which is the obstacle to peace in the Far East." He then asked that President Roosevelt meet Prince Konoye in Honolulu in spite of the fact that a Japanese "premier's going abroad would have no precedent in Japanese history."[21]

Ambassador Grew telegraphed Washington his support of a meeting with Konoye, stating that "it is an indication that Japanese intransigence is not crystallized completely owing

[20] Ibid., pp. 496–7.
[21] Memorandum of the interview in *Foreign Relations of the United States, Japan, 1931-1941*, Vol. 2, Dept. of State, Washington, D.C., pp. 560–4, as also quoted in Frederic R. Sanborn, *Design for War* (New York: Devin-Adair Company, Inc., 1951), pp. 347–8.

to the fact that the proposal has the approval of the Emperor and the highest authorities in the land."[22]

On August 27, Ambassador Nomura met with Hull and again, on August 28, met with both Roosevelt and Hull to restate Konoye's request for a meeting. Hull later wrote that Roosevelt read the message from Konoye "with interest and complimented the tone and spirit of it." Roosevelt, however, spoke of the difficulty of going to Hawaii and finally authorized Nomura to say to his government that "he would be keenly interested in having three or four days with Prince Konoye," possibly in Juneau. However, he avoided setting a date.[23]

Later that same day, Nomura called on Hull to try to fix a date, but Hull was evasive. On September 1, Nomura tried again, and in Japan Ambassador Grew, by request, asked Washington for a meeting about September 20. On September 3, Roosevelt gave Nomura a memorandum requiring the Japanese to agree in advance on all the unsettled problems between them. Orally he added that after such an agreement was made, he would have "to discuss the matter fully with the British, the Chinese and the Dutch. . . ."[24]

On September 4, Ambassador Grew received from the Japanese foreign minister a statement accepting earlier American proposals and also agreeing that Japan would interpret for herself rather than being bound by the meaning of the Axis pact with Italy and Germany. Grew, in sending this on to Washington, said that he believed this "is indicative of the earnest wish of the Japanese Government to achieve a basic settlement with the United States."[25]

The same day, in Washington, Nomura gave Hull a document agreeing fully with the American demands made on June 21, 1941. Hull then increased the demands and refused to set a date for a meeting until he "had approached the other interested governments."[26]

[22] Ibid., p. 565.
[23] Ibid., pp. 571-3; 576-9.
[24] Ibid., pp. 588-9.
[25] Ibid., pp. 608-9.
[26] Ibid., pp. 595-600.

The unfriendly reception Hull gave to what was a very drastic about-face by the Japanese and what must have seemed to them a great concession led to the withdrawal of the offer, with the face-saving explanation that it was Nomura's "personal and private views."

The Japanese began to believe that the United States was stalling. On September 6, in Tokyo at a top-level conference, it was agreed that every effort should be made for a peace settlement; but that "if by the early part of October there is no reasonable hope," they would prepare for war, with such preparations to be ready "toward the end of October."[27]

Prince Konoye that same evening met Grew secretly to discuss the problem Japan faced of mounting economic pressure and the resentment she felt against the countries exerting it. Grew, in transmitting the conversation to Washington, said that Konoye was prepared to accept Hull's principles and was confident all "questions at issue can be disposed of to our mutual satisfaction during the meeting with the President. . . ."[28]

To make a long story short, Japan finally agreed to interpret the Axis pact in such a way as to give the President complete leeway in going to war against Germany without Japanese reprisal.[29] Japan also agreed to American demands for peace with China, including "withdrawal of Japanese armed forces."[30]

Hull again delayed in agreeing to a meeting with Konoye. Thereafter, Grew cabled Hull that he should not expect exact agreement on every detail before the meeting, that if the United States dragged out the discussions, Japan "will come to the conclusion that the outlook for an agreement is hopeless and that the United States Government is only playing for time." Grew added, "The logical outcome of this will be the downfall of the Konoye cabinet and the formation of a military dictatorship which will lack either the disposition or

[27] Sanborn, *Design for War*, p. 369.
[28] *Foreign Relations of the United States*, Japan, Vol. 2, pp. 604–6.
[29] Ibid., pp. 626–9.
[30] Ibid., pp. 631–3.

the temperament to avoid colliding head on with the United States."[31]

Meanwhile, certain American military circles objected to a conference with Konoye unless Japan agreed in advance to withdraw from the Axis. Secretary of War Stimson also opposed the meeting with Konoye.[32]

After repeated attempts to get an idea from Washington about the possibility of a meeting or about what the United States would agree to, the crisis came in Japan. General Tojo on October 14 called upon Prince Konoye to resign. On October 16, the Konoye cabinet resigned.[33]

The Emperor, however, was unwilling to have war with the United States and ordered the armed forces to avoid war.[34] The new cabinet therefore continued to negotiate.

On October 24, Secretary of Navy Knox publicly announced that war with Japan was inevitable. The next day Grew cabled from Tokyo about the Knox statement, adding that war was not inevitable since "the present Japanese leaders are willing to give up their expansionist plans through armed forces if a workable understanding can be reached with the United States."[35]

The Roosevelt administration knew the position of the Japanese government at each step because the Japanese secret code had been cracked months prior to Pearl Harbor.[36] The administration knew of the deadline the Japanese had set for its envoys in Washington to achieve agreement. For example, a Tokyo dispatch on November 16, 1941 to Kurusu in Washington included the following:

> In our opinion we ought to wait and see what turn the war takes and remain patient. However, I am awfully sorry to say that the situation renders this out of the question. I set the deadline for the solution of these negotiations in my #736 and

[31] Ibid., pp. 645–50.
[32] Sanborn, *Design for War*, pp. 402–3.
[33] Ibid., p. 413.
[34] *Foreign Affairs of the United States*, Japan, Vol. 2, p. 697.
[35] Sanborn, *Design for War*, p. 419.
[36] *New York Times*, November 16, 1945.

there will be no change. . . . You see how short the time is. Therefore do not allow the U.S. to sidetrack us and delay the negotiations any further. Press them for a solution on the basis of our proposals and do your best to bring about an immediate solution.[37]

On November 25, Secretary Hull handed an ultimatum to the Japanese ambassadors in Washington in the form of American demands for resolving the impasse with Japan. Admiral Theobald described the situation in these words:

> These American proposals were absolutely devoid of diplomatic finesse. A far more subtle note resisting the Japanese-suggested solution would have been equally effective in breaking off the negotiations. The only possible conclusion is that President Roosevelt wanted to be absolutely sure that Japan's answer would be a declaration of war. . . .
> Everyone concerned recognized that this note put an end to the Kurusu–Nomura negotiations and that war was inevitable. Secretary Hull at once informed the heads of the Army and Navy that diplomatic negotiations had failed and that further action must be the responsibility of the Armed Forces.[38]

A member of Congress, Jeannette Rankin, said that the gist of the ultimatum was the requirement, made on September 3, 1941, that Japan accept the principle of "non-disturbance of the status quo in the Pacific."[39] "This requirement," said Congresswoman Rankin, "was the equivalent to asking Japan to guarantee the inviolateness of the white empires in the Orient, of which the British Empire comprised approximately 90 percent in both area and population."[40] Roosevelt, for example, was not concerned with the French rule of Indochina, but was disturbed at a shift to Japanese control.

An examination of the total record of American–Japanese relations reveals mutual guilt rather than sole guilt. Japan was dominated by the military which stood behind the civilian

[37] Decoded in the U.S. Department of the Navy, November 17, 1941. Theobald, *The Final Secret of Pearl Harbor*, p. 63.
[38] Ibid., p. 56.
[39] Department of State Bulletin, Vol. 5, No. 130, December 20, 1941, p. 538.
[40] *Congressional Record*, 77th Congress, 2nd Session, Vol. 88, Part 10, December 8, 1942, p. A4440.

government, ready to take over if the national interest as understood by the military did not prevail. Japan was not only seeking empire in Asia at the expense of weaker people but was trying to take over the possessions of the British, French, and Dutch in the Far East while these nations were weakened or defeated by the war with Germany. Japan's attempt to build an empire clashed with the economic interests of some business firms in the United States and with the nation's military or strategic interests in the Pacific. When Japan apparently was ready to capitulate to American demands and grant American and British interests an equal if not upper hand in most of Asia, this was not enough. Roosevelt, Hull, and Stimson wanted to involve Japan in war for other reasons, notably because of her alliance with Germany and Italy.

It can hardly be said by any objective mind that Japan was the aggressor in the war with the United States unless aggression is defined as the reaction of a nation to an intolerable situation that has been forced upon her. A week before the attack on Pearl Harbor, Congresswoman Rankin "asked a prominent non-Japanese oriental: 'Is the situation in the Pacific as serious at it appears?' 'Yes,' he replied, 'it is serious. Japan has no choice but to go to war or to submit to economic slavery for the rest of her existence.' "[41]

An ethical appraisal of the events preceding the attack on Pearl Harbor would have to conclude that the Roosevelt administration was interested in returning to the prewar colonialism of the West in the Pacific or in expanding American interests, rather than in justice for the Japanese or for the Indochinese, the Indonesians, the Indians, and the others in colonial empires. He did not, for example, ask of the British, the Dutch, or the French that they pledge the freedom or independence of India, Malaya, Burma, Indonesia, Indochina, or their other possessions. That Roosevelt was interested in maintaining British imperialism is obvious from the following excerpt from a note he sent on January 21, 1941 to Ambassador Grew in Tokyo:

[41] Ibid.

The conflict may well be long and we must bear in mind that when England is victorious she may not have left the strength that would be needed to bring about a rearrangement of such territorial changes in the western and southern Pacific as might occur during the course of the conflict if Japan is not kept within bounds.[42]

Apparently the aims of the Roosevelt administration in the Pacific were these: (1) To maintain the British, Dutch, and French empires in the Pacific; (2) To maintain the Open Door policy and extensive American influence in China; (3) To destroy Japanese power in the Pacific; (4) To use war with Japan as a pretext for entering the war in Europe.

Ironically, the first of these aims was not achieved. The British, Dutch, and French empires in Asia have been lost. The United States, however, has extended its influence into as many areas formerly held by the British, French, Dutch, and Japanese as possible. Only in Korea, Laos, Cambodia, and Vietnam has it been necessary for the United States to go to war, although American troops have been used for various purposes in Japan, Okinawa, Taiwan, and Thailand as well.

It is ironic also that the United States and the various realists who supported the Open Door policy in China as one of the reasons for war with Japan have had to accept the fact that war completely destroyed the Open Door. China as a result of the war has gone Communist. The United States, and the business interests so influential in American foreign policy, had a greater chance of doing business in a China temporarily under Japanese influence than they do with a China which is permanently Communist.

An ethical, as well as a political, appraisal that does not consider the probable consequences as well as the methods and motives of a given course of action is less than adequate.

Beyond this, the realists in and out of the Roosevelt administration supported a policy that gave no consideration to the necessity of social change or of improving economic con-

---

[42] Joseph C. Grew, *Ten Years in Japan* (New York: Simon and Schuster, Inc., 1944), pp. 362–3.

ditions for the people of Asia. Armed power became the American answer to all problems. One result of the war was the destruction of Japanese influence. The other was the weakening of Chiang Kai-shek's regime and the strengthening of the Chinese Communists. Both of these results in turn made possible the seizure of China and Manchuria by the forces of Mao Tse-tung. The further result is that a power struggle in Asia has developed between China and the United States. The one creative force that could play a non-Communist and non-American satellite role in Asia is nationalism. Yet the United States has become so addicted to military and/or economic domination that at a number of points it suspects non-aligned nationalism as being pro-Chinese, simply because nationalist leaders in Burma, for example, will not permit the United States economically or militarily to move into its country.

The consequences of World War II are still developing in Asia. In the meantime the realist myth persists in the United States that Pearl Harbor was an unprovoked attack, that American armed power had to be used against Japan in any event, and that such power in our enlightened hands was the only way of dealing with tyranny. It is fortunately increasingly obvious that the choice posed by realists between war and tyranny was not a genuine one. By our insisting on war with Japan, new forms of tyranny have resulted in various nations in Asia.

5

THE MUNICH MYTH

ONE OF THE MYTHS that sustains the whole realist thesis of power politics is summed up with one word—Munich. The myth is that World War II could have been prevented if France and Britain had acted decisively and militarily against Germany instead of trying to appease Hitler. Munich is the symbol of appeasement to which various meanings have become attached. These meanings include such ideas as appeasement being negotiation to avoid war, surrender without a fight, giving something away without cost to the other side, or any compromise with an adversary. The net impact of this myth is to discourage any approach to peace other than that of an uncompromising toughness based on overwhelming military power. The slogan No appeasement means no compromise, no bargaining—a dogmatic or inflexible position.

This myth survives partly because those who created it and continue to use it find it a convenient propaganda slogan to serve American power purposes. Actually, the myth of Munich rests on a falsification of history, or on subordinate myths that have to be believed on faith if the theory of Munich is to be upheld.

The first of these submyths is the notion that Britain, France, and Czechoslovakia were weaker militarily than Germany and that Munich was intended to buy time. The German army "had about forty-eight trained regular divisions," only three of them armored. Four others were motorized. Three infantry divisions were in East Prussia as "protection" against a Russian or Polish attack. The rest had to protect

Germany from a possible invasion by France and to advance into Czechoslovakia.[1]

Czechoslovakia had between thirty and forty divisions, which together with the French divisions made these two countries, even without British help, stronger than Germany.[2]

The German general, Jodl, testified at Nuremberg: "It was out of the question with five fighting divisions and seven reserve divisions in the western fortifications, which were nothing but a large construction site, to hold out against 100 French divisions. That was militarily impossible."[3]

Germany's weakness in relation to France, Czechoslovakia, and Britain was so serious that the German chief of staff, General Franz Holder, had plotted with a number of other generals "to seize governmental power by a military *putsch* centering in Berlin," and to hold and isolate Hitler. This plan was developed by September 12, a few weeks before the Munich agreement. But the Munich decision made it impossible and indeed dangerous with the new prestige Hitler had won.[4]

Telford Taylor, an American brigadier general, summarized the military situation in these words: "No matter how shoddy and dispirited the French Army might have been in 1938, as it proved to be in 1940, there is no question but that it could have marched with ease through [General] Adam's pitifully small forces and uncompleted defenses. To be sure, the German armies in the South might in the meantime penetrate Czechoslovakia, but by the time they were well into Bohemia they would have had a hard time getting out. . . . In almost every other vital respect the Third Reich was unready for a major conflict."[5]

Hitler was bluffing in terms of taking on France and Brit-

---

[1] Telford Taylor, *Sword and Swastika* (New York: Simon and Schuster, Inc., 1952), p. 209.

[2] Keith Eubank, *Munich* (Norman, Okla.: University of Oklahoma Press, 1963), p. 281.

[3] Telford Taylor, *Sword and Swastika*, p. 225.

[4] Ibid., pp. 218, 224.

[5] Ibid., p. 226.

ain, but his generals didn't know it. Hitler counted on no opposition from anyone except possibly the Czechs.

The reason Hitler believed there would be no war was his information from British leaders *long before Munich* that the British and French did not plan to try to prevent the incorporation of the Sudeten Germans into Germany.

Neville Henderson, the British ambassador in Berlin, assured Hitler in May, more than four months before Munich, that "France was acting for the Czechs and Germany for the Sudeten Germans, Britain was supporting Germany in this case."[6]

Henderson's next in command, Kirkpatrick, also told a German official: "If the German Government would advise the British Government confidentially what solution of the Sudeten German question they were striving after . . . the British Government would bring such pressure to bear in Prague that the Czechoslovakian Government would be compelled to accede to the German wishes."[7]

The reason for such British statements to the Germans was not British weakness or British betrayal of France, but a joint British–French policy decision made on April 28 and 29 in London. At that London meeting, Britain and France were divided.

Contrary to a second submyth, there was no basic unity among these two nations with respect to Germany. Daladier, the French premier, believed that "war could only be avoided if Great Britain and France made their determination quite clear to maintain the peace of Europe. . . ." He also said, "German policy was one of bluff. . . . We were at present still able to place obstacles in her path."[8]

The British, on the other hand, felt that the way to prevent war was to rectify the injustices of the Versailles treaty that brought Hitler to power. One of these, according to many

---

[6] A. J. P. Taylor, *The Origins of the Second World War* (New York: Atheneum Publishers, 1962), p. 162.

[7] Ibid.

[8] Ibid., p. 160.

influential Englishmen, was the German minority question. There were three million Germans in Czechoslovakia. They had been stirred to the possibility of reunion with Germany by the Anschluss with Austria. They were closely linked both ethnically and historically to the Austrians since they had been a part of the old Hapsburg empire.

A. J. P. Taylor, an able British historian, summarized Prime Minister Chamberlain's position:

> Timidity or doubt of British strength did not affect his calculations, though he had a natural dislike of war. He believed that Hitler could be won for peace; he believed also that Hitler had a good case so far as Czechoslovakia was concerned. Hence he was determined to act on these two beliefs, whatever the opposition at home or abroad. . . . Neville Henderson, the Ambassador at Berlin, was equally confident that Hitler could be won for peace. . . . Both Henderson at Berlin and Newton at Prague insisted that the Sudeten claims were well founded morally and that the Czechoslovakian government were making a genuine attempt to meet them.[9]

A third submyth which contributed to the Munich claims is the idea that no show of strength was made against Hitler. Hence, Munich was a failure of nerve at the last minute. This too is mistaken. There were those at the time who believed Hitler would back down before a show of strength. On May 20, Czechoslovakia recalled its reservists. The Czech army occupied posts at the frontier, and the government gave as its rationale for this that Hitler was about to invade. The Germans denied this, and the capture of their secret records at the end of World War II substantiated their denial.

This action had two immediate results. Hitler was thoroughly angered at the humiliation of Germany. He took the draft of a strategic directive prepared by General Keitel and "struck out the first sentence—which repudiated military action against Czechoslovakia. . . ."[10]

[9] Ibid., pp. 157, 158.
[10] Ibid., p. 166.

Those who advocate a show of force generally fail to understand that it can boomerang. It is often likely to make an adversary more determined. When a nation has a potential for developing a stronger force, a display of power by an adversary adds determination to sacrifice to achieve a superior force.

The second result of the Czech show of strength was to weaken British–French support for Czechoslovakia. The British told the French that France could expect support only in case of unprovoked aggression. French officials in turn told both the British and German ambassadors that "if Czechoslovakia were really unreasonable the French Government might well declare that France considered herself released from her bond."[11]

A. J. P. Taylor, in trying to explain the Czech action, wrote:

> It is more plausible that the Czech demonstration was undertaken to discredit appeasement and to show that Hitler would retreat before a show of force. . . . Some slight evidence suggests that the move was inspired by the tough members of the British Foreign Office who disliked the existing course. . . .[12]

About fifteen years earlier, the French had tried a show of force against the Germans by occupying the Ruhr. The occupation was intended to coerce Germany into an offer or settlement of reparations due France. German promises were duly made and later broken. The occupation was costly, had a bad effect on the French franc, and in 1924 led to the voters putting in power a left-wing coalition hostile to the French premier, Poincaré, who had made the decision about the Ruhr.

Although the French power action was temporarily and nominally successful, it too boomeranged. Stresemann, who came to power in Germany, was determined to revive German power in order to get revision of the Versailles treaty. The French, noting the high cost of their power thrust into

[11] Ibid., p. 165.
[12] Ibid.

the Ruhr and the negligible results, began to doubt the value of military coercion as such.[13]

A fourth submyth which sustains the whole Munich assumption is the idea that there was so much pacifism among the English and French people that Chamberlain and Daladier could not have gone to war over the Sudetenland. There is considerable truth to the idea that both of these leaders doubted their people would support a war move. But the reason was not pacifism. There were only a few pacifists in France, and even in Britain, pacifists were a tiny minority.

An astute observer of the times, the French citizen Raoul de Sales, wrote in his diary that the choice affecting most people was that of either Communism or Fascism. In his entry of October 4, shortly after Munich, he said:

> . . . there was a conjunction of blunders inspired by identical motives (fear of Communism, attraction of Fascism, etc.) ending finally in the present result. In short, this is a new stage in the great movement of reaction which established itself first in America when the New Deal began to lose ground some eighteen months ago, and later in France through the over-turning of the Popular Front. The pluto-democracies, as Gaydo calls them, are defending themselves by allowing themselves to be attracted by peace with the dictatorships.[14]

In referring to the dictatorship of Germany and Italy, he indicated that "the problem everywhere in the world is how to bring the working classes to heel [since this] is identified with the struggle against Communism. The attraction of Fascism is essentially that Mussolini and Hitler have 'resolved' the class struggle."[15]

Again in his entry of October 21, de Sales wrote: "Apparently the choice which obsesses Europeans, Communism or Fascism, is already made. . . ." He added:

> . . . there are too many people in France who really never accepted the socializing aspect of democracy. They had a nos-

[13] Ibid., pp. 50, 51.
[14] Raoul de Roussy de Sales, *The Making of Yesterday* (New York: Reynal & Hitchcock, Inc., 1947), p. 5.
[15] Ibid.

talgia for authority, that is to say for an order which would maintain the existing inequalities, would leave to the rich their riches, to the working classes their difficulties.[16]

It was this anti-Communism and fear of more power for the working class that led the Russians to believe that Munich was not a result of pacifism in the West or weakness on the part of Chamberlain and Daladier, but a desire to turn Hitler's aggressive intentions toward the Soviet Union. Czechoslovakia was in Eastern Europe and was a logical first step toward Russia. The East German and Czech governments, for example, on the twentieth anniversary of the Munich decision, issued the following statement: "The events following the signing of the Munich Agreement prove that Munich was an anti-Soviet plot . . . preparing aggression against the first Socialist state of the World."[17]

The Communist leaders of the USSR had some reason to form their judgment about Munich because the British and French acted as if Russia were not a part of Europe. The Russians had advocated a policy of collective security against Germany, but the British and French were not ready to include Russia in their collective discussion or plans. Stalin, after Munich, told the Eighteenth Party Congress (March 10, 1939):

> The majority of the non-aggressive countries, particularly England and France, have rejected the policy of collective security, the policy of collective resistance to the aggressors, and have taken up a position of non-intervention, a position of "neutrality". . . . The policy of non-intervention reveals an eagerness, a desire not to hinder the aggressors in their nefarious work: . . . not to hinder Germany . . . from embroiling herself in a war with the Soviet Union. . . .[18]

Although the mood among the leadership in Britain and France was anti-Communist rather than pacifist, it seems clear from the record that neither Chamberlain nor Daladier wanted Germany to go to war with Russia. They wanted to prevent

[16] Ibid., pp. 8, 9.
[17] Eubank, *Munich*, p. 296.
[18] Quoted in Frederick L. Schuman, *International Politics* (New York: McGraw-Hill, Inc., 1958), pp. 503–4.

war in Europe and maintain the status quo as nearly as they could without it. In spite of their anti-Communism, their preoccupation in the weeks prior to Munich was with Germany and not Russia.

If the propaganda about Munich being caused by pacifism, a failure of nerve, a lack of preparedness, and the like has no basis in fact, where then did such ideas originate?

Apparently, they originated in the difference between France and Britain, in the vacillation of France, and in Chamberlain's last-minute shift in strategy.

Chamberlain began with the idea that justice required self-determination for the Sudeten Germans, but before Munich, as a result of skillful diplomacy by Benes and an overplaying of Hitler's hand, British opinion was shifting to regard the Czechs rather than the Sudeten Germans as the underdog or oppressed. "Chamberlain wished to silence their opposition; and he therefore stressed the danger of war, not the justice of Germany's claims."[19]

On September 26, Hitler in a speech announced that German troops would occupy the Sudeten German territory by October 1. Chamberlain did several things. He had an envoy deliver this message to Hitler:

> If Germany attacked Czechoslovakia France would feel that she must fulfill her treaty obligations. . . . If that meant that the forces of France became actively engaged in hostilities against Germany, the British Government would feel obligated to support her.[20]

Yet, at the same time he urged France not to start an offensive.[21]

The second thing Chamberlain did was to appeal to Mussolini, who had real hesitations about supporting Hitler in Czechoslovakia. Mussolini appealed to Hitler, who responded that he would hold off occupying the Sudetenland another twenty-four hours to permit a four-power conference.

---

[19] Taylor, *The Origins of the Second World War*, p. 183.
[20] Ibid., p. 182.
[21] Ibid.

The third thing Chamberlain did was to go to Munich and together with Daladier agree to the dismemberment of Czechoslovakia. "The appearance of a *Diktat* was avoided. Right to the end, Hitler did not make demands; he graciously accepted what was offered by others." Chamberlain and Daladier did not even confer. They had made their decision months before.[22]

The reactions to Munich were varied. Chamberlain said, "I believe that it is peace for our time." Hitler asserted: "I have no more territorial demands to make in Europe." Churchill and other opponents of Munich felt that Germany had to be stopped; she was growing too strong and powerful. In response to this, Chamberlain called for more armaments, which seemed to belie his faith that Hitler would not go any further in his demands.[23]

However, the British government at the time thought Munich was "a triumph for British policy . . . not a triumph for Hitler . . . a triumph for those who had courageously denounced the harshness and short-sightedness of Versailles."[24]

Even the French did not believe they had surrendered their safety at Munich. They believed that the Maginot line was impregnable and that "a stalemate had been established in Western Europe."[25]

In fact, it was French military strategy as much as anything that foreordained the Chamberlain–Daladier decision at Munich, and not pacifist inclinations among the leaders or the people of either country. Eubank described the problem in these terms:

> If France had ever seriously intended to aid Czechoslovakia she would have made plans for an invasion of Germany. Such plans never existed and without an invasion of Germany to draw off Hitler's armies, the Czech forces were doomed. No plans for an attack on Germany existed in 1938 because

[22] Ibid., pp. 183–4.
[23] Ibid., pp. 187–90.
[24] Ibid., p. 189.
[25] Ibid., p. 188.

French strategy was defensive. The war of 1914–18 seemed to have proved the superiority of defense over offense.[26]

The French and Czech general staffs had not engaged in any joint planning, and it was not until June 18, 1938 that the Czech chief of staff proposed such joint studies.[27]

The Munich record simply does not support the realist conclusion that if power had been massed against Hitler at Munich, there would have been no world war. The problem was far too complex for such a simplistic solution.

The rise of Adolf Hitler, the growth of a strident German nationalism, and the events that culminated in the war are all rooted in the First World War, the Versailles treaty, and the whole power effort to maintain a victor's "peace."

These causes can be summarized as follows:

The Versailles treaty provided for substantial disarmament by Germany to be followed by disarmament by the other or victorious nations. The refusal of the other nations to follow suit led to a secret and then open rebuilding of German power.

The second major cause of World War II was economic. The Great Depression was world-wide and there was, as a result, poverty and crisis in Germany. Raymond Moley, after a conversation with President-elect Roosevelt in 1932, stated the connection between World War I and the depression:

> The World War had been financed in large part, both before and after 1917, by the billions of dollars of loans we had made and credits we had granted to the Allies. At the end of the war the Allies had proposed to draw from Germany, in the form of reparations, at least enough to pay back what they owed us. This fantastic burden of debt Germany could not discharge, even if she was permitted to export goods which competed with their own. At the same time we had found that our farmers and industrial producers could not continue to find expanding markets abroad as Europe's production reached and exceeded prewar levels. Hence we had lent Europe the money to buy our products, or, if you will, to pay us what she owed us.
> This jerry-built structure had begun to crumble the instant

[26] Eubank, *Munich*, p. 280.
[27] Ibid.

we ceased to make foreign loans, and the aftermath of its disintegration was political and economic crisis in Europe and the collapse of the system of international economics which had, up to that time, prevailed.[28]

Every German who suffered hunger or poverty or business failure blamed it on reparations. They blamed the inflation of 1923 and the depression of 1929 on reparations. A. J. P. Taylor wrote:

> These views were not held merely by the German man-in-the-street. They were held just as strongly by the most distinguished financial and political experts. The campaign against "the slave treaty" hardly needed the prompting of extremist agitators. Every touch of economic hardship stirred the Germans to shake off "the shackles of Versailles."[29]

A third factor that made the rise of Hitler and the war possible was the Communist strategy of fighting the Social Democrats and collaborating with the Nazis within Germany, while later collaborating with Hitler in the destruction of Poland.

A fourth cause of war was the whole system of collective security or collective power embodied in the League of Nations. The league was the heir of the older balance-of-power system whose military alliances and counteralliances precipitated World War I. The purpose of both the old balance-of-power approach and that of the league was to preserve the status quo. This meant that the league was formed by the victorious nations after World War I for the purpose of keeping "bad" nations in their place. Germany by definition was the bad nation while the British and French were the leaders of the good side.

The realists dub the League of Nations a failure because the United States did not become a member. Actually, this had nothing to do with the failure. The league failed for the same reason that any other system based solely or chiefly

---

[28] Raymond Moley, *After Seven Years* (New York: Harper & Brothers, 1939), p. 69.
[29] Taylor, *The Origins of the Second World War*, p. 47.

on military power fails. Military alliances exist either to prevent change or to challenge the status quo by war.

In a rapidly changing world or in a world where serious injustices exist, there must be some machinery or provision for necessary social and political change. The experience prior to World War I and also World War II was one of no provision for orderly change in the political pattern, no matter how much justice demanded it. Munich is a demonstration of this very fact. The only way for change to take place was by threat of military occupation or war.

The existence of a power system to maintain the status quo or to enforce the "peace" is therefore a challenge to any seriously aggrieved nation or group of nations to try to upset it.

The typical view held by realists is that Hitler was an evil genius who caused the war. They fail to see that Hitler was a direct result of their own policies and of their own theology that saw evil as something that could be restrained by superior armed power. They mistakenly saw power as being neutral, with its use by status quo powers as being good and its use by challengers of the status quo as being bad. They failed to see that power aimed at the maintenance of superiority over others is always evil. Governmental and intergovernmental arrangements that have no basis in the consent of those governed or of those participating in the treaties or intergovernmental arrangements are inevitably doomed.

The league had failed long before Munich, yet Munich was the logical result of a system that thwarted change. The British and French were confronted with the necessity for change compounded from their own sense of guilt over Versailles and their desire to avoid war. They used power to preserve their own status quo at the expense of a weaker nation. The Czechs were excluded from the Munich conference and informed by Daladier that they had to accept the decision.

Munich, instead of being simply an unusual act of betrayal, was a logical extension of the whole power philosophy which finds other nations expendable if such seems necessary to preserve the privilege or power of one's own nation. Munich, for example, was not out of harmony with the decision of Prussia, Russia, and Austria in the late eighteenth century to partition Poland. "This bargain at Poland's expense," wrote Frederick Schuman, "was the means of preventing a general war threatened by Austrian resistance to Russian aggrandizement against the Turks in the Balkans. When Austria later made additional claims to Polish territory, Frederick objected. The balance of power was peaceably preserved by the extinction of the Polish State. . . ."[30]

No one suggests that British–French acquiescence in the seizure of Ethiopia was a result of weakness or pacifism. The British navy could have closed the Suez or stopped the transport of troops. The fact was that neither the British nor the French considered Ethiopia worth a war. In similar fashion, the Sudetenland was not considered worth a European war. The British–French alliance and the status quo, they believed, would continue more securely if Germany got the Sudetenland than if this remained a center of agitation.

Munich was not the cause of World War II. Nor was it a byproduct of weakness, failure of nerve, or a principled pacifism. Instead, it was at the time a logical aspect of the whole game of Realpolitik, or realism. It was Realpolitik, or the use of armed power from 1918 on, in the defense of a victors' "peace" that caused the war. It was the failure in time to eliminate the injustices of Versailles and the economic deprivation made obvious in the Great Depression that rendered World War II unpreventable. This failure, while disturbing to many Germans as well as to others, did not seem to them an immediate forerunner of war.

[30] Schuman, *International Politics*, p. 78.

6

WORLD WAR II:
ILLUSIONS AND REALITIES

THE SECOND WORLD WAR itself is now surrounded with myths, partly as a result of wartime propaganda, partly as a result of the illusions of those emotionally involved. These myths include the following: The war was fought to end dictatorship; it was fought to save the Jews; it was fought to prevent world conquest.

These, of course, were not the reasons that Britain, France, the Soviet Union, or the United States entered the war. Britain and the United States, for example, were quite willing to ally themselves with tyrants such as Stalin and Chiang Kai-shek. Britain and the United States insisted on an end to dictatorship only in Germany, Japan, and Italy, the three who lost the war. Both nations refrained from war with Spain, even though Spain, a dictatorship, supported Hitler and sent a "blue legion" to fight against Hitler's major European adversary. Both nations collaborated with dictator-led Portugal and with dictatorships in Latin America. Their policy in the postwar period has shown no evidence of change.

Neither was the war fought to save the Jews persecuted by Hitler. Jews had been made the scapegoat by the political leaders of Germany as early as 1933 to keep the workers and peasants from blaming their lot on the industrialists and landowners. A one-day boycott of Jewish business occurred on April 1, 1933. Later, Jews were excluded from the army, from the civil service, and certain other work. In September 1935, Jews were deprived of citizenship, and their children were

84

excluded from the public schools. The first nationwide pogrom began in November 1938. During this time, none of the wartime Allies threatened war or other drastic action against Germany because of Jewish persecution. Neither did those nations take steps to transport from Germany those Jews who had no resources with which to travel to countries that might have received them. The British government even announced on May 17, 1939 that it would restrict Jewish immigration in its Palestinian mandate to ten thousand per year for the next five years in order to appease the Arabs. When the war was over, the European Jews who survived, for the most part, found themselves unwelcome in the nations that had fought against Hitler.

The record of events shows that the persecution of the Jews was used to good propaganda advantage by Hitler's opponents, but was not a reason for Allied intervention against Germany in 1939 or for U.S. involvement in 1941.

Actually, the war aggravated the predicament of the Jews. Prior to the war the anti-Semitism of Hitler and the Nazi party had been clearly demonstrated, but there was no policy of extermination. That policy was put into effect only after the war began and all fear of public opposition in other countries had lost its importance. Hitler indicated in January 1939 that war would result in the destruction of the Jews in Europe, rather than the destruction of Germany. Also in January 1939, before the war began, Hitler had instructed Heydrich to eliminate the Jewish "problem" by evacuation or emigration. When the war began on September 1, 1939 with an attack on Poland, about a fourth of Germany's 500,000 Jews had already left Germany. On the third of September, Britain and France entered the war. Nine days later a conference was held in Hitler's railroad car at which a decision was made to exterminate the Jews. In 1941 Himmler gave orders to build the huge concentration camps in Auschwitz–Birkenau. Other extermination camps were set up in Belzec, Treblinka, Sobibor, and Maidanek. It was only after the United States had entered the war in December 1941 and Allied bombing of Germany was increased that the Nazis began the program of systematic extermination of Jews.[1] The Wannsee conference, called by Heydrich on January 20, 1942, systematized and coordinated the policy of extermination. In 1942, four gas chambers and crematories were installed in Maidanek, which had originally been established in the fall of 1941 as a prisoner-of-war camp. Beginning in 1942, Jews were sent from various places in Europe to Belzec, Maidanek, and Treblinka for extermination.[2]

Prewar Nazi actions against the Jews rightly aroused the condemnation of millions of people around the world. But no British, French, Russian, or American leader proposed war against Germany in 1939 because of the first major pogrom, just as no white nation has proposed war against the Union of South Africa because of her racial policies, and no one proposes war against the Soviet Union for her anti-Semitism, which has been well documented in recent years. The war preceded the extermination of the Jews. Therefore the extermination was not a cause of the war nor of American intervention. The war also preceded the mass indignation of most non-Jews around the world. It is therefore quite likely that much of the indignation in the United States was a consequence of wartime propaganda induced by a desire to find additional justification for a war that was thoroughly abhorred by the overwhelming majority of Americans prior to the Pearl Harbor attack.

Nor can it be maintained that the war was fought for freedom. None of the wartime Allies had war aims that included the freeing of India, Burma, Indonesia, Algeria, or numerous other colonies. Likewise freedom from dictatorship was not

[1] Frederick L. Schuman, *International Politics* (New York: McGraw-Hill, Inc., 1958), p. 353.

[2] For information on dates, places, and other details of Jewish persecution, see Walther Hofer, ed., *Der Nationalsozialismus*, Dokumente 1935–45 (Frankfurt am Main, 1947). Also Cecil Roth, ed., *The Standard Jewish Encylopedia* (Jerusalem: Massadah Publishing Co., 1958–59) pp. 261, 391, 1250, 1395, 1835. Also see "The Jewish Question" in Guenter Lewy, *The Catholic Church and Nazi Germany* (New York: McGraw-Hill, Inc., 1964).

planned. In fact, the British and American war leaders at Yalta made a decision to turn Eastern Europe into a sphere of influence for the Soviet Union, then under the harsh dictatorship of Stalin. When the Allies talked of freedom, they meant a Europe and Asia that would be dominated by themselves rather than by Germany or Japan. In other words, it was to be a world in which the British would be free to keep India, Burma, Malaysia, Nigeria, and other colonies in subjection, but the Germans would not be free to do the same in Europe or the Japanese in Asia. The United States would be free to extend its economic holdings and control into Europe and Asia only if a German and Japanese monopoly could be prevented.

The other chief myth was that Britain and the United States were fighting to prevent world conquest. There were those in Britain and the United States who believed this, but such a thesis would not stand rational examination then or now. A study launched in March 1942 at the suggestion of President Roosevelt and reported in the February 4, 1947 *New York Times* stated:

> It is now perfectly clear that the Axis countries had not planned adequately beyond their initial aggressive thrusts. Their objectives in beginning wars on either side of the world were limited.
> The German attacks on Austria, then Poland, were limited, distinct actions, as were those of Japan in her attacks first in Manchuria, then on China.

The *New York Times* added: "Thus it was found that German war production in 1939, 1940, and 1941 was 'surprisingly low' either compared with its ultimate level or the production by Great Britain and Russia. The Japanese production also was 'surprisingly low.'"

Neither Germany nor Japan had enough personnel singly or jointly to occupy Europe and Asia and still have any force left to invade the United States, to say nothing of Latin America and Africa. Resistance movements everywhere in Europe and Asia were tying down armies that would have been needed for any ambitious plan of "world conquest." Hitler was unable even to cross the English Channel in 1940 to invade England. In 1940 Hitler put out "peace feelers" to see whether, in return for ending the war between Britain and Germany, the British would agree to a return of the former German colonies and to German hegemony over Western Europe.[3]

All this was true before the attempted conquest of the Soviet Union. The conquest and occupation of an enormous land mass, such as the Soviet Union, had proved impossible for Napoleon and for Hitler and would necessarily be impossible for any medium-sized nation that had to maintain troops in a dozen other hostile nations.

It is one thing to conquer the armies of a dozen nations and quite another thing to try to maintain indefinite control over them by military occupation, as Germany was beginning to discover. Violent resistance in countries such as France and Yugoslavia and nonviolent resistance in Norway and Denmark tied down scores of thousands of men in armies that a nation the size of Germany could not afford to keep indefinitely on garrison duty in addition to keeping other armies at home. If, on top of Western Europe, Germany had had to try to occupy the Soviet Union, it should appear obvious to everyone that the task was beyond her capability. There is an exception to such an estimate: if there had been a Nazi internationale or a substantial group in each country prepared to collaborate with Germany while maintaining their own national identity, fewer troops would have been necessary. But this was not the case. In Norway and France, Quisling and Pétain were unable to restrain the resistance movements and unable to guarantee the collaboration of their governments without the presence of German troops.

While it is theoretically possible that Germany could have maintained a longer sway over Western Europe than Russia has been able to maintain over such countries in Eastern Europe as Yugoslavia and Rumania, it is quite unlikely that the nationalist forces everywhere evident in Europe would have collaborated for very long, even unwillingly, with a

[3] Schuman, *International Politics*, pp. 477, 478.

dominant Germany or that a nation the size of Germany could have dominated the world.

If these myths are not a sufficient basis for the Allied participation in the war in Europe and Asia, there must be another one or more that constitute the real basis.

The first and most obvious reason for the British–French declaration of war against Germany after Poland was invaded was the Chamberlain note of March 30, 1939, which guaranteed the independence of Poland. That note stated that if "any action were taken which clearly threatened their independence, and which the Polish Government accordingly felt obligated to resist with their national forces, His Majesty's Government and the French Government would at once lend them all the support in their power."

However, the reason for the note to Poland was to forestall a Polish alliance with Germany, which Hitler sought, and to strengthen the Polish resolve not to yield to any German demands for territory. The British, however, felt that Danzig was not crucial to Polish independence; and was in fact a Free City with its own administration. Moreover, it was populated chiefly by Germans and had been German prior to Versailles. The British had also hoped for a softening of the Polish attitude towards Russia so that some cooperation might be possible in the event of difficulty with Germany.

Poland, however, was strongly against any association with the Soviet Union and against yielding even Danzig to Hitler. The French, on the other hand, wanted an alliance with the Soviet Union. The British were prepared to have such an alliance only if it were for the purpose of defending Poland. The British did not want to go to war with Germany if she attacked Russia without attacking Poland or if in alliance with Poland.

After prolonged discussions involving the Soviet Union, no pact was signed. Russia finally, on August 22, signed an agreement with Germany for mutual nonaggression, which also excluded Germany from eastern Poland and the Baltic states. Shortly thereafter, the British signed a formal alliance with Poland. But the British were also negotiating with the

Germans to forestall war. The Germans agreed that a crisis could be averted if they could establish negotiations with Poland about the return of Danzig to Germany and about a plebiscite in the Polish Corridor between Germany and East Prussia. These were terms which the British and French had favored for a long time. The Poles, however, refused to send a plenipotentiary to Germany.

The British were angered at the Polish obstinacy in refusing even to accept the German proposals. Since the British position was known to Hitler, he thought he had successfully divided Poland from Britain. He had already called off an attack on Poland to permit negotiations. On August 31, he decided to attack. The Polish ambassador in the meantime offered to talk, but the Germans knew he had orders not to engage in negotiations on any specific matters. The next day the Germans attacked.

On September 3, the British delivered an ultimatum to Germany, and when it was ignored, went to war. The French followed suit.

The Second World War began, then, because territory that formerly belonged to Germany was demanded, because Poland would not consider a plebiscite or negotiations looking toward any other solution. In short, there was no machinery for changing the injustice of the Versailles treaty.

The war also began because Britain and France, who would have been willing to grant German demands, were unwilling to have those demands fulfilled by war. They were bound by a military alliance to Poland. There was, however, a further factor. The Chamberlain government would probably have fallen if it had not gone to war. The mood in Parliament had shifted to recognize that a German victory would make Germany the chief power in Europe. If that happened, the British and French empires, especially their dominance in Europe and around the world, would be in jeopardy. British and French policy had kept Germany in check for two decades. A powerful Germany could not be expected to continue to bow to British and French dominance.

The basic issue at this stage was set forth in President Roosevelt's plea of September 29 to Hitler:

> The question before the world today, Mr. Chancellor, is not the question of errors of judgment or of injustices committed in the past. It is the question of the fate of the world today and tomorrow. The world asks of us who at this moment are heads of the nations the supreme capacity to achieve the destinies of nations without forcing upon them as a price the mutilation and death of millions of citizens. . . .[4]

President Roosevelt headed a status quo power, a victor at Versailles. He opposed war as a means of changing the Versailles verdict, but did not have an answer to satisfy Hitler, whose overriding purpose was to eliminate the injustices of Versailles and the humiliation of Germany. It is possible to assert that the war was caused by Adolf Hitler; but it is also quite likely that if Roosevelt had come to power in Germany, he would not have acted as the leader of a status quo power, but instead would have been responsive to the pressures for change.

It is also possible to say that if one accepts the thesis that the Versailles treaty did create injustice, did dismember and humiliate Germany, and did saddle her with reparations and a peace imposed by her British and French rivals, Hitler's strategy for change was one of avoiding global war. His strategy succeeded at first in that Austria and Czechoslovakia fell without war. At that point Raoul Roussy de Sales' diary has an interesting entry on October 28, 1938:

> Lunched with Walter Lippmann the day before yesterday. We agree that Hitler has invented a new form of war, the psychological war, a kind of Kriegspiel replacing the battles in which people are killed or cannons are fired. Hitler is building an empire with new methods which have not yet been understood by his adversaries. . . .[5]

[4] U.S. Department of State, press release, October 1, 1938, quoted in John H. Latane and David W. Wainhouse, *A History of American Foreign Policy* (New York: Odyssey Press, Inc., 1940), pp. 981–2.

[5] Raoul de Roussy de Sales, *The Making of Yesterday* (New York: Reynal & Hitchcock, Inc., 1947), p. 10.

The record of events up to the British and French entry into the war reveals that Hitler did not contemplate either a world war or a military confrontation with the British and the French. He did not at first think of war with Poland. A. J. P. Taylor wrote: "The destruction of Poland had been no part of his original project. On the contrary, he had wished to solve the question of Danzig so that Germany and Poland could remain on good terms."[6]

The threat implied in the Anglo–Polish alliance, which included the French, seemed to be another step in the Versailles pattern of encirclement of Germany. It was a challenge Hitler could not ignore. On March 25, five days before the Chamberlain note to the Polish government, Hitler issued a directive: "The Führer does not wish to solve the Danzig question by force. He does not wish to drive Poland into the arms of Britain by this."[7]

Hitler acted finally against Poland only after he felt that the British and French would not enter the war and only after he had concluded a nonaggression treaty with Russia removing her as a possible belligerent. Until the Polish campaign, Hitler's policy apparently was one of limited conquests short of war. The Polish invasion was also considered a limited conquest. In other words, there was a rational basis for German actions, which is contrary to the usual assumption that Hitler was simply a madman and that a world war was precipitated by his irrationality. His aims were exactly the same as those of his opponents in the terms of Realpolitik and avoidance of outright war.

The suggestion that there was a rational basis for German actions on the international scene does not condone them or condone the irrational action against minorities within Germany. It is set forth in defense of a widely held thesis in international relations that there is no "devil" theory to explain the crises in world politics. It is set forth also as one more indication that evil is not incarnate in one man or in one na-

---

[6] A. J. P. Taylor, *The Origins of the Second World War* (New York: Atheneum, 1962), p. 216.
[7] Ibid., p. 210.

tion. International crises that have roots in twenty to one hundred years of history, that involve rival claims to power and the inflicting or suffering of injustice, are so complex that it is impossible to maintain a theory of sole war guilt. The British, French, Americans, Poles, Japanese, Russians, and others share in the political and moral responsibility of World War II.

Once the war had begun and German victories rolled up, the war aims of the Allies shifted from an effort to preserve British–French power to an effort to prevent German conquest of Europe. With the defeat of France a note of desperation entered the picture. The war aim of Britain was survival until stronger Allies could be involved. Then when the Atlantic Conference was held and Churchill knew that the United States was unofficially fighting Germany and would soon be officially involved after war with Japan was brought about, there was another shift in war aims. Churchill and Roosevelt discussed plans for an Anglo–American force to police the world. They thought in terms of an Anglo–American peace imposed on the world. The *New York Times* of December 19, 1945 described the strategy of the two leaders, as revealed before the congressional Pearl Harbor Committee, as involving "an international police force composed of the United States and Great Britain." Sumner Welles, former undersecretary of state who was present at the Atlantic conference, also said "that the President thought it wise to have no more than an 'ostensible' joining of the small powers in this enterprise." The Welles' memorandum stated: "The President said it would have to be recognized that it would be ostensible since none of the nations mentioned would have the practical means of taking any effective or, at least, considerable part in the task involved."

The *New York Times* added: "Indicating that Mr. Roosevelt, and presumably Mr. Churchill as well, had little thought that Russia would emerge from the war with the immense power which she acquired, Mr. Welles' notes on the point disclosed no reference to the Soviet Union in the postwar machinery for keeping the peace."

This was clearly administration-thinking about the postwar

world since Secretary of Navy Knox reiterated it in a major address October 1, 1941, before the American Bar Association. In his speech he referred to Great Britain and the United States as controlling the seas and to "the impulses in American and British hearts for the common good and the advancement of civilization. . . ." He indicated that the maintenance "of safety and security requires the establishment and maintenance of adequate bases throughout the western world." Continuing in the same realist approach to power that precipitated World War II, he said that this means "that the great law-abiding peace-loving nations must take the power into their own hands and keep it there for a long time. . . ." They must provide "the essential might to enforce such a peace on those who are not willing voluntarily to pursue such a course."

Knox here outlined the idea of a huge powerful status quo nation preserving the status quo or another victor's "peace."

When the United States actually entered the war, Prime Minister Churchill remarked that with the combined strength of Britain and America, "we could subdue everybody else in the world."[8]

A prominent English editor, F. A. Voigt, in the September 3, 1943 issue of the magazine *The Nineteenth Century and After* wrote that "England fought to preserve the balance [of power]—for that reason and no other. The commonly accepted view that Germany made war to dominate the world is, in our opinion, mistaken. She wanted to be a world power, but world power and world domination are not the same thing. . . ."

Voigt, who was often the spokesman of Lord Vansittart, Britain's influential permanent undersecretary for foreign affairs and an advocate before Munich of a strong stand against Germany, added in comment on British and American aims in the postwar scene:

[8] Winston Churchill, *The Grand Alliance* (Boston: Houghton Mifflin Company, 1950), p. 607.

The United States are, at present, chiefly concerned with the prospects of long-term investment. Their greatest interest is in South America and, after South America, in China. Europe and North Africa come only third. The result in Europe may be an Anglo–American economic rivalry. But this does not make conflict inevitable. Great Britain and the United States have a common interest in the economic development of Europe. . . .

Speaking of the middle zone in Europe, Voigt added: "It would also have an expanding production and an even higher standard of living. It would be a market for British and American exports and a field for British and American investment."

It was not only British and American government spokesmen who foresaw Anglo–American domination of the postwar world. There were influential businessmen and publicists who saw that the real aims of the war included a new American imperialism. Henry Luce, the publisher of *Time, Life,* and *Fortune,* stated editorially in the February 17, 1941 *Life* that America was in the war to obtain from it a dominant position in the world, with billions of dollars of profit from trade. He entitled his editorial "The American Century."

The president of the National Industrial Conference Board, Virgil Jordan, on December 10, 1940, told the Investment Bankers Association of America:

Our government has committed the American community to participation in this war as the economic ally of England, and as her spiritual, if not her political, partner in her struggle with the enemies of the British Empire everywhere in the world, to help prevent, if possible, their destruction of the Empire, and if this should not be possible, to take her place as the heir and residuary legatee or receiver for whatever economic and political assets of the Empire survive her defeat. . . .

Whatever the outcome of the war, America has embarked upon a career of imperialism, both in world affairs and in every other aspect of her life, with all the opportunities, responsibilities and perils which that implies. . . . At best, England will become a junior partner in a new Anglo–Saxon imperialism, in which the economic resources and the military and naval strength of the United States will be the center of gravity. Southward in our hemisphere and westward in the

Pacific the path of empire takes its way, and in modern terms of economic power as well as political prestige, the sceptre passes to the United States.

. . . We may be afraid of the unfamiliar and forbidding word, imperialism, in connection with the commitment we have made. We may prefer, in the current American fashion, to disguise it in a vague phrase like, "hemisphere defense."[9]

Any ethical appraisal of the Second World War must ignore the propaganda designed to persuade the common people to support the real war aims. This propaganda is still being used by realists to support the world-wide American imperialism that has resulted from World War II.

In its crudest sense, World War II was fought to determine whether Germany should be dominant in Europe, and Japan in Asia, or whether Britain and the United States should be dominant throughout most of the world. Hitler wanted Germany to dominate Europe while eliminating the internal threat of political forces hostile to Nazism. Hitler's internal foes were the "internationalists" who maintained ties with the Soviet Union or with their fellow workers in France and other countries. When the Nazis established concentration camps in Germany immediately after Hitler came to power in 1933, the first occupants were the active opponents of Nazism, especially the leaders of the Socialist and Communist parties.[10]

Sometimes it is asserted that Hitler's actions were not conditioned by political realities or that he simply followed a program for world conquest set forth in *Mein Kampf*. Even in *Mein Kampf* Hitler considered England and Italy as possible partners in his goals and directed his chief venom against France and the Soviet Union. Hitler was also subject to the same power realities as others and could not with the limited German manpower dominate even temporarily much more than France and the smaller countries relatively close to Germany.

Japan, with her slogan of Asia for Asians, obviously wanted

[9] "War Aims in War Propaganda," *Propaganda Analysis*, March 27, 1941.
[10] Roth, *Standard Jewish Encyclopedia*, p. 391.

to emulate the earlier policy of the United States proclaimed in the Monroe Doctrine. But she also wanted to secure the British, French, and Dutch holdings in Asia while those empires were involved in what seemed like a losing war in Europe.

It is no defense of German and Japanese foreign or domestic policies to criticize the aims of their opponents. One of the mistakes of those who always support their nation's wars is to assume that criticism of their government's war policy is necessarily a defense of the enemy's position. It is essential to realize that war itself is the enemy and that the Second World War in Europe was a continuation of the First. It is necessary also to realize that Hitler was not the creator of war so much as he was the demagogue who capitalized on and headed the military, industrial, and nationalist forces that resented German defeat in World War I, the subsequent disarmament of Germany, the growth of Marxism, the hegemony of Britain and France, war reparations, and the economic crisis that began in 1929. The Hitler Youth and many of the older Germans looked forward to a new day in Europe when the shackles of Versailles would be broken and Germany would take the leadership in Europe. The Nazis even referred to their movement as *Deutsche Volkische Freiheits Bewegung* (German People's Movement for Freedom) because they thought in terms of freedom from the Treaty of Versailles, including reparations and foreign domination. That their program was not genuine liberation has been emphasized in numerous other books. It is therefore not necessary here to trace in detail the internal causes of German or Japanese war programs.

There is need, however, for a reevaluation of American power aims for entering the war, as contrasted with the altruistic claims that we entered to defeat the diabolical aims of Germany and Japan. Far from being a war fought for idealistic aims, the Second World War was a realist war fought to maintain and enhance the power of the economically dominant world powers. Of course, the fact that Germany and

Japan were totalitarian rather than liberal democracies permitted the myth that the war was fought for freedom, if one closed one's mind to the alliances with Stalin and Chiang Kai-shek.

Motivation, while important, should not be considered apart from the consequences of the war. If the war was fought to end authoritarian or totalitarian governments, the existence of such governments in Russia, China, Spain, Portugal, Eastern Europe, Southeast Asia, and Latin America indicates that the method did not accomplish the result. The United States itself adopted peacetime military conscription, a restriction on freedom hitherto employed by Germany and Japan, and then forced it on other postwar European countries. Germany and Japan were rearmed when regional military alliances were organized against Russia and China, the only nations capable of disrupting American world hegemony. In various ways Germany and Japan paid for American victory. Germany was dismembered as a result of war or postwar decisions and was forced to pay for the U.S. army of occupation. Korea passed from Japanese control to Russian and American control. Formosa, formerly Japanese, became a U.S. satellite ruled by a dictator.

Economically or militarily, United States' interests now occupy most of the countries in Western Europe and Asia once invaded by Germany and Japan and have also brought a number of former British and French colonies into the American orbit. The real war aims of American imperialism and world hegemony were thus to a large degree accomplished, even though they could be achieved only by a method consistent with the exploitation and destruction of millions of people.

7

POSTWAR PLANNING

DURING THE SECOND WORLD WAR there was extensive planning for the American world role after the war. One key aspect of this was a large military establishment that could, as Roosevelt and Knox had suggested, police the world. An expanded military establishment, top officers felt, would require some form of postwar military conscription. Accordingly, in July and August of 1944, a group of officers involved in the wartime planning were assigned to, and "spent most of their time" in, planning and "drafting legislation for compulsory military training."[1]

Shortly thereafter, a Citizens' Committee for Universal Military Training of Young Men was organized on Wall Street by persons who were prominent in industrial and financial circles. Secretary of War Stimson sent a letter of endorsement to this committee and also enlisted the support of the American Legion. At approximately the same time, James Forrestal, who had been president of the large investment banking firm of Dillon Read Company before entering Roosevelt's wartime administration, organized in 1944 the National Security Industrial Association. This was a group of industrial firms with substantial military contracts whom Forrestal brought together in order to ensure that "American business will remain close to the services."

Charles E. Wilson, president of General Electric, in an address to the Army Ordnance Association in January 1944,

[1] Roscoe S. Conkling, *The Case Against Compulsory Military Training* (New York: Post War World Council, 1945).

had already suggested an alliance between industry and the military and a permanent war economy which, in order to be successful, had to have a long term of continuing state of emergency as its base. He stated:

> First of all such a program must be the responsibility of the federal government. It must be initiated and administered by the executive branch—by the President as Commander-in-Chief and by the War and Navy Departments. . . . Of equal importance is the fact that this must be, once and for all, a continuing program and not the creature of an emergency. In fact one of its objects will be to eliminate emergencies so far as possible. The program must be insured and supported by the Congress. Industry's role in this program is to respond and cooperate . . . in the execution of the part allotted to it; industry must not be hampered by political witchhunts, or thrown to the fanatical isolationist fringe tagged with a "merchants of death" label.[2]

Wilson, however, doubted that the country would sustain such a program unless it were begun during the war. "The revulsion against war not too long hence will be an almost insuperable obstacle for us to overcome . . . and for that reason I am convinced that we must begin now to set the machinery in motion."

The war ended before peacetime conscription was adopted. Just two months before the wartime draft was due to end, Truman's secretary of state, James Byrnes, and secretary of war, Robert Patterson, appealed to Congress to renew it. In doing so they referred to the Russian refusal to withdraw Soviet troops from Iran according to wartime agreement. The State Department went so far as to indicate that Soviet armies were moving into Iran towards Teheran and also towards the Turkish border. On several occasions Byrnes or Truman insisted that conscription was needed "to prevent conflict in the Middle East."[3]

Actually, Soviet troops had not moved out of the Soviet area in Iran. Frederick Kuh, writing from London, reported

[2] Charles E. Wilson, "For the Common Defense," *Army Ordnance Magazine*, March–April 1944, p. 287.
[3] *New York Times*, March 22, April 7, May 17, 1946.

March 16, 1946 in the *Chicago Sun*: "British authorities have admitted there is no evidence whatever indicating that Red Army forces have moved beyond the Soviet area in Iran." A *New York Times* dispatch of March 21, 1946 from Berlin by C. L. Sulzberger said: "Certain diplomats believe that this crisis may have been deliberately seized upon by the United States Government to crystallize public opinion. . . ." Sulzberger added:

> The momentum of pro-Soviet feeling worked up during the war to support the Grand Alliance had continued too heavily after the armistice. This made it difficult for the Administration to carry out the stiffer diplomatic policy required now. For that reason, these observers believe, a campaign was worked up to attain a better psychological balance of public opinion to permit the Government to adopt a "harder line."

There was clearly a crisis for Iran, since the Soviet Union wanted to extend its influence and control into Iran. The case was taken to the United Nations, but while it was pending on the Security Council agenda and under real pressure from the council, Iran and the Soviet Union concluded an agreement for the evacuation of Soviet troops and the establishment of a joint Iranian–Russian oil company which would give the Soviet Union control of the company for the first twenty-five years of a fifty-year concession and equal control for the next twenty-five years. The agreement was signed April 4, 1946. After Russian troops had been withdrawn and Iranian troops had moved into the area evacuated by the Soviet Union, the Iranian Parliament refused to ratify the oil agreement.

Throughout the crisis there was no evidence that the United States planned to send a military force to Iran or otherwise risk war with the Soviet Union. Instead of using a military threat to induce Russia to withdraw, the United States and Britain relied on diplomacy and the mobilization of world public opinion. In the United States, however, the Iranian crisis was used to frighten the American people to get conscription. The draft extension was never needed since voluntary enlistments kept the Army at its authorized strength, and in March 1947, was not renewed by Congress.

In the meantime, it had become apparent in leading political, financial, and military circles in the United States that Great Britain was too weak to exercise her former influence or even maintain order at certain key points that had always been vital to British interests. Winston Churchill, on March 5, 1946, in an address at Fulton, Missouri, had urged an Anglo–American alliance to oppose the Soviet Union and liberate Eastern European peoples.

Churchill was countered by Secretary of Commerce Henry Wallace, who on September 12 asserted publicly in New York, "We should recognize that we have no more business in the political affairs of Eastern Europe than Russia has in the political affairs of Latin America, Western Europe, and the U.S.A." Wallace also said, "We must not allow national oil rivalries to force us into war."

In a letter to President Truman on July 23 he urged that the United States try to solve its problem with Russia by friendly action, such as a reconstruction loan, the sending of a trade mission, and a mutual effort to deal with long-term Soviet economic problems. He also said in the letter, which was made public on September 17, 1946:

> We should make an effort to counteract the irrational fear of Russia which is being systematically built up in the American people by certain individuals and publications. The slogan that communism and capitalism, regimentation and democracy, cannot continue to exist in the same world is, from a historical point of view, pure propaganda. . . . This country was for the first half of its national life a democratic island in a world dominated by absolutist governments.

A few days later, under pressure from Secretary of State Byrnes, the *New York Times*, and Congressional leaders, the President asked on September 20, 1946 for Wallace's resignation.

Then on March 12, 1947, President Truman announced, in what became known as the Truman Doctrine, that "it must be the policy of the United States to support free peoples who are resisting attempted subjugation by armed minorities or by outside pressure."

The occasion for the announcement to Congress was the decision by the British government, conveyed to the State Department on February 24, 1947, that on March 31 the British army would leave Greece and the British would cease their responsibility for that country. In Greece there had been widespread destruction by the war which was followed by a civil war between Communist-led guerrillas and right-wing forces.

President Truman could have extended economic aid, as he did and appealed to the United Nations. He could also have tried through diplomatic channels to enlist the support of the Soviet Union before announcing a policy so drastic. Or he could have assisted the Greek government while encouraging basic social change. Instead, he chose to announce a far-reaching policy of antagonism to the Soviet Union, stating that "nearly every nation must choose between alternative ways of life." He also laid down the policy that the United States would suppress armed revolution everywhere in the world—or at least everywhere that Communists might be suspected as being involved. In effect he allied the United States with status quo groups, however reactionary, so long as their opponents were either Communists or armed revolutionaries.

D. F. Fleming in his monumental two-volume work, *The Cold War and Its Origins*, describes the alternate plans available for dealing with the Greek situation, such as that of the Food and Agriculture Organization of the United Nations whose report set forth "a complete plan for beginning Greek rehabilitation, the real antidote to Communism." He also refers to the way Truman stood by while Churchill, contrary to republican sentiment in Greece, restored the reactionary monarch King George II to power, one of the factors that aggravated the situation Truman presumably wanted to correct.[4]

[4] D. F. Fleming, *The Cold War and Its Origins, 1917–1950* (Garden City, N.Y.: Doubleday & Company, Inc., 1961), Vol. 1, pp. 451–2.

Some senators addressed a series of questions to the State Department about the Truman Doctrine, one of which was: "How can America ask Russia to retire within its own national boundaries if America has no intention of remaining within her own?"[5]

At the time there were a number of persons who assumed that the American interest in Greece and Turkey was an interest in the Near East and its oil, that the Russians were interested in the Turkish Straits, and that the United States had to block any future efforts that Russia might make to control them. Others felt that the United States could have proposed the internationalization of the straits and of other strategic waterways, such as the Panama and Suez canals.

In any event the President chose to disregard other solutions and, at the outset of the Moscow Conference of Foreign Ministers, announced to Congress in the "Truman Doctrine" speech the beginning of the Cold War and of American world hegemony.

D. F. Fleming indicates that some action was essential if the danger of Communism filling the Greek political vacuum was to be averted, but that our declaration of support and our economic aid did not have to be anti-Communist and anti-Russian so as to declare "global political war." He adds: "Russia's satellites were helping the communist-led rebels in Greece, but Moscow gave no sign of throwing decisive strength into that struggle."[6]

While President Truman was announcing his doctrine, General George C. Marshall, who had been appointed secretary of state about two and a half months earlier, was representing the United States at the Moscow Conference of Foreign Ministers. The *New York Times* of April 30, 1947 described Marshall's presence at the conference in these terms:

> In the entire six weeks of the Moscow conference, however, Gen. Marshall apparently did not unbend. He was as rigid as the Washington Monument . . . though there were many outstanding questions between the United States and Russia and

[5] Ibid., p. 458.
[6] Ibid., p. 469.

the United States and Britain, he apparently made no effort to talk out these problems. . . .

The Army in the meantime, frustrated by the lapse of peacetime conscription, launched a nationwide campaign of fear. Colonel William Neblett, who was serving in the Pentagon at a high staff level and later served as national president of the Reserve Officers Association of the United States, described this campaign. He said: "The Pentagon line was that we were living in a state of undeclared emergency; that war with Russia was just around the corner, and that the safety of the nation was dependent on the speedy rebuilding of the lower ranks of Army, Navy, and Air with the Pentagon form of UMT."[7]

He added: "I know from my own knowledge of the men who worked up the fear campaign that they do not believe what they say. Their propaganda has always had the single objective to build a huge conscript professional military force of 10,000,000 men under the command of a professional General Staff."[8]

About the same time, the Marshall Plan for European recovery was being readied. There were apparently a number of motives for it. One was the need to provide Europe with aid so that thereafter she would be in a better position to buy products from the United States. Under-secretary of State Acheson had earlier noted that our exports were twice the amount of our imports and that other countries had to get dollars from somewhere to be able to pay the difference.[9] Another motivation was altruistic, to help a Europe that was destroyed by war. This was the moving factor in church support for the program.

The third motivation fit into the Truman Doctrine of cold war and containment. The Army wanted military allies and bases in Western Europe but knew that Europe had been so exhausted by World War II that no alliance was possible in

[7] William H. Neblett, *Pentagon Politics* (New York: Pageant Press, 1953), pp. 44–6.
[8] Ibid.
[9] Fleming, *The Cold War and Its Origins, 1917–1950*, p. 477.

her present state. One news commentator wrote at the time about the fear held "by our foreign policy makers that the Western Europeans would seek to declare themselves neutral in event of war between the world's two giants." He referred to the "clamor in Britain, France and the Lowlands for a neutral status, similar to that enjoyed by Eire during the late war and against granting the United States bases should conflict occur." He added that "by helping those countries to build up their economy, health, trade, and business and improve their living conditions, our policy makers believe a fighting spirit can be regained."[10]

Military spokesmen, such as Secretary of Defense James Forrestal and Secretary of the Army Kenneth Royall, told Congress on January 15 "that if the United States did not go through with the Marshall Plan for European recovery, it would be forced to spend an equal or greater amount of money on military preparedness."[11]

At first the military considered the Marshall Plan and conscription separate measures, but in March 1948, began to link them as "companion measures." When congressional reluctance to adopt them was apparent, the Army handed President Truman an intelligence report which portrayed "the Soviet Army as on the move" toward Western Europe.[12] The army war scare led to predictions that there would be "war before the harvest."[13] On the basis of this war scare, President Truman addressed a joint emergency session of both Houses of Congress on March 17, 1948 and asked for the immediate passage of the Marshall Plan, Selective Service, and Universal Military Training.

The Czechoslovakian Communist party's seizure of power a few weeks earlier seemed to lend substance to the Army intelligence report. But the Central Intelligence Agency within the week evaluated the Army's report as false. No report, how-

---

[10] Cecil Dickson, *Albany Knickerbocker News,* May 1, 1948.
[11] *St. Louis Post–Dispatch,* January 15, 1948.
[12] *Chicago Tribune,* June 9, 1948.
[13] Hanson Baldwin, *New York Times,* December 2, 1948.

ever, was made to the American people to dispel the idea of imminent war.[14]

In this climate of crisis, Congress adopted the Marshall Plan and Selective Service. *The U.S. News and World Report* on May 14, 1948 described the official manipulation in these words:

> President Truman is somewhat disturbed by the way the idea of imminent war with Russia hangs on in the country even after the official line has changed from war scares to more emphasis upon the prospect of peace.
>
> Gen. Omar Bradley, Army Chief of Staff, was out of step with the Government's new policy when he expressed the opinion that war prospects had risen in recent days. Both at the White House and in the State Department there is a backing away from that attitude now that the Marshall Plan is law. . . .
>
> War scares, encouraged by high officials only a few weeks ago, so alarmed the 144,000,000 U.S. public that top planners now are having to struggle hard to keep Congress from pouring more money into national defense than the Joint Chiefs of Staff regard as wise or necessary. It is proving more difficult to turn off than to turn on a war psychology.

Meanwhile, the Anglo–American Joint Chiefs of Staff had been taking steps to form a military alliance of countries on the English Channel to be known as the Western European Union. American military leaders, in conjunction with their Western European counterparts, then began discussions and joint planning for a larger alliance which would include Canada and the United States as well as Belgium, France, Luxembourg, the Netherlands, Italy, Portugal, Ireland, Denmark, Norway, and the United Kingdom. The treaty which authorized NATO was signed in Washington, April 4, 1949.

Although it might have been possible for the Soviet Union to accept the Marshall Plan as nonhostile, given its moderate wording and surface intent, the Truman Doctrine plus the linking of the Marshall Plan with an expanded armaments program in the context of talk of war with Russia made Soviet cooperation impossible.

[14] John M. Swomley, Jr., *The Military Establishment* (Boston: Beacon Press, 1964), pp. 64-5.

The Marshall Plan, peacetime conscription, and NATO, taken together, made technically possible the new global American empire which had been implicit in American planning since the German and Japanese expansion precipitated the showdown. There were three facets to this program. The first is well known as the containment of Communism so that the area in which "free enterprise" was forbidden would be sharply limited.

The second was the discouragement of democratic socialism in Western Europe. D. F. Fleming reports that "the conservative American businessmen who in the main managed the E.C.A. Program [the Marshall Plan] used their influence to discourage social reform." He added that "the effect of our economic intervention in Europe has been not only to oust the communists from the governments but to put the socialists out or decrease their influence," even though the *New York Herald Tribune* of January 14, 1948 rightly called democratic socialism "our strongest ally in Europe."[15]

The third is the growth of American investments overseas. After NATO had been established and the Marshall Plan had gotten well under way, American capital moved into Europe in a big way. Between 1950 and the summer of 1965, direct American investments (plants and equipment) in Europe reached a total of more than $12 billion, according to *Fortune*, "a 360 percent increase in only ten years' time."[16] By 1969 it exceeded $18 billion.[17]

In the Britsh islands, U.S. firms had a direct investment "estimated at $5,200,000,000 in 1965"[18] and $7 billion in 1969.[19] In Italy, the direct investments of U.S. business in-

[15] Fleming, *The Cold War and Its Origins, 1917–1950*, p. 501.

[16] Richard Austin Smith, "Nationalism Threatens U.S. Investment," *Fortune*, August 1965, p. 126.

[17] "How U.S. Industry Is Remaking the World," *U.S. News and World Report*, October 27, 1969, p. 58.

[18] James Reston, *Kansas City Times*, December 2, 1966.

[19] "How U.S. Industry Is Remaking the World," *U.S. News and World Report*, October 27, 1969, p. 58.

creased, from 1950 to 1965, 150 percent to $800 million,[20] but by 1969, totaled more than $1.2 billion.[21]

In France, American manufacturers' direct investment continued to rise, as it did elsewhere. In 1965, the estimated direct investments were $243 million; in 1966, $286 million; and in 1967, $345 million. At first the French government tried to prevent new American industry from buying or building plants in France. "Having failed to persuade her partners in the Common Market to adopt a common policy on restriction of American investments," said the *New York Times* of January 16, 1967, "France decided that her own barriers were futile. [For example,] an auto plant built just outside her own borders will by July 1, 1968 be able to sell its output in France without tariff barriers—while France loses out on the employment and tax revenue offered by the new plant."

A French writer in the April 1966 *Foreign Affairs* wrote that the danger of war inherent in Stalinist postwar policy has largely disappeared. "In contrast the economic invasion by the United States is a clear and present danger." He referred to the size of American investments in Europe and the power of American big business as "the beginning of the colonization of our economy." After indicating how France's only large electronics firm had passed "into the hands of General Electric which competes on the world market with another American firm, I.B.M.," he added, "thenceforth the centers of decision in a vital sector, not only in the economic sense but for the national defense, were no longer in France but in the United States."[22]

There is a correlation between the rapid growth of U.S. investments overseas and the presence of American troops.

[20] Richard Austin Smith, "Nationalism Threatens U.S. Investment," *Fortune*, August 1965, p. 126.
[21] "How U.S. Industry Is Remaking the World," *U.S. News and World Report*, October 27, 1969, p. 60.
[22] Gaston Defferre, "DeGaulle and After," *Foreign Affairs*, April 1966, pp. 440-1.

Business Week in 1959 described the military–economic base for these investments:

> . . . the economic cards still are stacked somewhat in favor of Western Europe and Japan. A good part of the gold and dollars being accumulated today in these areas comes from U.S. military expenditures—troop pay and local procurement for U.S. forces stationed in Western Europe and Japan. . . . For U.S. investors abroad, whether they have put money into European stocks or into production facilities in Western Europe or Japan, the new business boom abroad provides a pleasant prospect. In fact, it probably will lead to still further investment in these areas, both direct and portfolio.[23]

The United States has maintained more than three hundred thousand troops in Western Europe where NATO has been operating. Prior to 1950, the largest U.S. investments were in Latin America and Canada. The Canadian portion remained the same at the end of 1965, the Latin American proportion had decreased, but the European investments had almost doubled.

In Japan, where approximately fifty thousand American troops have been stationed, U.S. direct private investments at the end of 1965 totalled $676 million, according to the U.S. Department of Commerce,[24] but Fortune magazine asserts that they may be three times this amount, since the Department of Commerce uses book value rather than market value for such American investments overseas.[25] "Over 400 U.S. companies are now doing business in Japan. . . ."[26]

In Taiwan, where the United States has had about fifty thousand troops, now only ten thousand, about five hundred American manufacturers are doing business and the First National City Bank of New York and the Bank of America

[23] "Booming Free World Sets Pace For U.S.," Business Week, October 17, 1959, pp. 28, 30.

[24] Overseas Business Report, October 1966 (OBR 66–70) U.S. Dept. of Commerce, Washington, D.C.

[25] "The Business Globe," Fortune, October 1956, p. 93.

[26] "How U.S. Industry Is Remaking the World," U.S. News and World Report, October 27, 1969, p. 60.

have established branches to handle U.S. trade.[27] By the end of 1967, American investments reached $130 million, chiefly in electronics, chemicals, and petrochemicals.[28] "Americans lead the investment" in Taiwan said the July 6, 1968 *Business Week* and the Taiwan government has "received more than $4 billion in American military and economic assistance" over the past fifteen years. According to the same source, U.S. military spending has accounted for 5 percent of the island's gross national product. But "the fact Taiwan is effectively buffered from Red China by the U.S. Seventh Fleet," says *Business Week,* is what "makes it attractive to skittish investors." The net result is that U.S. military activity has had a decisive effect on Taiwan's economy.

In Korea, where the United States maintains a force of about fifty thousand, there were twenty-five American companies with investments of $41 million in 1965. In 1966, over one hundred American companies sent agents to South Korea to investigate investment possibilities.[29] Cotton textile manufacturing is the largest Korean industry. The Korean Cotton Textiles Export Association indicated that they "are required to buy raw cotton . . . only from the U.S.A. . . . all of the imported cotton comes from the United States. In 1967 Korea was able to import 387,814 bales of American cotton, costing $41,310,000 . . . and 49,000 bales of usual marketing requirement raw cotton, costing $6,370,000 from the U.S.A."[30]

The first American soldiers in Thailand were few in number when they arrived in 1950. By May 1968, they numbered forty-seven thousand. Major U.S. government construction projects, chiefly air force bases, a new seaport, and a highway system, have cost about $1 billion. There has been a corresponding increase in U.S. firms doing business in Thailand in the period following World War II from a handful to

[27] *New York Times,* January 20, 1967.
[28] Ibid., January 19, 1968.
[29] Ibid., January 20, 1967.
[30] Ibid., January 19, 1968.

about one hundred American corporations and affiliates in 1967.[31]

U.S. business investments in Thailand were thirteen times greater in 1969 than they were in 1961 and are still growing. [32]

The little nation of Singapore has a total American investment of about $100 million which *Fortune* calls the largest influx of new investment from any nation.[33]

Asian investments have been growing steadily but are well behind Europe, Canada, and Latin America. On a world basis, between 1958 and 1968 U.S. manufacturers expanded their overseas capacity 71 percent compared with 72 percent in the United States, but the biggest share of such expansion will continue to be in Western Europe as it has been in 'the last 20 years.'[34]

A major portion of the income produced from such overseas investments returns to the United States. "Repatriated dividends and interest, together with royalties and management fees," said the National Industrial Conference Board, "amounted to 76.1 percent of the income earned in all industries in 1965." This means that about $4 billion returned to the United States. The total earned income from all U.S. direct investments abroad amounted to 60.8 percent of the total U.S. private investment in 1965.[35]

This growth in American investments overseas, or U.S. economic imperialism as it can be called, seems to be directly related to the cold war against the Soviet Union. Every evidence of Russian extension of influence into other countries was used to authenticate claims in the United States that the Soviet Union was intent on world conquest. These claims, however, were used to justify an American effort to assert

[31] *Christian Science Monitor,* October 12, 1967.
[32] John Deedy, "News and Views," *Commonweal,* September 26, 1969, p. 578.
[33] Peter Simms and Rush Loving, Jr., "New Tides in an Island Nation," *Fortune,* August 15, 1969, p. 82.
[34] "More Capital Goes Abroad," *Business Week,* August 9, 1969, p. 38.
[35] *Roadmaps of Industry,* no. 1558, November 15, 1966.

world control since the only way to thwart Soviet power, according to realist theory, was to preempt it with American power. Since the United States had the capability and the Soviet Union did not, it was American economic power and U.S. military garrisons around the world that established an effective American world hegemony. But the cold war is not the only reason for the increase in American business investments overseas. The federal government has established the U.S. Agency for International Development (AID). This agency guarantees American investors overseas up to 100 percent against losses they suffer through war, expropriation, insurrection, and currency inconvertibility. AID also guarantees investments up to 75 percent for other losses, including ordinary commercial failure.

There has been direct influence by American businessmen in the formulation of U.S. military and governmental policy. Such financial and industrial leaders as James Forrestal, Douglas Dillon, Nelson Rockefeller, John Foster Dulles, Averill Harriman, Robert A. Lovett, Charles E. Wilson, and William H. Draper have had a virtual monopoly on key government positions in the State, Defense, and Treasury Departments.

Business leaders who do not occupy government posts have also had tremendous influence on government policy. The Business Council, which is an overall group of corporate executives and board chairmen, has direct access to key government figures. A *New York Times* dispatch said:

> Most of the Council members have had extended personal dealings with [Lyndon] Johnson and they feel he respects and understands them. . . . The Council's role as consultant to the Government has expanded enormously since Johnson has been President and is continuing to expand.[36]

Business influence upon Congress was evident also in the testimony in 1960 of business leaders before the Senate Government Operations Subcommittee. Thomas J. Watson, Jr.,

[36] *Kansas City Times*, October 24, 1966.

head of the International Business Machines Corporation, told the committee: "We are in a critical contest with the Soviet Union. Therefore, we must be willing to accept any sacrifices necessary to win." Watson asked that public discussion of defense matters be limited with debate on controversial subjects remaining behind closed doors. He added, "I do not agree with people who suggest that we must not push our economy to any point necessary in competing with the Soviet. . . ."[37] Other business leaders appeared before the same committee to ask for greater sacrifices to deal with the Russians. They were Robert A. Lovett, former secretary of defense, and Robert C. Sprague, a former presidential adviser on security.[38]

Watson's International Business Machines system operates in eighty-seven countries and has nineteen foreign manufacturing plants. It was ranked thirty in the top fifty military prime contractors in the fiscal year 1968, and in the fiscal year 1969, it was twenty-seventh in the list of top military prime contractors, with a total of $257 million.[39]

Many of these business interests are directly involved in promoting the cold war and formulating cold war policy. The Crusade for Freedom and its affiliate Radio Free Europe, which operates the largest radio stations in Europe, are joint CIA–big business enterprises. Each of its ten directors is a major Wall Street figure.[40]

Business leaders also serve on the Foreign Intelligence Advisory Board which is given detailed information about the CIA's plans and procedures, information which is not made available to the Senate Foreign Relations Committee.[41]

Early in the cold war, Charles E. Wilson of the General

[37] *New York Times*, February 26, 1960.
[38] Ibid.
[39] "Defense: Who Pulled in the Big Ones," *Business Week*, November 8, 1969, p. 130.
[40] Victor Perlo, *The Empire of High Finance* (New York: International Publishers Company, Inc., 1957), p. 305.
[41] Richard J. Barber, "The New Partnership: Big Government and Big Business," *New Republic*, August 13, 1966.

Electric Company, who also served as Defense Mobilization Director, commended the Newspaper Publishers' Association for their cooperation in printing

> millions of words laying down the premise . . . that the free world is in mortal danger. . . . If the people were not convinced of that it would be impossible for Congress to vote the vast sums now being spent to avert that danger. . . . With the support of public opinion as marshalled by the press, we are off to a good start. But the mobilization job cannot be completed unless such support is continuous. . . . It is our job—yours and mine—to keep our people convinced that the only way to keep disaster away from our shores is to build America's might.[42]

The predictions made during World War II of American world control, of the United States falling heir to the British Empire and becoming the world policeman, have come true. These predictions, of course, did not take into account the possibility of a powerful postwar Russia or of China's passing under Communist control. There have been many other unintended consequences of World War II, such as the development of nuclear power, the cold war, the Korean War, the destruction of the British, French, and Dutch empires, the economic prosperity of Japan and West Germany, the war in Vietnam, the development of Israel, and Arab–Israeli tensions.

The intended consequences of American world dominance, or, as some prefer to call it, "leadership," could not of course have been outlined in detail prior to the war. It was assumed that the British and other empires would probably continue, that China would remain in friendly hands, and that Germany, Japan, and the Soviet Union would be no obstacle to Anglo–American world hegemony. Everywhere except in the Soviet Union it was assumed that American industrial, financial, and military power in collaboration with the British or as successor to the British would be decisive.

The growth of Soviet power in the postwar world was in part a problem for U.S. dominance and in part a foil by which to extend U.S. dominance. The cold war and the alleged threat of Soviet world control made it politically and "morally" possible for the United States to extend its power into various parts of the world to "forestall" Communist power. The Soviet Union made it possible for the American people to accept peacetime conscription, NATO and other military alliances, the military–industrial complex, and the huge taxation required to meet its demands.

The consequence of World War II and the cold war, however, was not Soviet control, as cold war propaganda steadily asserted, but American control. Nearly half of the 3.407 million in the armed forces of the United States were overseas in 1969. The Pentagon maintains some military presence in at least sixty-eight foreign countries and has four hundred thirty-two major military installations overseas. Of these, forty-eight are in Japan, which is not threatened by any other nation. The United States also maintains centers for training personnel from the United States and other countries in counterrevolutionary warfare. The American navy patrols every ocean, and there are military missions on every continent. The American business community is the decisive economic factor in country after country around the world.

The consequences as well as the intent of American realists who planned and promoted and provided the intellectual rationale of the American power role are essentially imperialistic. They have used the whole problem of Communism as a foil for the development of a Pax Americana and a foreign policy that suppresses social change.

8

ORIGINS OF THE COLD WAR

COMMUNISM AND CAPITALISM are both dynamic. Communists want to see the spread of Communism to other countries, just as American businessmen want to see the philosophy of free enterprise accepted everywhere. Communism, however, is not simply a philosophy or an economic system; it exists in nation–states as well. The Soviet Union does not exist to promote Communism, though it frequently does so. There are Russian national interests which sometimes fit into and sometimes jeopardize efforts to spread Communist influence into other countries.

The existence of Communism in the Soviet Union and China has in fact served the interests of those realists who want to promote American world hegemony. They have tended to explain Soviet and Chinese foreign policy in terms of a Communist program or conspiracy to control the world. The only way to deal with such a conspiracy is to contain it by American power throughout the world, and this means American military power and alliances throughout the non-Communist world.

There have been a number of Russian and Chinese actions over the years that make credible the belief that they would like to dominate neighboring nations or curb U.S. power or extend their influence into other continents. Nevertheless, the allegation of Communist conspiracy overlooks three basic facts. The first is the nationalist differences between such countries as Russia, China, and Yugoslavia. The second is the relative weakness of both the Soviet Union and China in the postwar period when the conspiracy theory was formulated. Frederick Schuman described the devastation of Russia during the war in these words:

> The cost of victory was staggering. Among the citizens of the USSR, 38,000,000 were driven from their homes; 7,000,-000 soldiers, sailors, airmen, partisans, and civilians died in battle, succumbed from wounds, or perished from starvation, forced labor, torture, or mass extermination behind enemy lines; increased death rates and decreased birth rates attributable to the war probably meant the loss of another 8,000,000 lives at least. Soviet casualties were ten times those of all the other Western United Nations combined. Property damage was estimated at 679,000,000,000 rubles. The destruction included 6,000,000 buildings in 1,700 devastated cities and 70,000 ruined villages, including 84,000 schools, 43,000 libraries, 31,000 factories, 13,000 bridges, and 40,000 miles of railway track. Also lost were 7,000,000 horses, 17,000,000 cattle, 20,-000,000 pigs, 27,000,000 sheep and goats, etc. The USA would have suffered a comparable disaster if 9,000,000 Americans had been slain, with 27,000,000 homeless and most of the area east of the Mississippi occupied and devastated.[1]

The third fact is that there is a rational explanation of the events that have been used by realists to justify a devil theory or a "Communist plot" at the root of major postwar problems.

A look at Soviet foreign policy will reveal that it is shaped basically by Russian national interests, even though it is at times conditioned by Communist ideology. Traditional Russian policy has included at least four factors: (1) Efforts to get access to the oceans through a warm-water port. This is still Soviet policy, even though the problem is not quite so urgent in the days of air travel and large cargo planes. (2) The need to industrialize and to gain equality with, or supremacy over, Western technology. (3) Russian nationalism has had in it, both under the czars and the Communists, a strong messianic tendency, which is at the root of her expansion. In czarist times this led to simple territorial expansion, whereas under the Communists there has been an effort to extend Soviet influence via Communist movements in other countries. (4)

[1] Frederick L. Schuman, *International Politics* (New York: McGraw-Hill, Inc., 1958), p. 512.

Since Russia has no natural boundaries to protect her, she has always had an abnormal emphasis on military defense, which for a land power meant a huge army. Under the Communists this defense program has included a program of coexistence and efforts to achieve world disarmament. Since the Communists have taken power, the fear of capitalist encirclement and of war being waged against her by the West has been a dominant factor in Soviet policy, leading to nuclear and missile development as well as efforts to obtain and hold buffer states.

American foreign policy has similarly been guided by at least four main concerns: (1) An effort to prevent war coming to the United States by using the oceans as barriers. (2) A policy, known as the Monroe Doctrine, designed to keep unfriendly foreign powers out of the Western Hemisphere. (3) Both of these have been modified or expanded with the advent of planes and missiles which make oceans less of a barrier. As a result, the United States has not only developed radar and air defenses but has expanded the Monroe Doctrine virtually to a world-wide level so as to try to exclude hostile foreign influence, notably Russia and China, from territory or spheres of influence not accepted as their own. This is a policy aimed at Russia, China, and Cuba, but not at Yugoslavia, for example. The vehicle for this policy is a system of military alliances, overseas military garrisons, subversive activities by the Central Intelligence Agency, foreign economic aid, and other economic pressures. Instead of conquest of other countries, the United States seeks formal acceptance of the U.S. military presence and U.S. foreign policy by the various states allied with her. (4) Commercial trade everywhere in the world and governmental aid of American business interests in acquiring factories, raw materials, and other property overseas, as well as in promoting the distribution of American products. This has included various activities to prevent nationalization, socialization, or the exercise by other countries of dominant economic rights.

The purpose in listing these foreign policy goals is to suggest that the fundamental problems that exist between the

United States and the major Communist nations are not totalitarianism versus democracy, nor atheism versus religion, nor even ideology, but military and economic rivalry.

The cold war can be viewed from an American nationalist perspective, or it can be viewed from a nonpartisan position aimed at understanding why each nation has taken the course of action it has. An ethical perspective, as distinct from a narrow partisan position, will necessarily be concerned with such understanding and with an effort to arrive at more truth than one perspective alone will bring.

The key to Russian action from 1945 on is evident if we note that three nations—the Soviet Union, Great Britain, and the United States—won the war, the Soviet Union having suffered the greatest losses. The Russians might have assumed that the postwar world would be run according to a three-power design. Instead, the United States began to insist on a two-power world, or rather an American world in which Britain was the junior partner.

Among the early factors which led the Russians to believe the United States was hostile to her as a partner were the following:

1. At Potsdam in July 1945, while the war in Asia was still raging, the United States presented a statement which asserted that the Yalta agreements about Eastern Europe were not being carried out. The United States proposed that the governments of Rumania and Bulgaria be reorganized along what were essentially Western lines. The next day, Molotov, the Russian foreign minister, attacked Western democracy as exemplified in Greece where Anthony Eden insisted there had been international observers to watch the elections. However, before the observers had been invited to come, the political power of the left-wing forces had been effectively broken. Molotov quoted British and American newspapers to demonstrate that there had been greater excesses in Greece than in Bulgaria or Rumania.[2]

[2] D. F. Fleming, *The Cold War and Its Origins, 1917–1950* (Garden City, N.Y.: Doubleday & Company, Inc., 1961), p. 290.

The Western powers had claimed that the Soviet Union was crowding out Western influence in Bulgaria and Rumania. Molotov, in turn, claimed that Soviet influence was being crowded out of Italy. "The exclusion of the Soviet Union from all voice in Italian matters was . . . a bad precedent for common action by the Big Three elsewhere."[3]

2. During the war the United States trusted one of its Allies, the British, with information about our atomic bomb program but not the other major ally, the Soviet Union. During that war, our agreement with the Russians was that they would enter the war with Japan three months after the European war ended. The Potsdam declaration with respect to Japan was prepared by the United States and accepted by the British and Chinese but was released for publication before the Russians were consulted. A copy was sent to Molotov by special messenger. Later that day, Molotov telephoned to ask that it be held up two or three days. Byrnes' explanation was that the USSR was not yet at war with Japan and "we did not want to embarrass the Soviet Union." Molotov, however, insisted that the USSR should have been consulted.[4]

3. The war in Europe ended May 8, and the Russians were to enter the war against Japan on August 8. The U.S. timetable for invading Japan had previously been November 1, but under forced steam American scientists were instructed to have the atomic bomb ready in early August. The purpose apparently was to knock Japan out of the war before Russia could come in or make anything other than a token participation.[5]

President Truman, evidently in order to divert attention from the real situation, said that he had directed the use of the atom bomb to save the lives of two hundred thousand

[3] John C. Campbell, *The United States in World Affairs 1945-1947* (New York: Harper & Brothers, 1947), p. 54; Fleming, *The Cold War*, p. 290.

[4] James F. Byrnes, *Speaking Frankly* (New York: Harper & Brothers, 1947), pp. 205-9.

[5] P. M. S. Blackett, *Military and Political Consequences of Atomic Energy* (London: Turnstile Press, 1948), pp. 119-23; Philip Morrison, review of Blackett's book in *Bulletin of the Atomic Scientists,* February 1949, p. 40.

American soldiers. He publicly said that he would again order the bomb dropped if it were necessary to preserve "the welfare of the nation [and] democracy.[6]

The responsible military leaders, such as General Dwight D. Eisenhower, Admiral Ernest King, and General H. H. Arnold, had stated prior to the bombing their belief that it was unnecessary to drop the bomb.[7]

The Japanese had already proposed surrender, but on condition that the emperor be retained. Stalin reported this to Truman at Potsdam, since the Japanese had asked the USSR to relay the message to the United States. Joseph Grew, then undersecretary of state, told President Truman on May 28, 1945 that a Japanese surrender would be improbable unless the president publicly guaranteed that such surrender would not eliminate the emperor and his constitutional monarchy. Truman referred Grew to Secretary of War Stimson, who said that "for certain military reasons, not then divulged, it was inadvisable for the President to make such a statement at that juncture. . . ."

As a result, Truman omitted any reference in the Potsdam declaration to the retention of the emperor. Very significantly, after the two bombs were dropped, Secretary of State Byrnes gave to the Japanese the assurance previously denied.[8] This demonstration of power, though not necessary for the Japanese surrender, could have had only three possible purposes: to test the bomb on live targets; to crush and punish Japan; and to demonstrate to the Russians how dangerous and superior our power could be.

4. Another problem that arose between the United States and the USSR involved the Russian request for a $6 billion credit to help reconstruct their badly destroyed country. The Truman administration discussed this request with the Russians but kept delaying on a decision by claiming it had no

[6] *New York Herald Tribune*, April 7, 1949.

[7] Gar Alperwitz, "Why We Dropped the Bomb," *The Progressive*, August 1965, pp. 11–4.

[8] Harry Paxton Howard, "Days of Infamy," *Liberation*, December 1959, pp. 7–10.

authorization from Congress. It seemed to the Russians quite clear that nothing was being done to get the authorization. D. F. Fleming wrote: "In the later days of the Cold War most people applauded our slowness to help bind up Russia's wounds. Why arm 'the enemy'? Yet the reflection cannot be excluded that the grant of a large credit to Russia might have changed much of the postwar atmosphere—if it could have been made in good spirit."[9]

There are numerous other illustrations of the way American actions contributed to a hardening of the Russian attitude towards the United States. There had been misunderstandings and suspicions on both sides during the war, but it seems clear that when the war ended, the Soviet Union was not thinking of a cold war. In July 1944, for example, at the Bretton Woods Conference where plans were worked out for the Bank for International Reconstruction, the Soviet Union, at the suggestion of the United States, raised her contribution from an earlier ceiling of $900 million to $1.2 billion.

When the Truman Doctrine, to which reference has already been made, was announced and subsequent anti-Communist action taken, such as forcing Communists out of the French and Italian governments, the reaction in Eastern Europe was predictable. The Communists moved almost immediately to liquidate the right wing in Hungary and Bulgaria.[10]

Frederick Schuman writes:

> In 1944–46 the men of Moscow envisaged the extension of their power to the Elbe and the Adriatic in terms of semi-democratic, "bourgeois" coalition regimes. . . . This relatively tolerant conception was abandoned only when Bevin, Byrnes, Churchill and Truman made clear their resolve to challenge the whole Soviet position in Eastern Europe, to roll back the "Iron Curtain," if possible to the old frontiers, and to embark on the economic rehabilitation and military rearmament of Western Europe against the Red Menace. Moscow's response to the Truman Doctrine and the Marshall Plan was to organize the Com-

[9] Fleming, *The Cold War and Its Origins, 1917–1950*, p. 293.
[10] Ibid., p. 461.

inform (September, 1947) . . . to impose 100% Communist regimes—with the process culminating in the Czechoslovak Communist coup of February 1948.[11]

The Czechoslovakian coup deserves special consideration. The background of this coup lies in two crucial actions involving the West. The first of these was the Munich agreement by which Czechoslovakia was given to Hitler. The Czechs, consequently, mistrusted the West and tended to look to the Soviet Union. President Benes in December 1943, for example, went to Moscow to form an alliance with the Russians. The Soviet Union recognized the Benes government in exile rather than one proposed by the Czech Communist leader, Gottwald. The result was a Soviet-sponsored Czech government during a war in which Western leaders had abandoned the same Czech government leaders.

The second crucial action was a decision made by high American officers to let the Soviet armies liberate Prague. At Teheran and Yalta a decision had been made to let Eastern Europe, including Czechoslovakia, be within the Soviet sphere of influence. When General George Patton's U.S. Third Army crossed the frontier into Czechoslovakia, General Eisenhower, on the advice of General Marshall not "to hazard American lives for purely political purposes," ordered Patton's troops to stop about sixty miles short of Prague. The German armed forces in Europe surrendered May 7, 1945, but the Russians did not reach Prague until May 10.[12]

As a result, Soviet armies liberated Czechoslovakia from Hitler's armies. They were hailed as liberators; they seized key positions in communities throughout the country, and encouraged the idea of a political coalition between Communist and non-Communist parties. Vacant farms and jobs in factories were distributed by Communist leaders. The labor unions, as they were reorganized after the war, were controlled by the Communists.

[11] Schuman, *International Politics*, p. 550.
[12] Keith Eubank, *Munich* (Norman, Okla.: University of Oklahoma Press, 1963), p. 293.

A further result of all this was the Communists' success in the first election in 1946 when they took more than a third of the seats, got 49 percent of the popular vote, and became the strongest political party. During the first two years, they behaved like a Western democratic party, with a share in the cabinet.

> In this period Czechoslovakia was the marvel of most observers. Its government was led by Communists, but it remained a democratic country. Freedom of press and speech continued. All the controversial literature of the West could be purchased freely and in great variety. Travellers who visited the country reported no evidence of a police state.[13]

In 1947, when the Communist party of the Soviet Union decided to reject the Marshall Plan and to have all Cominform countries do so, a cleavage developed between the Communist and the other parties in Czechoslovakia. The handwriting was on the wall, and it appeared that the Czech Communist party would make a poorer showing in the 1948 elections than it had in 1946. The Communists, among other things, began to put more of their men into the police, who were controlled by the minister of the interior, a Communist. The non-Communist parties objected to this padding, which in Slovakia alone amounted to fifteen hundred Communists being added to the police force. When the cabinet learned that the last eight non-Communist regional police commanders in the Prague area had been retired or transferred, they voted to instruct the minister of the interior to reinstate the eight. He refused and was supported by the Communist premier, Klement Gottwald. The ministers of three parties, twelve in all, resigned in protest, expecting to be backed by President Benes and the Social Democrats.

During these days of crisis, Valerian Zorin, Soviet deputy foreign minister, came to Prague to advise the Communists. The American ambassador, Laurence Steinhardt, who had been in Washington, had earlier explained to Peter Zenkl, a

[13] Fleming, *The Cold War and Its Origins, 1917–1950*, p. 491

non-Communist leader, that the non-Communists could not expect American aid. Jan Masaryk, the foreign minister, and others had tried to get a large loan from the United States to build up Western influence in the country, but they were turned down.[14] Contributing also to the psychological situation of abandonment by the West was the decision at Teheran, which still stood, that Czechoslovakia was to be within the Soviet military sphere.

The combination of this atmosphere with the poor health of Benes, the Communist control of the police and of the labor unions, and the mobilization of a workers' militia made the coup possible. It is impossible to discuss the Czech situation, however, without referring to the emotional feeling and conviction on the part of all Czechs that the real danger was a revival of German militarism, and for that event they needed Russia's future support.

The Czech coup seemed like a great betrayal to the West and was one of the factors that helped make a tough line in the United States more possible. Yet Czechoslovakia had already been written off by the United States, and almost nothing was done to encourage the democrats there. From a power standpoint, Czechoslovakia a year before the coup was no more of an asset to the United States than she was after the coup. But to the Czechs the loss of liberty was great, and to the United States the Czech coup was another opportunity to blame the Soviet Union for what was in large part an American responsibility.

Although there were a number of serious U.S. actions which caused or contributed to the Russian reaction in Eastern Europe, it must not be assumed that the Soviet Union does not share in the causation of the cold war.

At Yalta, for example, the United States, the USSR, and the United Kingdom agreed to form in Eastern Europe interim governments broadly representative of all democratic elements in the population and to hold free elections. The Russians de-

---

[14] Andrew Gyorgy and Hubert P. Gibbs, *Problems in International Relations* (Englewood Cliffs, N.J.: Prentice-Hall, Inc., 1955), p. 33.

manded and the American leaders agreed that Soviet troops should occupy key centers like Prague and Berlin. This gave overall control in Eastern Europe to the Soviet Union. Between 1945 and 1948, local Communist party organizations gained more local control of Albania, Bulgaria, Czechoslovakia, Hungary, Poland, and Yugoslavia.

Except in Czechoslovakia, where there was genuine democratic government until 1948, the Russians did not keep the Yalta agreement about free elections and a democratic government. The Soviet Union interpreted the agreement as involving non-Communist elements in a pro-Communist or puppet government.

The Soviet Union had also decided unilaterally that the new Poland should include most of East Prussia and other parts of Germany beyond the Neisse and Oder rivers. Truman and Churchill protested this at Potsdam, but without success.

From the standpoint of power politics, it would be naive to expect Russia to permit a Western-oriented group of governments in territories she had conquered, just as it would be naive to expect the United States to encourage pro-Communist governments in territory we had liberated. Yet this action on the part of the Soviet Union was one of the early sources of friction that led to a hardening of the U.S. attitude towards Russia and a general feeling on the part of the American public that we were behaving in a more "moral" fashion than the Russians.

American leaders were not united, however, in blaming Russia for what happened in Poland. Admiral Leahy, for example, indicated that "he had left Yalta with the impression that the Soviet Government had no intention of permitting a free Poland, and that he would have been surprised had the Soviet Government behaved any differently than it had."[15]

The Russians also wanted a Soviet base in the Turkish

[15] Fleming, *The Cold War and Its Origins, 1917–1950*, p. 267.

Straits and two provinces in Turkey and sought to be named trustee of an Italian colony in North Africa.

There was no doubt about Stalin's ruthless rule in the Soviet Union, nor about his suspicion of the West. He held to a doctrine of inevitable conflict between capitalist countries, based on what he believed was the inherently aggressive tendency of modern capitalism. Although he yielded many times to Western requests, he was adamant on numerous occasions and suspicious of Western postwar plans. This suspicion was not lost on Western leaders, especially inexperienced and impatient negotiators like President Truman, who were equally suspicious of the Russians.

Since the chief point of irritation in 1945 and 1946 was the Soviet action in Eastern Europe, it is well to examine this briefly. There are four possible explanations of such action. The whole effort to bring Eastern Europe under Soviet control can be interpreted as a desire for security from possible aggression. By controlling Eastern Europe and having Soviet armed forces in those countries, Russian frontiers were in effect moved westward so that war, if it came, would be fought on former enemy territory. In similar fashion, by keeping American troops in Western Europe, the United States moved its frontiers eastward.

A second possibility is to interpret Soviet moves in Eastern Europe as an ideological step calculated to eliminate Western influence and to indoctrinate the people with Communism.

A third value of Eastern Europe to the USSR was evident in the way the Soviet Union used the economic resources of those countries to rebuild the Soviet economy that had been damaged during the war.

Finally, it is obvious from a look at the map that Eastern European countries bordering on the Mediterranean, the Adriatic, and the Baltic have been the objects of Russian expansionist policy for years, the success of which would provide access to warm-water ports.

Another major source of controversy between the United States and the Soviet Union was Berlin. When the war ended,

Germany was divided into four zones and Berlin into four sectors with the United States, USSR, United Kingdom, and France respectively controlling the four zones and sectors. Berlin was located entirely within the Soviet zone. During the war, but after the decision had been made to establish the zones of occupation, the State Department wanted a guaranteed access to Berlin. The U.S. military, however, made the actual decision and had a veto over the State Department. Military planners, with an arrogance of power, felt they could handle the Russian armies and decided to leave such matters for settlement at the military level in June 1945. It was this military decision that made the Berlin blockade possible and cost millions of dollars and more than a score of American lives.

In 1945 the Soviet Union apparently did not intend to incorporate Berlin into the USSR sphere of influence; it rejected a U.S. request that it feed Berlin which would have put it under effective Russian economic control.

There was an agreement at Potsdam in 1945 that Germany should be operated as one economic unit. The French, who were not present at Potsdam, and the Russians had suffered great losses as a result of German invasion. They were in a serious situation in 1945 and 1946 and as a result took food and industrial products from Germany, including items from the American zone—a practice to which the United States had agreed. This meant that the British and Americans who had to feed Germans in their respective zones were also bearing the cost in the other two zones. Here again, it was faulty planning in the United States that made possible the Russian and French actions. From 1944 on, there was conflict over the Morgenthau plan, which assumed that the only postwar function of American policy in Germany was punitive. Under this plan Germany would have been divided into smaller states. The War Department supported the Morgenthau plan against a more moderate line advocated by the State Department. As a result, Roosevelt issued a directive forbidding any policy settlements over Germany during the war. When Germany surrendered in May 1945, there were still policy problems to be worked out.

At Potsdam policies were established, but the compromise on reparations was unsatisfactory to the Soviet Union, and France was not even involved. The Russians kept wanting more reparations. Then in April 1946, the Soviet Union established in her zone a Socialist Unity party as an effort to get more control of the situation at a grass-roots level.

On January 1, 1947, the British and Americans declared their zones an economic unit and tried to convince the French to join with them. It was not until June 1948 that agreement was reached among the British, American, French, and Benelux nations to form a West German government.

This decision to partition Germany into western and eastern governments was the overall cause of all subsequent Russian efforts to drive the West out of Berlin.

D. F. Fleming wrote:

> On the basis of logic the Soviet position was strong. If the West was formally splitting Germany into two parts, then it should abandon its position in Berlin, which was 125 miles deep in the Soviet zone. If partition was accepted, the West should not attempt to maintain an artificial outpost in Soviet Germany. . . . On the other hand the Allies had a clear legal right to be in Berlin, even if they had neglected to reserve means of access.[16]

In early 1948 the four powers began negotiations for a new German currency. These broke up on March 20 after the Soviet representatives demanded and were refused a report on the Western negotiations in London that later led to the establishment of the West German government. On March 30 General Lucius Clay announced a plan for currency reform in the joint British–American zones. On March 31 the Soviet military administration stopped the movement of military passenger trains to Berlin unless baggage and passengers could be checked by its personnel. Thereafter, no freight was permitted to leave Berlin.

[16] Ibid., p. 506.

The Western powers attempted to establish a uniform currency; when this seemed impossible to achieve, given Soviet reactions to the planned establishment of a West German government, the three Western military governors advised their Russian counterpart that they would, in their three zones, institute currency reform on June 18 "but that the measure would not apply to Berlin."[17]

On June 23 Soviet currency measures were put into effect, and on June 24, in spite of the earlier promise, the Western powers made the Western currency legal tender in Berlin. On that day, June 24, 1948, the Soviet military stopped all rail traffic between Berlin and the Western zones. In this way the Berlin blockade began.[18]

Many nations feared the blockade would lead to war. The skillful handling of the Berlin airlift, together with the sympathy aroused for a beleaguered city and skillful propaganda by the United States, tended to influence world opinion against the Soviet Union. The Russians have ever since been blamed for the blockade, although the record of events shows, at the very least, mutual responsibility for the causation of the whole incident.

With few exceptions, government spokesmen, political scientists, theologians, and others who claim the name *realist* have blamed the Soviet Union and especially a Communist master plan, for the cold war. President Truman on March 17, 1948, in his address to Congress calling for a renewal of conscription, asserted that "one nation"—Russia—was responsible for preventing a "just and honorable peace" and for destroying "the independence and democratic character of a whole series of nations in Eastern and Central Europe."

An effort to be ethically objective instead of narrowly partisan would lead to the rendering of certain other judgments:

[17] General Lucius D. Clay, "The Berlin Blockade," an excerpt of Chapts. 19 and 20 of his *Decision in Germany* (New York: Doubleday & Company, Inc., 1950), reprinted in Gyorgy and Gibbs, *Problems in International Relations*, p. 87.

[18] Gyorgy and Gibbs, *Problems in International Relations*, pp. 86-8.

1. The Soviet Union was not solely or perhaps even largely responsible for the cold war.

2. The United States failed at a number of points to plan adequately for the future, relying instead on military and economic power to correct policy failures.

3. The United States in its affluence and power saw the much poorer Soviet Union as the only potential rival, instead of being concerned about allaying her security fears and assisting in her economic plight.

4. Military and economic power interests in the U.S. combined Soviet aggressive tactics or responses with selected portions of Marxist–Leninist philosophy to show a pattern of world conquest which could be thwarted only by U.S. power throughout the non-Russian world.

5. The United States, after conceding to the Russians a sphere of influence in Eastern Europe, judged Soviet actions there by American standards, but refused to be concerned about any other standard of judgment for American actions in those parts of the world claimed as an American sphere of influence.

In other words, the cold war is a product of many causes, including an ethical failure to understand the problems of others and to be concerned about those problems.

9

THE KOREAN WAR

EUROPE HAS NOT BEEN the only center of East–West or Communist–capitalist rivalry. Asia has been not only a cold-war battleground, but the scene of shooting wars as well.

Many Americans assume that the various problems and hostilities in the Far East are a result of the various Communist governments in Vietnam, North Korea, and China. In one way or another the presence of Communism is the explanation offered for the unsettled state of affairs in Asia. Such an assumption, of course, overlooks such long-existent problems as poverty, Western colonialism, Japanese imperialism, lack of industrialization, and nationalism.

If, however, there is any key to the fact of Communism in China and Korea, it is the American policy during World War II of unconditional surrender of Japan. That policy is responsible for the refusal by the Truman administration to accept the conditional surrender of Japan, conditional only on the maintenance of the emperor and his constitutional monarchy. The refusal to accept that conditional surrender when the war in Europe ended led to three further events: Russian entry into the war against Japan and consequent Russian occupation of Manchuria and North Korea; the explosion of atomic bombs over Japan and the consequent nuclear rivalry; the flowing of Chinese Communist troops into the power vacuum created by the destruction and expulsion of Japanese power without orderly transition to an all-China government.

Korea is a case in point. When the war with Japan ended, North Korea came under Russian control as a result of a decision by the U.S. Army. A State Department publication reports that "a military decision, adopted with a view to effecting the surrender of Japanese forces in Korea, provided that Japanese troops north of the 38 degree parallel in Korea should surrender to Soviet forces and that those south of the 38 degree parallel should surrender to United States forces."[1]

Russian troops entered Korea on August 10, but U.S. troops did not enter until September 8. On September 6, two days before General John R. Hodge landed in Korea, a new People's government had been set up in Korea under the leadership of a Korean liberal, Lyuh Woon Hyung. The *Korean Times* of September 5, 1945, which was distributed to the Americans as they entered Korea, said, "the people cooperated with the leaders of the Provisional Korean Commission, headed by Mr. Woon Hyung Ryu." (This was the Japanese version of the leader's name.) The party was later called the Korean People's Republic. Professor Alfred Crofts of the University of Denver's history department, who was a high-ranking officer in the U.S. military government in Korea at the time, wrote of Lyuh Woon Hyung: "It is apparent that he was fully supported in the South and would easily have united the country. [Instead] the People's Republic was destroyed and Lyuh assassinated; Syngman Rhee was imported from America to lead an implacable anti-Northern and anti-Russian regime which would keep the nation permanently divided and guarantee an American base on the Asian continent."[2]

Another account states that "many prominent Korean leaders joined together in setting up a People's Republic in the capital Seoul, with connections throughout the country, including the Russian zone." This same account added that these leaders, headed by Lyuh Woon Hyung, "organized local committees to preserve order and they convened a national congress in Seoul attended by representatives from all

[1] U.S. Department of State, *Korea, 1945 to 1948*, Far Eastern Series 28, No. 3305, (Washington, D.C., October 1948), p. 3.

[2] Professor Alfred Crofts to John M. Swomley, Jr., April 25, 1967, enclosing copies of two pages from the *Korean Times*, September 5, 1945.

parts of Korea, which on September 6 proclaimed the People's Republic. In northern Korea these local committees were being formed with the sanction of the Russian occupying forces." In the South the Japanese "did not impede the formation of the Republic, but on the contrary granted its leaders special facilities. . . ."[3]

Representatives of the Korean People's Republic were sent to meet General Hodge, but he refused to cooperate with them! Instead, he announced that he preferred to work with the previous Japanese administration "to facilitate the occupation."[4]

General Hodge not only refused to cooperate; he issued a a statement that "directed my occupation forces and the Military Government of Korea that the activities of any political organization in any attempted operations as a government are to be treated as unlawful activities. . . ." Hodge had earlier insisted that "military government is the only government in Southern Korea." Since the People's Republic refused to dissolve and continued to insist it was the people's government, it was treated as unlawful.[5]

In this way the U.S. Army effectively prevented a popular political unification of the two zones, preferring instead to negotiate later with the Russians in an effort to form a unified government.

Meanwhile, in October 1945, Syngman Rhee was flown from Washington, D.C., in an army plane. Rhee was more conservative than the American military and hence close to extreme right-wing groups in Korea. The rightist groups rallied around him, and he was made chairman of the Representative Democratic Council, appointed February 14, 1946, to act as an advisory group to the commanding general. "Since the appointees were almost all right-wing conservatives, the leading liberals refused to participate. . . ."[6]

[3] George M. McCune, *Korea Today* (Cambridge, Mass.: Harvard University Press, 1950), p. 46.
[4] Ibid., p. 47; *New York Times*, September 10, 1945.
[5] McCune, *Korea Today*, pp. 49–50.
[6] Ibid., p. 50.

The Russians, on the other hand, set up no formal military government, but after allowing the People's Republic Committee to function, finally in February 1946, united all the political groups including the Communist party into a single political New People's party. There was ample evidence, according to one scholar, that "the Russians actually did permit the Koreans of their choice to exercise real authority whereas in the American zone, the Korean employees of Military Government were allowed little power and no authority."[7]

At Moscow in December 1945, the foreign ministers of the United States, the Soviet Union, and the United Kingdom agreed that an all-Korean provisional democratic government should be set up. Then, at a joint conference January 16 to February 5, 1946, the U.S. military command tried to get Korea consolidated into an administrative and economic unit. "The Soviet Command, however, . . . insisted that the administrative and economic integration of the two zones of occupation must await the formation of the provisional government envisaged under the Moscow agreement."[8]

The Moscow agreement had provided for a four-power trusteeship of Korea by the United States, United Kingdom, USSR, and China for a period of up to five years. Since the Koreans interpreted such trusteeship as tantamount to the trusteeship formerly exercised by Japan, most of the political groups in Korea except the Communist party had opposed the Moscow agreement.

In a joint United States–USSR commission meeting between March 20 and May 8, 1946, the Soviet Union "took the position that the Joint Commission should consult, in connection with the founding of a provisional Korean government, only those Korean parties and social organizations which had supported agreement."[9]

In April and May 1947, after an exchange of letters between Secretary of State Marshall and Foreign Minister Molo-

[7] Ibid., pp. 51–2.
[8] U.S., Department of State, *Korea, 1945–48*, pp. 3, 4.
[9] Ibid., pp. 4, 5.

tov, the State Department said, "It appeared that the Soviet Government was willing to modify its position on the question of eligibility of Korean parties and social organizations for consultation. . . ." As a result the United States and USSR "directed the Joint Commission to resume its work."

The Joint Commission reconvened on May 21, 1947. At first it seemed that the two delegations had worked out a formula for resolving the issue, but in early July the Russians reverted to their former position.[10] The reason for the Russian action was apparently twofold. The Russians had proposed that in South Korea only 118 rather than 425 of the political groups be consulted in the formation of the government. The groups at issue were "rightist who had shown little disposition to cooperate with the Joint Commission. . . ."[11]

Molotov gave a second explanation of the changed position when he stated that:

> The parties and organizations of Southern Korea which support the Moscow decisions are being subjected on the part of the American authorities . . . to the severest restrictions and cruelest persecutions, which contradicts democratic principles and is entirely out of accord with the decision of the Moscow Conference. The premises of such parties and organizations are being seized by police authorities; their leaders and members are being arrested; press organs are being closed.[12]

While the United States and USSR were trying to work and plan for an all-Korean government, General Hodge, in December 1946, in the South appointed forty-five members of a ninety-member Interim Legislative Assembly and arranged for the other forty-five to be elected. Those elected were chiefly rightist supporters of Rhee.

Also in December 1946, the Communist party joined with a large group from the People's Republic party to form the Labor party. Lyuh Woon Hyung refused to go along with the merger of his party with the Communists, but nevertheless

[10] Ibid., p. 6.
[11] McCune, *Korea Today*, p. 66.
[12] A. Wigfall Green, *The Epic of Korea* (Washington, D.C.: Public Affairs Press, 1950), p. 87.

would not attack those who did collaborate with the Communists.[13] As the leading compromise candidate for head of an all-Korean government, he was invited by General Hodge to join the Interim Legislative Assembly; he refused the invitation "because the members were not elected by fair means."[14]

On July 19, 1947, Lyuh Woon Hyung was assassinated, presumably by rightists associated with Syngman Rhee.[15] A campaign against leftists in South Korea ensued, which was the basis for the Molotov statement already mentioned.[16]

The Soviet Union on September 26 proposed that Soviet and American "troops be withdrawn simultaneously during the beginning of 1948 and that the Koreans organize their own government without outside assistance." The United States, however, opposed the ending of the occupation and indicated that the United States would refer the whole matter to the UN. In the UN, the Russian proposal for troop withdrawal was defeated, and the U.S. proposal for elections to create a national assembly was accepted.[17]

The election was to be held not later than March 31, 1948. In South Korea it was actually held on May 10, 1948. The leftist and middle-of-the-road parties opposed and actually boycotted the elections, so that chiefly two rightist parties participated. During the election campaign, 589 persons were killed and over 10,000 rioters "were processed in police stations."[18] This suggests that coercion and terror were used to obtain the election results. Rhee was elected by the new assembly to be president of the government.

On September 9 a Supreme People's Council was elected in North Korea and on September 19 the Soviet Foreign Office informed the U.S. embassy in Moscow "that all Soviet forces

[13] Hugh Deane, "Death of Lyuh Woon Hyung," *The Nation*, September 6, 1947.
[14] Green, *The Epic of Korea*, p. 76.
[15] Deane, *The Nation*.
[16] McCune, *Korea Today*, p. 67; Deane, *The Nation*.
[17] U.S., Department of State, *Korea, 1945–1948*, pp. 6–9.
[18] McCune, *Korea Today*, pp. 229–38.

would be withdrawn from Korea by the end of December 1948."[19]

In this way Korea was permanently divided. Under Syngman Rhee's leadership, South Korea became a police state. The army began to usurp police functions and, said the July 3, 1949, *New York Times*, "have been exercising the power of summary arrest without warrant." There was inflation and an almost complete loss of civil liberty. U.S. officials began to have serious doubts about Rhee, and on April 7, 1950, Secretary of State Acheson in a note to Rhee warned him of the loss of American aid unless he held elections as were required by the South Korean Constitution. When the elections were held on May 30, 1950, Rhee was effectively repudiated; only 47 Rhee candidates were elected while more than 120 of the 210 assembly seats went to anti-Rhee elements.[20]

Less than a month later, Syngman Rhee was saved by a war that began on June 25 with an invasion from North Korea. There are those, however, who assert that it was Rhee and his South Korean forces who started the war. The Russian delegate Vyshinsky, on October 29, 1952, told the United Nations Political and Security Committee that as much as twelve months before the outbreak of war "there had been numerous armed incidents in the area of the Thirty-Eighth parallel. All these incidents were initiated by the South Koreans." He added, "In June, 1949, the South Koreans dispatched seven battalions of infantry, equipped with mine throwers and heavy artillery into North Korean territory and began the occupation of various positions there."[21]

Vyshinsky could well have been right, for Ambassador Philip Jessup of the United States reported in April 1950: "The boundary on the 38th parallel . . . is a real front line. There is constant fighting. . . . There are very real battles, involving perhaps one or two thousand men."[22]

[19] U.S. Department of State, *Korea, 1945–1948*, pp. 21–2.

[20] D. F. Fleming, *The Cold War and Its Origins, 1950–1960*, (Garden City, N.Y.: Doubleday & Company, Inc., 1961), Vol. 2, p. 594.

[21] *New York Times*, October 30, 1952.

[22] U.S. Department of State Bulletin, Vol. 22, No. 564, April 24, 1950, p. 627.

The *New York Daily Compass* of July 10, 1950 reported that "border clashes have taken place almost constantly since the withdrawal of Soviet and U.S. troops from the parallel." North Korea claimed that South Korean army and youth corps units had raided the North 1,863 times between January 21 and December 15, 1959. "It listed 432 engagements in 13 northern counties. South Korean authorities likewise have reported a succession of raids from the North as well as many attempts to supply guerrillas. Last summer, U.S. officers declared that responsibility for violation of the parallel was about equally divided between North and South."

The same article by Hugh Deane also reported that the North Korean defense minister had told a Pyongyang rally February 8 that the duties of the army were, among other things, "to adjust the territory of our Fatherland and to liberate the people in the southern half."

On March 1, 1950, Rhee, in a speech at Seoul, talked of liberation of the North: "We shall respond to the cries of our brothers in distress." He added that "some of our friends across the sea" had warned him against invading the North, but "in our demand for the redemption of our conquered land we shall not much longer be without allies." On May 6, in a broadcast to the North Koreans, Rhee said that he could not "liberate" them at the moment because of "international complication" but that the opportunity would come "in the not too distant future."[23]

The *New York Herald Tribune,* as early as November 1, 1949, reported that Sihn Sung Mo, South Korea's defense minister, "said today that his army is ready and waiting to invade Communist North Korea, but has been restrained by American officials." Mr. Sihn said, "If we had our own way we would, I'm sure, have started up already. But we had to wait until they (American government leaders) are ready. They keep telling us, 'No, no, no, wait. You are not ready.' "

Another dispatch from Seoul in the May 30, 1950 *New York Herald Tribune* quoted Brigadier General William L. Roberts, head of the American military mission there, as say-

[23] Hugh Deane, *Daily Compass*, July 11, 1950.

ing, "The Communists will probably engage in some limited action, but at this point we rather invite it." He added, "It will give us target practice."

Whether these threats were more than words, or whether they revealed a course South Korea actually took is likely to be the subject of indefinite speculation. When the United States took the war to the UN Security Council to get support for action already being taken by the United States, Yugoslavia voted no because she did not believe there was enough information available to determine who had caused the war. Similarly, Egypt and India did not vote. Action was taken by the minimum majority of seven, solely on the basis of South Korean reports and without any effort to get the North Korean version.[24]

The United States assumed that Russia was behind the attack, though Russia's absence from the Security Council where she could have vetoed UN participation argues for another interpretation. Russia had been staying away from the Security Council meetings for two months in protest against the exclusion of the Chinese Communist delegate. The basis for the United States assumption was that North Korea as a Russian protectorate would not have moved without Russian consent.

The origins of the Korean war seem even now to be a mystery. An intelligence officer at MacArthur's headquarters told a group of correspondents that "the North Korean Army had not carried out the mobilization plan at the time the war began. . . ." Only six divisions were ready for combat as over against the thirteen to fifteen called for by their war plans. Moreover, the situation in South Korea was so bad that D. F. Fleming wrote, ". . . All the responsible agencies of our government agreed that Communist prospects for taking over South Korea without war were good if not excellent." Fleming adds, "There was also an impression at MacArthur's Headquarters when the war broke out that the South Koreans had begun it." There had been a phone call received at headquarters, and the official who received it, according to John

[24] Fleming, *The Cold War and Its Origins, 1950–1960*, p. 602.

Gunther, "came back and whispered, 'A big story has just broken. The South Koreans have attacked North Korea!' "[25]

On the other hand, as the evidence of the war revealed, the South Korean army was not very well equipped for heavy fighting. As Hanson Baldwin pointed out in the *New York Times* on July 10, 1950, there was fear on the part of American authorities that any heavy weapons would fall into the hands of the Communists. Morever, if the South Koreans had such material they could not be kept from invading the North.

A Senate committee hearing discovered, as a result of questioning John H. Ohly, acting director of Mutual Defense Assistance, that the National Security Council had in March 1949 adopted a policy of giving South Korea "just enough arms to maintain internal security" but not enough to deal with the North Korean army.[26] Apparently, the top military and foreign policy advisers of the administration feared Syngman Rhee's threats of invading the North more than they feared an invasion from the North.

Secretary of State Acheson, on January 12, 1950, in an address to the National Press Club, announced government defense policy on the Far East as including the Aleutian Islands, Japan, the Ryukyus, and the Philippines. Korea and Formosa were on the other side of his "defensive perimeter." Acheson also said, in reference to them, that if other parts of Asia were attacked, "the initial reliance must be on the people attacked and then upon the commitments of the entire civilized world under the charter of the United Nations. . . ."

In this fashion the North Koreans knew that the United States would be ultimately, though not initially, involved. Moreover, the Soviet Union, if it were involved in planning or advising the invasion, knew that the United Nations would be involved, and, if it wanted the invasion to succeed, should

[25] Fleming, *The Cold War and Its Origins, 1950–1960*, p. 599.
[26] *Congressional Record*, 81st Congress, 2nd Session, Vol. 96, Part 16, July 5, 1950, p. A4912.

have been present at the UN Security Council meeting to veto the decision to intervene.

Hanson Baldwin, the military analyst for the *New York Times*, in a story appearing in that paper on June 27, 1950, indicated that the key to the invasion was the "unpopularity of the Syngman Rhee government," which was evident, not only among civilians, but in the "revolt of one regiment and defections and desertions in other military units." He added, "In other words the attack upon Southern Korea seems to be in thorough accord with the principle of Marxist military philosophy in that armed force is to be used preferably as a coup de grace against a nation of people weakened by internal subversion, economic distress and political instability."

The United States had provided South Korea with $495.7 million in military and economic aid between the end of the war in 1945 and the North Korean invasion of June 25, 1950, of which $53.7 million was Economic Cooperation Administration shipments; the rest was military.[27]

It seems evident from the record of events that there was a mutual responsibility for the outbreak of the Korean War. The U.S. Army, with customary shortsightedness on political matters, thwarted an obviously popular effort to develop a unified government, and hence set itself against the most powerful force in Korea, the pent-up nationalism that broke forth after decades of Japanese rule. If the South Koreans wanted to reunify their country, it must be presumed that the North Koreans had similar aims. Both groups might have acted in this respect without the consent of their Russian or American sponsors.

The second military government error was to assume that right-wing extremists like Syngman Rhee and his colleagues were better able to provide an alternative to Communism than more moderate leaders who believed in land reform and other measures designed to win the loyalty of the common people.

[27] *Congressional Record*, 81st Congress, 2nd Session, Vol. 96, Part 9, August 16, 1950, statement by Senator Tydings, p. 12589.

The third error was the assumption on the part of both the United States and the Soviet Union that Korea was theirs to dispose. It is obvious that both the United States and the Soviet Union wanted to use Korea for their own power purposes. As Professor McCune pointed out: "The underlying reason for the failure of negotiations was the clash of opposing powers: The United States was determined to create a Korean government favorable to its interests; the Soviet Union was equally determined to provide for a Soviet-oriented Korean nation.[28]

In a joint meeting of the Senate Armed Services and Foreign Relations Committee, Senator Ralph Flanders asked General Omar Bradley whether the military felt that "this world-wide struggle is primarily a struggle for power." Bradley self-righteously replied: "On our part our struggle is not for power, it is for peace. On the part of Russia it is a struggle for power and the spread of Communism." Senator Flanders added, "Now that is a satisfactory answer, of course, from our standpoint, but [we should try to keep from] the minds of neutrals or half-hearted nations that this is primarily a struggle for power—we should be very careful to avoid expressions which support that idea instead of its being a struggle between two ideologies, two sets of ideas." To this General Bradley agreed, saying, ". . . we should make it plain on every occasion that this is no imperialist move on our part. . . ."[29]

The question of power struggle and imperialism is not easily dismissed by words. More than fifteen years after the war in Korea ended, the United States still had about fifty thousand troops in Korea and was using South Korean troops in Vietnam in the tradition of other imperialist powers.

If the Korean army was strong enough to supply fifty thousand troops for fighting for the United States in South Vietnam, there was no need to maintain fifty thousand U.S. soldiers in Korea unless U.S. military and political bodies regard this as a useful military base for control of the North Pacific.

[28] McCune, *Korea Today*, p. 62.
[29] *New York Times*, May 24, 1951.

The question of Korea, of course, cannot be considered apart from China since it was Chinese armies that intervened in the Korean War. The official Chinese version of that intervention was given to Edgar Snow by Premier Chou En-lai. Chou pointed out that after China went Communist, the Truman administration stated that the United States would not interfere in the internal affairs of China and that Taiwan was an internal Chinese matter. The United States acknowledged that Taiwan was Chinese in 1945. Chou added:

> After war broke out in Korea in June 1950 Truman changed the policy and adopted a policy of aggression toward China. While sending troops to Korea the United States at the same time dispatched the Seventh Fleet to the Taiwan Straits and exercised military control over Taiwan. *Beginning from that time the United States started new aggression against China.* . . . Shortly afterwards United States troops in Korea showed the intention of crossing the Thirty-eighth Parallel and pressing on toward the Yalu River (China's frontier), and because of this, the Chinese Government could not but warn the United States Government that we would not stand idly by if the United States troops crossed the Thirty-eighth Parallel, and pressed on toward the Yalu River. This warning was conveyed to the United States Government through the Indian Ambassador. The United States Government disregarded this warning and United States troops did . . . press on toward the Yalu River.[30]

The Chinese must have known that General MacArthur, who directed the advance to the Yalu, had spoken in Seoul in 1948 of unifying Korea and implied the destruction of Chinese power. He said of the thirty-eighth parallel: "This barrier must and will be torn down. Nothing shall prevent the ultimate unity of your people. . . ." Then speaking of complex "issues," he added, "The manner in which those issues are resolved will determine in large measure not only the unity and well being of your people but also the future stability of the continent of Asia." The only way of providing for future stability for the Asian continent in MacArthur's eyes in-

[30] Edgar Snow, *The Other Side of the River: Red China Today* (New York: Random House, Inc., 1961), pp. 88–9.

volved, as D. F. Fleming put it, "the destruction of Communist power in Asia."[31]

General MacArthur, in fact, disobeyed a directive of the Joint Chiefs of Staff who had "stated that as a matter of policy no non-Korean ground forces should be used in the northeast provinces bordering the Soviet Union or in the area along the Manchurian border." MacArthur on October 24 informed the Joint Chiefs that he planned to use non-Korean troops in the border areas. Within a few weeks Chinese troops had come into the war.[32]

There were apparently three reasons for the Chinese intervention. The first, as Harrison Salisbury pointed out in the December 11, 1950 *New York Times* after talking with Moscow diplomats, was a fear born of Western and Japanese attempts to crush the Soviet revolution following the First World War.

> Interpreting present-day developments in the light of the history of the Soviet Revolution, China's Communist leaders might regard the possibility of armed intervention by the United States and other capitalist powers as one of the greatest potential threats to consolidation of their revolutionary new social system, it is felt.

They also remembered their recent "bitter experience with Japanese imperialism."

A second reason was strategy. Just as the United States would not wait for enemy forces in Mexico to cross the Rio Grande, so China apparently preferred to fight her adversary on Korean rather than on Chinese soil, as she feared would become necessary. A spokesman sent by China to the United Nations, Wu Hsiu-chuan, stated in his November 28, 1950 UN address that "there is only a narrow river between Korea and China, [and the U.S. forces] have directly threatened China's security. . . ." He added:

[31] Fleming, *The Cold War and Its Origins, 1950–1960*, p. 595.

[32] Leland M. Goodrich, "The United Nations and the Korean War: A Case Study," M. Andrew Gyorgy and Hubert P. Gibbs, eds., *Problems in International Relations* (Englewood Cliffs, N.J.: Prentice-Hall, Inc., 1955), pp. 249–50.

From August 27 to November 10, 1950, the military aircraft of the United States aggression forces in Korea have, for ninety times, violated the territorial air of Northeast China, conducted reconnaissance activities, strafed and bombed Chinese cities, towns and villages, killed and wounded Chinese peaceful inhabitants and damaged Chinese properties.[33]

A third reason for Chinese intervention was the reluctance to stand by and watch another Communist country destroyed without aiding her. Wu Hsiu-chuan in his UN address also said:

The Korean People's Democratic Republic is a country bound by close ties of friendship to the People's Republic of China. Only a river separates the two countries geographically. The Chinese people cannot afford to stand idly by in the face of this serious situation brought about by the United States Government aggression against Korea. . . .[34]

The Chinese intervention was a shock to the American military. Hanson Baldwin at the time wrote, "There is no question that as of today the United Nations forces suffered a very definite defeat in Korea. . . ."[35] Although the United States subsequently retrieved some of its military losses and the war ended in stalemate, the Chinese intervention marked a turning point for the United States. Baldwin, who is very close to the Pentagon, wrote that in Asia "any political solution will be founded upon power. The Asian respects power, and power—Asian power, anti-Communist power—is what must be developed."[36]

Among the power efforts the United States undertook following the Korean War were the building of a strong military force in South Korea, a military alliance with and rearmament of Japan, the formation of SEATO, the garrisoning of Taiwan, the sending of military advisers and aid to a government installed by American leaders in South Vietnam and the stationing of troops also in Thailand. In addition the

[33] *New York Times*, November 29, 1950.
[34] Ibid.
[35] *New York Times*, December 8, 1950.
[36] Ibid.

United States has kept the Seventh Fleet and powerful air force units in Asian waters.

A second Far Eastern crisis grew out of the Korean War and the earlier Chinese civil war. When Mao Tse-tung and his followers conquered China, Chiang Kai-shek and his troops fled to Taiwan. That island had been a Japanese colony from 1895 to 1945. The Chinese Nationalists under Chiang took it over and exploited it as conquered territory. The Taiwanese protested in 1947, and the Nationalists systematically executed thousands of those involved. In 1949, when Chiang arrived with his troops, it became the base for a rival China, signifying that the civil war in China had not ended. During the Korean War the U.S. Central Intelligence Agency, under a cover name, Western Enterprises, Inc., organized a series of commando-type raids against the mainland. These were launched from Quemoy and the Tachens, islands which were occupied by Chiang's troops. These attacks, made with the protection of the Seventh Fleet, were authorized by the CIA and the Pentagon without knowledge by or authorization of the President or the Congress.[37]

These raids continued until 1954. In January 1953, President Eisenhower announced that he had decided to free Chiang from earlier restrictions so that he could attack the mainland. Chiang, still protected by the Seventh Fleet, began bombing and shelling the Chinese mainland, ports, and ocean shipping, using ships and planes supplied by the United States. In December 1954, Eisenhower signed a military alliance with Chiang Kai-shek.

In January 1955, the mainland Chinese bombed the Tachens and captured a small island just north of them. Tension mounted, and there was danger of war. The chairman of the Joint Chiefs of Staff, Admiral Radford, Air Force Chief, General Twining, and Navy Chief, Admiral Carney favored bombing China. The only dissenter, the Army Chief,

[37] Stewart Alsop, "The Story Behind Quemoy," *Saturday Evening Post,* December 13, 1958.

General Ridgway, was backed by President Eisenhower, and the United States retreated from the brink of war.

Taiwan continues to be a police state under military rule protected by the U.S. fleet. Communist China continues to want it. The Taiwanese, however, maintain a government in exile in Tokyo, hoping to get rid of Chiang and his rule and achieve independence.

The Korean War has perpetuated rather than resolved the divisions of Korea. It has resulted in the long-term extension or overextension of American power into northern Asia. The overextension became obvious when, in January 1968, an American spy ship, the *Pueblo*, was captured in or near North Korea's coastal waters; the United States was unable to stop the capture or secure the immediate release of the vessel or its crew. It became obvious then that the United States could not fight a limited war in Vietnam and at the same time become involved in military action in Korea. Both nations were thousands of miles from American shores and next door to China.

The Korean War and its aftermath, as well as the American support of Chiang Kai-shek in Taiwan and the continued occupation of other islands, lend credence to the charge that the United States has tried to take over the former Japanese empire as well as incorporate into its sphere of influence those territories formerly held by the French in Asia. American action can thus be viewed as an expansion of the American empire as well as occupation of territory near China in order to contain Chinese influence.

10

LATIN AMERICAN POLICY

FOR MANY YEARS American diplomatic and military policy in Latin America has been used to maintain business dominance by United States interests. Major General Smedley D. Butler, a key figure in the U.S. Marine Corps, described American policy in these words:

> I spent thirty-three years and four months in active service as a member of our country's most agile military force—the Marine Corps. I served in all commissioned ranks from a second lieutenant to major general. And during that period I spent most of my time being a high-class muscle man for Big Business, for Wall Street, and for the bankers. In short, I was a racketeer for capitalism. . . .
>
> Thus I helped make Mexico and especially Tampico safe for American oil interests in 1914. I helped make Haiti and Cuba a decent place for the National City Bank boys to collect revenues in. . . . I helped purify Nicaragua for the international banking house of Brown Brothers in 1909–1912. I brought light to the Dominican Republic for American sugar interests in 1916. I helped make Honduras "right" for American fruit companies in 1903. In China in 1927 I helped see to it that Standard Oil went its way unmolested.
>
> During those years I had, as the boys in the back room would say, a swell racket. I was rewarded with honors, medals, promotion. Looking back on it, I feel I might have given Al Capone a few hints. The best *he* could do was to operate his racket in three city districts. We Marines operated on three continents.[1]

The policy of military intervention was supplemented by resident American military forces known as military missions. These missions trained Latin American officers and men,

[1] *Common Sense*, November 1935.

with the result that Latin American armies were tied to the United States by such training and the provision of equipment. On May 19, 1926, Congress authorized military missions to all countries in the Western Hemisphere, which basically meant Latin America. Later, on June 4, 1938, it also authorized the Navy to train Latin American naval forces. In early 1946 there were seventeen military missions in thirteen countries. In the fiscal year 1947/48 the appropriation for these missions was $1.24 million.

The use of military missions and equipment made it possible for U.S. military officers to influence Latin American governments through the officer group in each country. The *Washington Post* on June 28, 1947 editorially criticized the United States military program, saying:

> We conclude that the whole thing is dangerous from beginning to end, and we should rue the day that we inaugurated this arms traffic, set up our military missions as the dominant element in our representation to Latin American countries and elevated the status of Latin American military staffs as the dominant element in those countries.

In 1947 the United States persuaded Latin American countries to sign a military defense treaty known as the Rio Pact. Subsequently, at the request of General George C. Marshall, Congress adopted a new program of military aid, which was expanded in 1952 to $65 million annually.

U.S. military aid encouraged the Latin American officer corps to engage in politics. The army became the power behind nearly every Latin American government. Since Latin America was not threatened by aggression from Europe or Asia, American military missions interpreted hemisphere defense as both the prevention of internal change and the destruction of revolutionary movements that threatened U.S. economic control. It is the military missions and the Latin American military staffs who judge what constitutes internal subversion.

The Latin American military establishments are not composed of professional military men in the sense that they are objective servants of whatever government is in power. They generally represent and are drawn from class or regional or ethnic groups. They are therefore not usually strong enough to impose their wills on their respective nations but must have the support of other interests, such as the corporations, banks, and landed aristocracy. In each nation there are numerically small but financially powerful groups whose interests are best served by cooperating with the North American miiltary–industrial complex.

When labor unions can provide the balance of power for a military or former military man, as was the case under Peron's leadership in Argentina, some military leaders will cooperate with labor for their own power reasons. But more often military governments suppress the efforts of labor to assert power. During my teaching assignment in Buenos Aires in 1969, the military government, headed by General Juan Carlos Ongania, used the threat of military conscription to try to stop a railway strike and used the threat of guns, prison, and other sanctions to avert a general strike. Workers for three years had had their wages frozen, while there were no similar restrictions on prices to be charged by either Argentina or North American corporations. A number of labor unions had also been "interevened," which means that the military had displaced elected union leaders in an effort to run the unions directly. Nevertheless, during a period of a little more than three years the Ongania government was challenged by four general strikes, by student demonstrations, and by extensive damage to property. Again and again military leaders referred to outside agitators or direction from a foreign source when the problem was one of cost of living and of military suppression.

One of the clearest acknowledgments of the real problem in Latin America was set forth in a study prepared in October 1967 for the Subcommittee on American Republic Affairs of the U.S. Senate Committee on Foreign Relations.

> The rationale set forth for the present military assistance and arms sales programs does not stand up under close scrutiny. The threat to internal security allegedly posed by the forces of international communism has been distorted and exaggerated.

Castro's Cuba has only a limited capability for subversion; the Soviet Union and the orthodox Communist Parties of Latin America are not currently provoking social violence and the proviolence unorthodox Communist Parties, encouraged by Red China, have very limited influence. The principal threat to internal security in Latin America comes from suppressed populist forces, and the United States military assistance program is contributing to that suppression in all those countries with military regimes, or with unrepresentative civilian regimes sustained by the military.

American foreign policy in Latin America could be illustrated by events in many countries, for American interests are extensive throughout Central and South America. Guatemala and the Dominican Republic, however, are celebrated cases of U.S. intervention, and illustrate somewhat different ways in which the North American policy operates in the South.

In Guatemala in 1944 a nonviolent revolt led by students and other middle-class elements, with the acquiescence of the United States, which was preoccupied by war in Europe, unseated Jorge Ubico, a despot who had ruled Guatemala since 1931. The first democratically elected president, Juan José Arevalo, was a university professor and moderate socialist. He began a policy of encouraging labor organization, ended forced labor, and was able to get a social security law adopted. He legalized the Communist party, but gave it no real opportunity for power. Similarly, he refused to permit the U.S. oil companies to enter and exploit Guatemala. His successor, Colonel Jacobo Arbenz Guzman, who was democratically elected, took office in 1951.

Arbenz was hampered by inexperience and lack of organization and accepted any support he could get, including that of the small Communist party, which a U.S. Senate investigating committee estimated included about one thousand members. The Guatemala Workers' party, which was Communist and influential in the labor unions, became a part of the government coalition, but it did not control the government.

The Arbenz government adopted a number of laws, including agrarian reforms, which seriously affected U.S. business interests. The Guatemalan economy was linked so closely to the United States that 77 percent of its exports went to and 65 percent of its imports came from the United States. The three main enterprises in that nation of almost three million people were American owned. The United Fruit Company employed about twelve thousand persons. United Fruit was also the major stockholder in the second industry, the International Railroad of Central America. The third was Empresa Electrica, the only large producer of electric power in the country. Since so many Central American countries are one-crop economies, they are agriculturally dependent on the United States. Guatemala's chief crop, coffee, accounted for 82 percent of its exports.

When the Arbenz government expropriated 160,000 acres of uncultivated lands belonging to United Fruit and offered in payment only $609,572 instead of the $16 million demanded by the company, John Foster Dulles and the State Department backed United Fruit. A campaign was launched in the United States to label Guatemala "Communist" and to permit broad action against the Guatemalan government. John Foster Dulles's law firm had prepared the United Fruit Company's 1930 and 1936 contracts with Guatemala. His brother, Allen Dulles, who was director of the U.S. Central Intelligence Agency, had been president of United Fruit. The assistant secretary of state for inter-American affairs, John Moors Cabot, and his family owned stock in United Fruit.[2]

A Guatemalan military officer, Colonel Castillo Armas, with the aid of the Central Intelligence Agency, gathered and equipped an invasion force in neighboring Honduras. Armas had been close to the U.S. Army for years. He had studied at Fort Leavenworth, Kansas, in 1945 and 1946, and in 1947 had spent three weeks lecturing at West Point. When it became apparent that Honduras was being used as a base for armed invasion, Guatemala tried to forestall it by proposing in May 1954 that Honduras join with her in a pact of friendship and nonaggression. Honduras turned down the

[2] John Gerassi, *The Great Fear in Latin America* (New York: The Macmillan Company, 1965), p. 241.

offer and instead signed a military assistance pact with the United States.

After Guatemala had been denied the right to buy arms from the United States or its allies, she bought a shipload of weapons from Czechoslovakia. The shipload from Czechoslovakia was pointed to as proof of Communism in the Guatemalan government; there were further U.S. efforts to bar arms shipments to Guatemala, and large supplies of arms were shipped to Honduras and Nicaragua. John Foster Dulles, who normally showed little interest in Latin American affairs, flew to Caracas in March 1954 for a meeting of the Organization of American States (the Rio Pact group). Dulles insisted upon action against Guatemala and the Communist threat he saw there. The Latin Americans, "firmly committed to the principles of non-intervention and convinced that the Communist threat was not urgent," responded with the Caracas Declaration against Communism in the Americas but did not name Guatemala or commit themselves to any action against the Arbenz government.[3]

When Colonel Armas's troops invaded the country, he was opposed by the Guatemalan peasants. But Arbenz did not arm the people, as the Communists had wanted. Instead he stepped out of office in June 1954 at the request of a group of army officers to whom he turned over the government, proclaiming Colonel Carlos Enrique Diaz President of Guatemala. Diaz and his fellow officers had consulted with the U.S. ambassador, John E. Peurifoy, before Diaz decided to take over the presidency. Diaz was acceptable to Arbenz because they were both graduates of the Guatemala Military Academy and because Diaz had in 1953 made a public declaration of his support for the land and other reforms of the Arbenz administration. However, Diaz's first official act was to announce suspension of the constitution during the emergency.

John Peurifoy, who had a reputation as a troubleshooter, had attended the United States Military Academy at West

[3] Edwin Lieuwen, *U.S. Policy in Latin America* (New York: Frederick A. Praeger, Inc., 1965), p. 90.

Point and was close to the whole army program of military diplomacy in Latin America. When Peurifoy, after being in touch with the rebel forces under Colonel Armas, met a second time with the first military junta headed by Colonel Diaz, he indicated the need for a change in leadership. The July 1, 1954 *New York Times* reported it in these words:

> In the dramatic climax of the negotiations, Col. Diaz announced he and Col. Sanchez were resigning for the peace of the country. Col. Monzon and two other Army officers strode in. The situation was tense. According to eyewitnesses, Mr. Peurifoy leaned back and crossed his arms over his chest where he had a shoulder holster. A United States Marine aid in civilian clothes edged nearer the envoy, fearing bullets might fly.

When Colonel Monzon, who announced he was taking over leadership of a new junta, requested Peurifoy to sit in on talks with Colonel Castillo Armas, Peurifoy refused, saying the United States did not want to be involved.

However, when the two colonels appeared to be fighting over junta leadership during their talks in San Salvador, Peurifoy flew to the meeting. The July 3, 1954 *New York Times* described it as follows:

> Col. Castillo Armas was known to have demanded the primary executive role. But the formula that Mr. Peurifoy had largely developed and pushed for in the strongest possible measure consistent with the "good offices" of the United States, eventually gained approval. . . . Five copies of the final declaration were passed around the table for signature. When this had been done, Colonels Monzon and Castillo Armas, unsmiling and in what seemed an agonizing personal tension, embraced while camera bulbs exploded.

In addition to Peurifoy and the U.S. ambassador to El Salvador, six United States armed forces officers were present to aid in the talks.

Colonel Armas became the new dictator of Guatemala with Peurifoy's help and remained in power until 1957 when he was assassinated.

The United States was understandably concerned with the danger of Communism in Guatemala, but it took no action to prevent it by ending the exploitation of that country by the

United Fruit Company. It is even doubtful that the United States would have acted against a government friendly to Communists if the Agrarian Reform Law had not been adopted.

As soon as the revolution was over, the U.S. government brought an anti-trust suit against the United Fruit Company. The suit charged that the United Fruit had attained a monopolistic position in the banana trade by obtaining control of nearly all of the land in Central America used for growing bananas. "Almost from its inception," the complaint charged, "United has exercised a policy of ownership or control of all or a major portion of the railroad facilities in the banana producing countries of Central and South America except Ecuador." The suit was brought for domestic reasons, in line with similar efforts of the U.S. government in those days to break up cartels or efforts to achieve monopoly control.

It is unfortunate that action was not taken earlier for foreign policy reasons as well. The suit did not end United Fruit's exploitation of Central America. In fact, Armas destroyed the constitution and reforms of Arevalo and restored the United Fruit property.

The Guatemala incident is significant in its revelation of the way American business, the State Department, and the military cooperate to maintain the status quo, including American domination in Latin America.

Eleven years later the United States was involved in a similar effort to keep the Dominican Republic under control.

The Dominican Republic story could begin either with the assassination in May 1961 of General Trujillo, a dictator for thirty-two years, or with the election of Juan Bosch as president in December 1962. Bosch had campaigned on a platform of land distribution; increase in the wages of farm workers; and development of cooperatives, new industry, and public works. After his election, Bosch found it virtually impossible to get U.S. aid. One of the major obstacles to support from Washington was the 1963 constitution, the first in the republic's history to be written and adopted by democratic processes. Justice W. O. Douglas of the U.S. Supreme Court was one of the consultants on what kind of constitution it should be. In general, it was a constitution for a secular state and thus alienated some key Roman Catholic elements. It also provided for industrial and agrarian reform and hence alienated important business interests. The *Washington Post* and *I. F. Stone's Weekly* disclosed that during the 1965 negotiations in Santo Domingo to form a new government, the United States applied pressure to revise certain articles of the constitution. "One target is Article 19 which gives workers a right to profit-sharing in both industrial and agricultural enterprises. Another is Article 23 which prohibits large land holdings. A third is Article 25 which restricts the right of foreigners to acquire Dominican land. Another is Article 28 which requires landholders to sell that portion of their lands above the maximum fixed by law; the excess holdings would be resold to the landless peasantry."[4]. The *Washington Post* reporter, Dan Kurzman, reported that the United States wanted the constitution amended to exempt owners of sugar plantations and cattle ranges.[5] The constitution legitimized divorce, secularized education, and omitted reference to the 1954 Concordat with the Vatican— three items that were objectionable to the Papal Nuncio, Emanuele Clarizio.

It was this "liberal" constitution which the forces of former President Juan Bosch believed would prevent the growth of Communism in the Dominican Republic. But it is also this constitution's curtailment of capitalism and Roman Catholic control of the state that led to charges in 1963 that the Bosch regime was pro-Communist. The charges made against Bosch were made by an ardent Roman Catholic, Colonel Wessin. Wessin and a Roman Catholic army chaplain issued an ultimatum to President Bosch when it became clear that Bosch intended to restrict Catholic political activity.[6] Wessin was

---

[4] *I. F. Stone's Weekly*, May 31, 1965.

[5] *Washington Post*, May 25, 1965.

[6] Edwin Lieuwen, *Generals vs. Presidents: Neo-Militarism in Latin America* (New York: Frederick A. Praeger, Inc., 1964), pp. 58–60.

described in the April 30, 1965 *New York Times* in these words:

> As a deeply religious Roman Catholic, he instituted the teaching of Catholic doctrine to troops of the Dominican Army. He also lectured on Communist theory and on methods of detecting subversion. It was his violent anti-Communism that led him to see something sinister in the moderate position Dr. Juan Bosch had assumed toward the Communist and other left-wingers when he was President.

The May 7, 1965 *Time* magazine added that Wessin "instituted mandatory Sunday mass for recruits." Wessin and other army officers also objected to the social reforms that Bosch was instituting because these would eat up some of the budget traditionally reserved for the armed forces.

Bosch became the first freely chosen democratic president in thirty-eight years in December 1962. President Kennedy's administration moved immediately to make this country "the showplace of democracy" under the Alliance for Progress. When a military revolt led by General Wessin ousted President Bosch nine months later, the Kennedy administration suspended diplomatic relations and halted economic aid.[7]

Yet the Kennedy administration participated in the overthrow of Bosch by training those who carried out the revolt against him. Edwin Lieuwen wrote:

> . . . the United States-trained police joined the army in ousting President Bosch, following which both the police and the antiguerilla units, trained during 1963 by a forty-four man United States Army Mission, were used to hunt down Bosch's non-Communist partisans in the name of anti-Communism.[8]

Apparently there was more than training involved, for it has been asserted that the Dominican armed forces acted only after word from the Pentagon.[9]

Shortly after President Johnson came to power, he reversed

[7] *New York Times*, May 15, 1965.

[8] Lieuwen, *Generals vs. Presidents*, p. 127.

[9] John Bartlow Martin, *Overtaken by Events: The Dominican Crisis from the Fall of Trujillo to Civil War* (Garden City, New York: Doubleday and Company, Inc., 1966), pp. 504–5; Sam Halper, "The Dominican Upheaval," *The New Leader*, May 10, 1965.

some of the Kennedy policies towards Latin America and returned to the older policy of more cooperation with Latin American military groups and North American business interests. Johnson recognized the military group that had ousted Bosch and had installed Donald Reid Cabral as president.

Reid, who was one of the oligarchs, quickly abandoned the 1963 constitution and Bosch's various reforms.

On April 25, 1965, the Reid group, supported by the Johnson administration, was overthrown by a group of army leaders who wanted to restore constitutional rule and Bosch to the presidency.[10] When they began this revolt on April 24, 1965, President Johnson alerted U.S. airborne troops and ordered a Marine force to land. The Air Force and Marines, led by General Wessin, fought against the pro-Bosch army units; on April 26, the new pro-Bosch regime, led by Colonel Caamano, armed about three thousand civilians.

President Johnson got word to Bosch, who was in exile in Puerto Rico, that he would not be permitted to return. There was a common belief that the appearance of Bosch would ensure the success of his partisans.

On April 27, the U.S. Navy began evacuating Americans. On April 28, General Wessin's forces began to lose. U.S. Ambassador W. T. Bennett, who had been in the United States and who was flown back to Santo Domingo, sent a cable to President Johnson asking for U.S. Marines. Five hundred marines were landed, and the next day, April 29, General Wessin requested United States assistance in restoring law and order in Santo Domingo.[11] President Johnson, in his news conference on June 1, 1965, said that the plea for troops came "from the entire country team made up of the Ambassador, CIA Director, USIA, Army, Navy, and Air Force. . . ."

The *New York Times* and some other papers reported that, despite Johnson's public profession of neutrality in the struggle, the U.S. embassy helped to form a junta and the U.S. Marines openly assisted it in defeating the Bosch

[10] *New York Times*, April 26, 1965.
[11] *New York Times*, May 1, 1965.

forces. The *New York Times* of May 20, 1965 spoke of the junta forces achieving "military victory in the northern section of the city, in an offensive visibly supported by United States troops." American paratroops "engaged in fierce fighting against the rebel forces." Earlier, the *New York Times* of May 11 reported that U.S. Marines had been working with Dominican soldiers and that "the psychological warfare resources of the United States Information Agency and of the military assist the national council [the military junta] headed by Brig. Gen. Antonio Imbert Barreras, who was picked by the American Embassy."

The reason for such direct military intervention was explained in terms of preventing a Communist takeover of the country. At the very beginning of the U.S. intervention, the April 30 *New York Times* reported that a high-ranking U.S. Navy officer had said the marines were there "to see that no Communist government is established in the Dominican Republic." In support of its thesis that there was danger of Communist control of the revolution, the administration made public a list of fifty-five Communists and pro-Communists who "were playing an important role in organizing mobs among the rebels as well as carrying out much of the paramilitary action."[12] The counter evidence included the *New York Times* report that "there was no indication that the Communists were initially involved in the coup but it was noted that the three principal Communist groups in the Dominican Republic had come out in favor of a return of Mr. Bosch."[13]

Colonel Caamano, the leader of the Bosch forces, stated, "I am completely sure that a dictatorship of the left is infinitely worse than one of the right"; and the colonel's chief aide, Mr. Aristy, asserted that the Dominican revolution had been painted leftist as wrongly as had the Mexican revolution in its first days.[14] Former President Bosch has also denied that it is a Communist-led movement. He said, "This was a

[12] *New York Times*, May 6, 1965.
[13] *New York Times*, April 28, 1965.
[14] *New York Times*, May 11, 1965.

democratic revolution smashed by the leading democracy of the world, the United States."[15]

The *New York Times* of May 15, 1965, in commenting on a U.S. envoy's claim that the Bosch forces had been taken over by Communists, said that these "assessments were not shared by many embassy officials or by other American and foreign observers here." James Goodsell of the *Christian Science Monitor* wrote, "I tried to locate several of those whose names were on the [U.S.] list [of Communists]. I was not successful. . . . I could find no evidence that they were anywhere in . . . key command positions. . . . The top rebel command is in the hands of non-Communist elements who fiercely proclaim their opposition to Communism."[16]

The other big issue in the Dominican invasion arose because President Johnson acted in violation of Article 15 of the Charter of the Organization of American States, which denies the right of any state or group of states to intervene "for any reason whatsoever," and Article 17 which says no state may be occupied militarily "even temporarily," directly or indirectly, "on any grounds whatever."[17]

President Johnson did not consult the OAS until after marines were landed. In fact, the inititative for consultation was taken by a committee of the OAS.[18] On May 6, the OAS, at the request of the United States, agreed to recruit a military force to go to the Dominican Republic to give the action there an international appearance and forestall United Nations intervention.

The U.S.-sponsored resolution was approved by a bare two-thirds majority after the group agreed to let the Dominican junta representative cast a vote. Some nations abstained, including Venezuela, whose instruction to vote no arrived after the official vote was taken.[19]

In spite of all U.S. diplomatic and military efforts,

[15] *New York Times*, May 8, 1965.
[16] Samuel Shapiro, "Santo Domingo: Can We Withdraw," *Nation*, May 24, 1965.
[17] *New York Times*, May 5, 1965.
[18] *New York Times*, May 27, 1965.
[19] *New York Times*, May 7, 1965.

Mexico and Venezuela, Uruguay and Chile were outspoken in their opposition to the U.S. action.[20]

Even after the OAS had agreed to intervene in the Dominican Republic in an effort at peacemaking, there was bitterness against the United States. The *New York Times* of May 19 stated: "Some members of the OAS team were also reported to have been irritated at the Johnson Administration for having sent a presidential mission to try to work out a coalition government."

The Johnson administration had decided to downgrade the earlier Communist allegations and form a coalition government of the military junta and the Bosch forces that had originally been called Communist-dominated. The official explanation was that the Communist elements had been isolated as a result of United States intervention.[21]

Critics of the president say he either received inaccurate information or acted impetuously. In any event, no overt Communist attempt to take over the rebel forces was revealed; President Johnson, eager to prove himself right, sent FBI agents to the Dominican Republic.

A Washington dispatch in the *Kansas City Times* of May 26, 1965 stated: "One line of speculation here holds that the FBI would reach the same conclusions as the CIA on Communist infiltration of the rebels, and thus give the administration ammunition to answer charges of its critics that it intervened too precipitously."

Newspapers of May 11 reported that General Wessin at the United States' urging had resigned from the armed forces in order to ease the political climate in the Dominican Republic. "After word of General Wessin's resignation was received, the Papal Nuncio, Msgr. Emanuele Clarizio, borrowed the helicopter of the United States Ambassador, W. Tapley Bennett, Jr., to fly to San Isidro airbase," which was Wessin's headquarters.[22]

Shortly thereafter, General Wessin decided not to resign.

[20] *New York Times*, May 7, 1965.
[21] *New York Times*, May 19, 1965.
[22] *New York Times*, May 11, 1965.

The May 15 *New York Times* stated that General Imbert had decided to keep him in the junta.

A five-nation peace committee of the OAS, in protesting the U.S. effort to form a coalition government, said: "It is up to the Dominicans and to them alone in the exercise of their national sovereignty and the principle of self-determination of peoples to choose a political administration to adopt the government that best meets their democratic aspirations."[23]

The OAS attitude was reflected in the unwillingness of most nations to send troops to the Dominican Republic. The *New York Times* of May 18 said: "Thus far only three nations—Honduras, Nicaragua, and Costa Rica—have committed troops and their contributions come to less than 500 men." *I. F. Stone's Weekly* on May 31, reported: "The OAS force we are trying to muster as our mercenaries is made up entirely (except for 20 policemen from Costa Rica) of forces supplied by the military dictatorships we helped install in Brazil, Honduras, and Nicaragua." By June 5, the *New York Times* was able to report, "The inter-American peace-keeping force is now made up of 14,600 United States troops . . . and 1,560 men from Brazil, Costa Rica, Honduras, Nicaragua, and El Salvador." The inter-American force was at least technically under the command of a Brazilian, General Hugo Penasco Alvin, who was involved in the overthrow of President Goulart in 1964 for alleged leftist leanings.

The Johnson administration, after it had downgraded the Communist charges against the Bosch forces, sent a mission headed by McGeorge Bundy to get the opposing groups together in a coalition. When the Bundy mission failed, Johnson turned to a three-man committee which was to be composed of a Brazilian, Ellsworth Bunker from the United States, and the Costa Rican ambassador.[24] The Costa Rican refused to serve and was replaced by a man from El Salvador. Three months later, on September 4, 1965, President Johnson

[23] *New York Times*, May 20, 1965.
[24] *New York Times*, June 1, 1965.

announced that a provisional government under the leadership of Dr. Hector Garcia Godoy had been installed.

The Johnson administration was acting on behalf of powerful economic interests in preventing social reform in the Dominican Republic. Men who were active in the Democratic party, some of them key figures in Americans for Democratic Action, had a financial interest in the Dominican Republic. They included Abe Fortas, who for twenty years was a director of Sucrest Corporation, a large sugar refinery dependent on Dominican sugar; A. A. Berle, Jr., who was chairman of the board of Sucrest for many years; Ellsworth Bunker, a former president of National Sugar Refining Corporation; and J. M. Kaplan, molasses magnate. There were also other interests, including North American banks and the Roman Catholic hierarchy, who would gain from having someone other than Bosch in power.

Bosch was subsequently permitted to return to the Dominican Republic to campaign for the 1966 elections, but the candidate of the United States, the church, the armed forces, and the oligarchy, Joaquin Balaguer, won easily. Bosch remained in his heavily guarded headquarters throughout, believing that even if he won, he would not be permitted to govern.

Both the Kennedy and Johnson administrations were determined to keep the Dominican Republic safe for U.S. business interests. The former was prepared to accept Bosch, believing that he could eventually be manipulated, whereas the Johnson machine did not feel a liberal facade was necessary. It was only necessary to convince the American people, which could be done with talk of Communism and the need to preserve "freedom."

Throughout the armed invasion by the United States, and the other efforts to ensure a government acceptable to American business, President Johnson spoke in traditional moralistic terms. On June 3, 1965 he said: "Over the years of our history our forces have gone forth into many lands, but always they returned when they were no longer needed. For the purpose of America is never to suppress liberty but always to save it." Again on June 6, 1965, he said: "The might of America lies in the morality of our purposes and their support by the will of our people of the United States."

In startling contrast the *New Statesman* of England, after comparing U.S. actions to Soviet actions during the Hungarian revolution, asked: "Why should the Americans escape international opprobrium if the Russians were rightly condemned before world opinion."

The significance of the Dominican Republic incident is not simply the direct U.S. military intervention and all that it means in terms of American colonialism, but in the way the United States was able to manipulate the Organization of American States. The United States was able to control the votes of enough countries in the OAS to secure nominal intervention by the OAS to support American foreign policy. As President Johnston stated on May 28, 1965, "For the first time in history the Organization of American States has created and sent to the soil of an American nation an international peacekeeping military force. That may be the greatest achievement of all."[25]

A report in the *Kansas City Star* of June 1, 1965 from Santo Domingo revealed that this "great achievement" was to all practical purposes to label the OAS as a U.S. puppet: "There are no announcements from the U.S. embassy, only from the OAS which has now become the spokesman for the outside world. But the moves are widely understood to be American moves. . . ."

The Guatemalan and Dominican Republic incidents illustrate a startling fact: Those who determine American foreign policy are not prepared to permit determination by Latin American nations of their own destiny. On the surface the U.S. position is opposition to the extension of Communism, but this has been alleged even when there was no threat of a Communist takeover, as evident in the Dominican

[25] U.S. Department of State, Inter-American Series No. 92, No. 7971, October 1965.

Republic. The real issue appears to be the threat of any social change that would lead to expropriation or serious restriction of American-owned business. Ironically, it is the virtual impossibility of social change with American approval that tempts Latin Americans to consider collaboration with Communists.

11

CUBA

THE CUBAN REVOLUTION that brought Castro to power is thought by many Americans to have been a result of superior Communist intrigue and planning to get a foothold in the Western Hemisphere. It is seldom placed in the perspective of long-term American policy towards Cuba. Neither is Castro's Communism understood as an evolving reaction to events, including U.S. actions.

The Castro seizure of power was really a revolution against American policy in Cuba. That policy began when the United States went back on its Spanish–American wartime pledge, adopted by Congress on April 19, 1898:

> The United States hereby disclaims any disposition or intention to exercise sovereignty, jurisdiction or control over said island, except for the pacification thereof, and asserts its determination when that is accomplished to leave the government and control of the island to its people.

During the American military occupation under General Wood, a constitutional convention was called in Havana. While working on the constitution and treaty to govern future relations with the United States, the Cubans were handed a set of articles known as the Platt Amendment. The U.S. Congress had already adopted this amendment, which provided that the "U.S. may exercise the right to intervene for . . . the maintenance of a government adequate for the protection of life, property and individual liberty. . . ." The significant word was *property*. The amendment also provided that Cuba must sell or lease to the United States land for naval stations. Given no choice but to accept it, the Cubans included the Platt Amendment in the Cuban Constitution and in the permanent treaty with the United States.

During the occupation, which ended May 2, 1902, the land laws imposed on Cuba wiped out the communal lands and laid the foundations for vast acreages to be owned by U.S. corporations, leaving many Cubans landless.

American troops intervened in 1906, 1912, 1917, and 1920. Having established the pattern of intervention, it was possible for American political and financial advisors to control the government without troops.

When General Gerardo Machado was overthrown in 1933 after having ruled despotically since 1924, Dr. Ramon Grau San Martin became president. Under his leadership a moderate reform program was adopted which included an eight-hour day, a minimum wage for cutting sugar cane, an agrarian reform program, and a reduction in electricity rates. As a result, the administration of Franklin D. Roosevelt, which had abrogated the Platt Amendment, withheld recognition of the Grau government during its four months in office. Thirty naval vessels, including two large battleships, were sent to Cuban waters. In September 1933, Sergeant Fulgencio Batista seized control of the army. Early in October Sumner Welles, who had been sent to Cuba to look after U.S. business and government interests, told Batista that "in my judgment he was the only individual who represented authority in Cuba," that his opposition to "radical elements . . . had brought to his support the great majority of the commercial and financial interests of Cuba." With this encouragement Batista moved into the United States camp and in January 1934 forced the Grau government to resign.[1]

The coalition which took office as a result of American diplomacy was recognized within five days after President Mendieta took office. In March 1952, three days after the

[1] Samuel Shapiro, *Invisible Latin America* (Boston: Beacon Press, 1963), p. 73.

Cuban army had been strengthened by a U.S. military assistance pact, Batista seized control of the government by a coup d'état after he saw he could not win a free election. That same month, we recognized the Batista regime, although the presidents of both houses of the Cuban Congress had denounced the Batista takeover and a young lawyer named Fidel Castro had, three days earlier, filed a petition with Cuba's constitutional court asking that the new regime be declared illegal.[2]

Fidel Castro launched his first military attack on July 26, 1953, was defeated, imprisoned, and later amnestied. During the second stage of the Castro revolution, which began in November 1956, the United States continued to supply Batista with arms until March 1958, when an arms embargo was declared. The United States military missions, however, continued to train Batista's troops even after the embargo was imposed.

On January 1, 1959, before the revolution was complete, Batista left Cuba; his forces surrendered the next day.

In the early years of the Batista regime, the Communists cooperated with Batista. Rafael Rodriguez, the present editor of the Cuban Communist party's newspaper and, during the Batista regime, a leading Communist, served in the Batista government as a minister without portfolio, with special responsibilities for education. It was the same Rafael Rodriguez who, toward the end of 1958, was sent by the Communist party as an emissary to Castro to pledge Communist support of his revolution. It is important to remember that the Communists were not in on the Castro revolution when it started. They climbed on the Castro bandwagon after it seemed likely he would win. Rafael Rodriguez has served the Castro government in a number of capacities. He reorganized the faculty, structure, and curricula of the University of Havana and each week has delivered from three to five ideological lectures to government employees, student groups, and TV audiences.[3]

[2] *I. F. Stone's Weekly*, August 8, 1960.
[3] Max Frankel, *New York Times*, November 27, 1960.

Immediately following the revolution, Castro turned the government over to Manuel Urrutia, a former judge, who included in his cabinet persons committed to democracy and to friendly relations with the United States. One of these, Rufo López-Fresquet, the minister of the treasury, now in exile in Puerto Rico, has written that Castro was not a Communist and did not receive assistance from the Communists in launching the revolution. But Castro was strongly anti-American as a result of his experiences in the sugar cane fields and his knowledge of U.S. support of Batista.[4]

In the early days of the Castro regime, the Communists were doing all they could to establish themselves in key positions but did not succeed in taking over. In those days Castro apparently had hopes of some collaboration with the United States. There have been published reports of a request to the Export–Import Bank for a $3 to $4 million loan for road-building equipment and reports of a proposed $1 million barter deal of Cuban chrome for corn to meet food shortages.[5]

In February 1959, one month after he came to power, Castro sent a three-man mission to Washington to see whether financial aid could be secured to bolster Cuba's depleted reserves and to make a program of industrialization possible. "The mission was cordially received but went away empty-handed."[6]

Castro himself wanted to come to Washington but could not get an official invitation. In April 1959, he was invited by the National Press Club to speak to the Washington newspaper correspondents. In spite of the fact that this was an unofficial invitation, he brought with him his ministers of the treasury and the president of the Cuban National Bank. Secretary of State Christian Herter met him in a hotel room rather than in his State Department office—so as to emphasize that he was not being received officially by the Eisenhower

[4] Rufo López-Fresquet, *My Fourteen Months with Castro* (Cleveland: The World Publishing Co., 1966), pp. 159–63.
[5] *I. F. Stone's Weekly*, August 8, 1960.
[6] Ibid.

administration. President Eisenhower snubbed Castro by leaving Washington "for no other reason than to play golf in Georgia," which, wrote Rufo López-Fresquet, "was a diplomatic discourtesy." Castro instead had an interview with Vice President Nixon that left Castro angry because, as he indicated, Nixon spent the entire time upbraiding him.[7]

Castro had instructed his financial advisers who accompanied him not to ask for financial aid on the ground that it was a good-will trip and that it would be better for the United States to offer aid "without our asking for it."[8] A number of Cubans in exile believe that Castro was so hostile to the United States from the beginning that he merely wanted an excuse to claim that the United States was not willing to help finance the Cuban revolution. Yet some who hold to this also indicate that even the Communists in Cuba wanted U.S. help in industrializing the island. López-Fresquet, a fervent enemy of Castro's, also says that "the policy of the U.S. should have been directed toward denying Castro the chance to present Americans as enemies of social, political and economic progress in Cuba." Instead the United States collaborated with "Batistianos" at least until the Bay of Pigs invasion.[9]

Whatever Castro's motives, his Washington trip did not improve relationships. A month later the Castro government passed a law confiscating property belonging to Batista supporters. In May 1959, the Agrarian Reform Law was decreed. That reform permitted private landlords to keep 900 acres of land with payment for any excess to be made in 4.5 percent bonds redeemable in twenty years. The value of the land was to be determined by the owners based on the tax appraisals they made of their own property. If their land was in rice, cattle, or sugar cane, they could keep up to 3,300 acres. Castro said at the time that he was "only trying to move from Feudalism to enlightened capitalism." When the law was carried out, officials ignored its provisions and seized

---

[7] López-Fresquet, *My Fourteen Months with Castro*, p. 169.
[8] Ibid., p. 106.
[9] Ibid., pp. 164, 166, 170, 171.

machinery, trucks, and other equipment, often without providing receipts for what was taken. Eventually, Castro dispossessed everyone and did not give the peasants any land. The state became the owner of all land.[10]

A year later, in June 1960, three big American oil companies in Cuba—Texaco, Shell, and Standard Oil of New Jersey—refused to refine Soviet oil which the Cuban government was importing as a result of a trade agreement made with the USSR in February 1960. The Cuban government insisted, and the oil companies retaliated by cutting off oil from Venezuela. The U.S. Congress in July 1960, in reaction, cut off the rest of the 1960 sugar import quota, about seven hundred thousand tons. The USSR agreed to buy this quota, and China agreed to take five hundred thousand tons each year for the next five years.

Castro retaliated on August 6 and nationalized the U.S.-owned electric company, telephone company, oil refineries, and sugar mills. The nationalization decree said, in effect, that the U.S. government would decide whether the U.S. companies would be paid. Parts of the proceeds of the sugar above 3 million tons sold in the United States thereafter would be used to pay off the confiscated property. In September 1960, the U.S.-owned rubber companies, grocery chains, and banks were nationalized. On October 19 the United States retaliated with an embargo on all exports to Cuba except medicines and some types of food. By October 25 everything American worth confiscating had been taken; 166 American-owned companies had been nationalized.

It is worth noting here that the September 26, 1960 *New York Times* carried this report: "Despite the Castro government's increasing economic dependence on the Soviet bloc, it voted against the Communists at the United Nations last week in support of an African–Asian resolution backing Mr. Hammarskjold in the Congo crisis." It is also worth noting that Cuba participated in the neutralist conference that met in Belgrade under Yugoslav leadership.

But the U.S. embargo further pushed the Cubans into the

[10] Ibid., p. 115.

eager arms of Russia and China, though Western Europe and Canada were still trading with Cuba.

Nevertheless, Cuba did not become Communist in any ideological or other fashion. Two independent socialist writers, Leo Huberman and Paul M. Sweezy, reported after several weeks' visit in Cuba, in March 1960, that "this is the first time—ever, anywhere—that a genuine socialist revolution has been made by non-Communists!" Their explanation of Communist participation in the Cuban revolution follows.

> The leadership for its part, finding that the Communists work hard for the Revolution, not on their own terms but entirely within the framework of policies laid down by the leadership itself, has no objective reason for rejecting their support or quarreling with them—quite the contrary. And having no well articulated ideology of its own, either Communist or anti-Communist, it has no subjective reason either.[11]

Castro, his colleagues of the July 26th movement, the army, and the masses of the people apparently thought of the revolution neither in Communist nor in anti-Communist terms.

Well before the expropriation of American-owned business, and before any Communist attempt to take over the revolution, the Eisenhower administration in late 1959 decided to give the green light to the CIA to organize Cuban exiles, train a military force, and plan an invasion of Cuba.[12] The CIA was involved in such planning in spite of a statement by the deputy CIA director, General C. P. Cabell, to a Senate Internal Security Subcommittee that the CIA did not consider Castro either "a Communist party member or even pro-Communist. . . ."[13]

This decision was made and carried out in violation of the UN Charter which binds all members, not only "to refrain . . . from the threat or use of force against the territorial integrity or political independence of any state," but also "to avoid giving assistance to the aggressor." It also was a viola-

[11] Leo Huberman and Paul M. Sweezy, "Cuba, Anatomy of a Revolution," *Monthly Review*, July, August 1960, pp. 150, 154.
[12] William Shannon, *New York Post*, April 9, 1961.
[13] López-Fresquet, *My Fourteen Years with Castro*, p. 168.

tion of American law forbidding anyone in the United States to prepare for or finance or take part in "any military or naval expedition against the territory or dominion of any foreign prince or state . . . with whom the U.S. is at peace. . . ."

In late 1959, the Castro government, whether aware then of the invasion plans or not, asked Britain to sell it jet fighters. The British, after consultation with the State Department, turned down the Castro request. The December 4, 1959 *New York Times* quoted the Cuban ambassador in London as saying that Cuba now intended to buy these planes "wherever they can be purchased." The Soviet Union became the major source for Cuba's military planes.

After Kennedy came to power, serious differences of opinion developed over the Cuban invasion plans. The Central Intelligence Agency had backed one Cuban refugee faction led by Varona, who had the backing of American business interests and who was alleged to have pledged to return Cuban property to American business interests. The man A. A. Berle, a former assistant secretary of state, is alleged to have wanted in a position of leadership was Manuel Ray, the leader of a rival and more left-wing but anti-Communist faction. Ray was apparently devoted to carrying through the social successes of the Castro revolution but without the Communists and without Castro.[14]

A third group included Senator J. W. Fulbright and Chester Bowles, then undersecretary of state, who were opposed to the invasion itself. Kennedy vacillated but in the end, just two weeks before the invasion, decided not to permit U.S. forces to be used in connection with the invasion.

There were apparently a number of reasons for President Kennedy's willingness, despite misgivings, to permit the abortive Bay of Pigs invasion of April 1967 to proceed. The invasion project had been jointly planned by the United States Joint Chiefs of Staff and the CIA. The CIA presented alterna-

---

[14] See also *Time*, January 27, 1961; *Washington Post*, March 22; *I. F. Stone's Weekly*, April 17; *New York Post*, April 9.

tive invasion sites to the Joint Chiefs who recommended Trinidad to President Kennedy. When Kennedy turned down Trinidad, the Joint Chiefs chose the Bay of Pigs. An associate of President Kennedy, Theodore Sorenson, asserted that Kennedy went along with the invasion chiefly because he could not accept the political and psychological consequences of stopping the invasion and partly because "he felt that his disapproval of the plan would be a show of weakness inconsistent with his general stance."[15]

Tom Wicker of the *New York Times* reported on July 23, 1965 that Kennedy "was ever confronted with the question from the plan's advocates whether he would be less resolute against Castro than the Republican Administration that had conceived the invasion scheme."

Richard M. Bissell, Jr., who was in charge of planning the invasion for the CIA, reported that the Cuban exiles who were to carry out the invasion "were the most powerful military force between Mexico and Panama and it is entirely possible that they might have tried to seize a base in Nicaragua, Honduras or Guatemala; there is not the slightest doubt that they could have defeated any Guatemalan force."[16] Bissell indicated that there was no plan agreed upon for dealing "with this armed, highly motivated unit in case the operation were cancelled."[17] Tom Wicker of the *New York Times* concluded that the project became a "sort of Frankenstein's monster that once created, went out of control."[18]

The events surrounding the Bay of Pigs invasion demonstrate that American foreign policy is not always pursued as a result of policy decisions by top leaders of government. Decisions have frequently been made by CIA and military leaders that force the hand of the president.

Throughout this whole period, the Communist party in Cuba was gradually strengthening its position in the government. The *New York Times* of August 2, 1960, in a long

[15] Tom Wicker, *New York Times*, July 23, 1965.
[16] Ibid., July 22, 1965.
[17] Ibid., July 22, 1965.
[18] Ibid., July 23, 1965.

analysis of the Communist activity, said: "The Communist Party in Cuba has made no effort to preach Communist doctrine among Cubans, preferring to gain quiet acceptance and respectability while moving its members and sympathizers into important positions."

Castro himself had said, "Our revolution is humanist, not Communist," but by the summer of 1960, the Castro regime was saying in a shoulder-shrugging way, "Let them call us Communists if they want to."

Huberman and Sweezy explain this refusal of Castro to be concerned about the charge of Communism:

> . . . they have correctly recognized that to attempt to "prove" their non-Communism is to set foot on the road to disaster. This is how it works: You begin by denying that you are a Communist. Your baiter counters with a statement to the effect that "that's what you say, but you cooperate with Communists and follow policies of which they approve. How do I *know* you are not a Communist? You must prove it." If you accept this challenge you are lost. The first step is to refuse to cooperate with Communists, and in order to carry this through you have to establish political tests to determine who is a Communist. The witch hunt is on. Next you must alter your policies to differentiate yourself from them, and the best way to achieve this is to become once again a client of the United States. But for Latin America this means precisely embracing the status quo ante, renouncing all possibility of "doing what needs to be done."[19]

On December 2, 1961, a UPI dispatch from Miami asserted that Castro had said in a speech that "he really has been a dedicated Communist since his college days but he concealed his views so it would be easier to seize power." Since the UPI office in Havana was closed during the night hours, UPI got its story instead from a Cuban exile in Miami who monitored the Castro speech. Even this initial report, which stated that Castro "disclosed that his political creed had been developed over many years, starting with his college days," was rewritten in New York. The rewrite stated, "Castro has been a dedicated Communist since his college

[19] Huberman and Sweezy, *Cuba: Anatomy of a Revolution*, p. 162.

days."[20] What Castro actually said was that he was not a Marxist while a student but became one only after he came to power.

"Both the A.P. report from Havana and the record of the U.S. Foreign Broadcast Monitor," said the *New York Post* of December 14, 1961, "support the view that Castro recited a rambling tale of his political evolution in which he never even acknowledged present Communist membership but described his gradual drift to the Marxist–Leninist creed."

C. L. Sulzberger confirmed in a report from Havana, published in the November 7, 1964 *New York Times*, that Castro was not a Marxist–Leninist until after the Bay of Pigs invasion. He reported Castro as saying that during his guerrilla warfare against Batista:

> I did not clearly see that a social revolution would collide directly with the U.S.A., that the antagonism arising from this would produce the concrete events of later years.
> Had I understood the imperialist phenomenon, I would then (not later) have truly become a Marxist–Leninist. But to reach that point I had to have two years of armed conflict (against Batista) during which I saw U.S. planes being used to attack the defenseless population causing measureless suffering.
> A year of revolutionary government would have to pass before experience made us genuine Marxist–Leninists. We announced the socialist nature of our revolution after the attacks by CIA planes bearing Cuban markings (April, 1961) on the eve of the Bay of Pigs.

It was American foreign policy operating without ethical commitment and on behalf of a military–industrial elite that persuaded Castro that he should accept the philosophy that elite abhors. Those who fear the worst in any effort to disturb the status quo often tend, by their reaction, to create the situation they fear.

Castro, although subscribing to a Marxist approach, refused to let his revolution be controlled by the Communist party (PSP). In March 1962, after Castro saw that Anibal Escalante, the party's organizing secretary, was trying to put

[20] *New York Post*, December 14, 1961.

Communists into all the key positions, Castro attacked sectarianism "and broke the power of the PSP so effectively that it has never come back." Instead Castro supported the Partido Unificado de la Revolucion Socialista de Cuba (PURSC), which was an outgrowth of selection by working groups, such as those of factories, farms, and public utilities, of those who "were supposed to be their best men and women."[21] It is a Cuban elite organization designed to carry out, without any governing responsibilities, the purposes of the revolution in much the same way as have the Communist party in the Soviet Union, the Fascist party in Italy, and the Nazi party in Germany.[22]

Herbert Matthews of the *New York Times*, after a number of assignments in Cuba, wrote:

> The belief fostered by Washington and the Cuban exiles that Fidel Castro is a prisoner of the Cuban Communist apparatus or a puppet of Moscow is a myth. He is, by character, incapable of accepting orders or even advice. The path he has chosen forces him into a conformity to most of the needs and desires of the Soviet bloc, but that is a different matter.[23]

According to Regis Debray:

> Fidel Castro says simply that there is no revolution without a vanguard; that this vanguard is not necessarily the Marxist-Leninist party; and that those who want to make the revolution have the right and the duty to constitute themselves a vanguard, independently of these parties.[24]

This means that instead of a world-wide Comunist party, the ruling party in any future revolution or socialist state would be developed out of the leadership that won the guerrilla or other warfare—as was the case in Cuba.

During the years following the Castro revolution, the

---

[21] Herbert L. Matthews, "Return to Cuba," *Hispanic American and Luso-Brazilian Studies*, Bolivar House, Stanford University, California, 1964.

[22] Ibid.

[23] Ibid.

[24] Regis Debray, "Revolution in the Revolution?" *Monthly Review* (sp. ed.), New York, July–August 1967, as quoted in *Problems of Communism* (Washington, D.C.: Government Printing Office, January–February 1968), p. 9.

United States tried repeatedly to get the Organization of American States to back its position on Cuba. It achieved only partial success until the Kennedy announcement of the Cuban–Russian plans for long-range missiles on Cuban soil. In the Punta del Este Conference in Uruguay in January 1962, where the United States wanted to expel Cuba from the Organization of American States, the United States used economic aid as a bribe. The *New York Times* of August 1, 1962 reported that the United States, which had earlier refused to continue an economic aid program in Haiti, promised at Punta del Este "to resume aid expenditures when Haiti agreed to cast a crucial vote to exclude Cuba from participation in the inter-American system."

The *U.S. News and World Report* of December 18, 1961 reported that projected U.S. loans to Mexico, who voted against intervention in Cuba, and loans to other countries that abstained in the vote at the December meeting of the OAS were being reviewed.

When the Kennedy administration received evidence that Russian missile bases were being set up in Cuba, President Kennedy, on October 22, 1962, announced the quarantine of Cuba. In addition, he mobilized American forces for "a global response for whatever counter-measures the Russians may make."[25]

The quarantine action included the stopping and, if necessary, the sinking of Russian ships or planes taking missiles to Cuba.

President Kennedy announced a decision to take this quarantine action before he put the issue up to the UN or the OAS. The UN and the OAS were thus faced by unilateral action before they could meet. Moreover, in the Kennedy speech the announcement that we were prepared to present our case in the OAS and the UN was coupled with this qualifying phrase: "without limiting our freedom of action." The only legal basis the United States had for its action was that the UN Charter allowed for regional security arrangements. After the

[25] *Kansas City Times*, October 25, 1962.

announcement, the OAS formally acted to back the United States.

Premier Nikita Khrushchev, in an exchange of letters with President Kennedy and in a public statement, proposed dismantling Russian bases in Cuba if the United States would dismantle its bases in Turkey. Legally, U.S. missiles in Turkey could be justified only on the ground that Turkey and the United States are in a regional security arrangement, NATO. But if countries as far from each other as Turkey and the United States are in the same region, presumably Russia and Cuba could be in a regional security arrangement. Russia and Cuba, however, avoided any effort to include Cuba in the Warsaw Pact.

Although there was a technical basis for U.S. missiles in Turkey to be aimed at Russia, the Cuban incident revealed the double moral standard. The United States could have missile bases in the proximity of Russia to defend Turkey, but Russian bases could not be set up near the United States to defend Cuba.

President Kennedy refused the offer of mutual dismantling of missiles, and a further exchange of letters took place. The crisis ended when Khrushchev, in a broadcast on October 28, agreed to dismantle the bases in Cuba. In that broadcast he acknowledged Kennedy's letter of October 27 giving "assurance against an invasion of Cuba" as soon as United Nations inspection in Cuba showed that the bases were dismantled.

American officials, as well as public opinion, viewed the missile bases in Cuba as an effort by the Russians to extend Soviet military and political influence into Latin America. Castro and Khrushchev, however, suggested a different rationale. Castro believed on the basis of intelligence reports that the United States was getting ready in 1962 to invade Cuba. He asked the Russians for the missiles, saying, "We showed them in an incontrovertible way that an invasion was being planned."[26]

[26] Matthews, "Return to Cuba."

Premier Khrushchev on December 12, 1962, in a major foreign policy address to the Supreme Soviet of the USSR, gave his rationale. This rationale in brief was that the United States was contemplating an invasion of Cuba, that the Soviet Union supplied missiles and bombers for defensive purposes "so that the American imperialists, if they really decided to invade, realized that the war which they threatened to start stood at their own borders, so that they realized more realistically the dangers of thermonuclear war." According to this rationale, Soviet rockets would not have been sent to Cuba if there had been no threat of invasion. Therefore, when the president of the United States was willing to promise that there would be no invasion, there was no need to keep rockets in Cuba. If it is argued, said Khrushchev, that the United States forced the USSR to back down, "These people should say that the United States too was compelled to yield the settlement of outstanding issues between states, without war, by peaceful means."

It is interesting to note by way of digression that in the United States, the extreme right wing accepts this portion of Khrushchev's analysis that the Soviet Union got a major victory, in the promise of no invasion, from the Cuban affair. The tough crowd in the United States who believe that a brink-of-war approach is the way to conduct diplomacy are, together with the right-wing extremists, implicated in all the invasion plans, training camps, and the military threat to Cuba. So in one sense their policy created the situation which caused the Russians to precipitate the crisis that enabled Kennedy to claim credit for forcing a Russian backdown. The Russians apparently accomplished their purposes, and the United States as a result has foregone the invasion advocated by the tough crowd.

However, the viewpoint cannot be completely discounted that Russia put rockets in the Western Hemisphere as a bridgehead for Soviet political and military penetration in much the same way that U.S. bases have created and sustained American interests in various parts of the world. Yet, Castro's reaction to the Russian decision to dismantle bases seem to belie this. He was angry and admittedly humiliated by the decision taken without consultation with him.

Only in April and May 1963 did the Cubans and Russians resolve their differences over the removal of missiles. In a joint communiqué, the Russians recognized the Cuban regime as "socialist" but with a special status of independence. Cuba did not join the Warsaw Pact or Comecon, nor did it condemn Albania. It decided "to maintain fraternal links with the entire socialist world. . . ." While affirming its support of coexistence—the Soviet position—it subsequently refused to ratify the Nuclear Test Ban Treaty, which was an illustration of Soviet–American cooperation.[27]

One important political and ethical issue in the missile confrontation was the legal one. Where did President Kennedy get the authority under international law to enforce a blockade or quarantine in time of peace? Article 51 of the United Nations Charter permits defense only in the case of armed attack. If it is argued that nations have a right to blockade or quarantine or go to war to prevent the establishment of weapons on the soil of another sovereign nation, then this is an argument for preventive war. None of the churches that have adopted statements against preventive war came out against the Kennedy action as mobilization for that purpose.

The U.S. argument was that the Russian weapons were offensive missiles as distinct from defensive weapons such as antiaircraft missiles. But this argument could hardly be sustained without admitting that U.S. missiles in Asia and Europe are offensive weapons against neighboring China and Russia. American military men speak of their missiles as deterrents. Why should this not be true of Russian missiles on Cuban soil? To raise the question is to reveal that the U.S. position was based on superiority of power rather than on any legal or ethical base. Kennedy did not, as the UN

[27] Kevin Devlin, "The Permanent Revolution of Fidel Castro," *Problems of Communism* (Washington, D.C.: Government Printing Office, January–February 1968), p. 3.

Charter provides, take the dispute to the UN or the OAS until after he had acted to set up the quarantine.

The missile confrontation and the pro-Soviet posture of Cuba need never have taken place. At least the question needs to be raised as to whether the United States could have produced a different result in Cuba if it had acted with less hostility. Samuel Shapiro wrote:

> More skillful American diplomacy might have caused events to move in a very different direction, especially in the early months of 1958 when Castro's thinking had not yet hardened. . . . It is easy to forget now that Fidel's first cabinet was made up of moderates and even conservatives; that his first visit abroad was to the United States; that in 1959 he sponsored a multi-million dollar publicity campaign to attract American tourists; that he promised to pay (in bonds) for the land taken by the Agrarian Reform Law; that he continued to pay interest in dollars on Cuban bonds traded on the New York Stock Exchange for two years after coming to power; that he still insists that he is willing to reimburse American owners of expropriated property if Cuba is allowed to earn dollars by selling sugar to the United States.[28]

The fundamental issue in early Cuban–American relations was whether Cuba had a right to regulate or even expropriate property or corporations owned by North Americans. The United States under a more enlightened administration finally recognized Mexico's right to expropriate oil property, but only because of the insistence of our seventy-year-old ambassador in Mexico, Josephus Daniels. Daniels refused to let the oil companies dictate policy. As a result, the United States and Mexico have friendly relations and American business is able to invest in Mexico subject to her governmental restrictions.

So long as the United States insists on its sovereignty in making decisions, it is only just that the rights of other smaller nations be respected when they make decisions they deem essential to the well-being of their peoples. The United States pursues this policy with respect to reactionary regimes in

[28] Shapiro, *Invisible Latin America*, p. 96.

South Africa and South America; it can afford to acknowledge the rights for left-of-center governments. Unfortunately the diplomatic relations of the United States with Latin American nations are governed more by the temporary interests of the large corporations than by the long-range interest of the peoples of either North or South America.

The goal of American foreign policy as evident in our actions in Guatemala, the Dominican Republic, and Cuba is not, as our leaders have frequently said, a peaceful world in which democracy has a chance to develop, but a world subordinate to our will. We set the stage for similar actions by other great powers instead of trying to change either the moral basis for national action or the procedural basis for resolving disputes within a strengthened United Nations. When the United States engages in such actions where it has the power to enforce its will, there is no moral basis on which it can condemn similar invasions by the Soviet Union or China. The Soviet invasion of Czechoslovakia in 1968 can be justified by the vague term *national interest* in much the same way as the American "national interest" is used to rationalize an invasion of Latin American countries.

12

SOUTHERN ASIA

Asia is not simply a battleground for mainland China and the United States. There are parts of Asia where nationalism is proudly opposed to both American and Chinese control. Some countries, like Burma and India, have pursued a neutralist policy to avoid military entanglements with the great powers. Others have been subject to the pressure or invasion of one great power, while being ignored by the other. Two countries where the United States has made little or no effort at military control have faced Chinese armies: Tibet and India.

China had claimed Tibet for centuries. Tibet, however, was a concern of Great Britain's during her rule of India because she feared that Russia might control Tibet and gain access to India. In 1904, a British colonel named Younghusband forced on Tibet the Lhasa Convention under which Tibet would not permit any concession to a foreign state without British consent. In 1906, Britain and China signed a Peking Convention which said that no nation except China could have concessions in Tibet. A year later a British–Russian agreement recognized Chinese authority in Tibet both with respect to foreign relations and general overall control. During the 1911 Chinese Revolution that brought Sun Yat-sen to power as head of the Chinese Republic, the Tibetans seized the opportunity to get rid of Chinese control. When China tried to reestablish control, Britain told her to stay out of Tibet.

In 1914, representatives of the three nations met at Simla in India. The Simla Convention provided that Tibet was to be autonomous under the general suzerainty of China. China

186

was not to interfere with her internal affairs, and both Britain and China were to station a limited number of troops in Tibet. Sir Arthur McMahon, Britain's representative, drew a line on a map from Bhutan to Burma which roughly followed the Himalayan peaks. The line, however, was never surveyed or marked on the ground. The Indian government claims the McMahon line as a part of the Simla Convention. China denies that it was even discussed and asserts that it was determined "behind the back of the representatives of the Chinese Central Government. . . ." In any event the Simla Convention was repudiated by the Chinese government of that day. The Chinese Communist government now points out that "the Simla Treaty . . . was not formally signed by the representative of the then Chinese government, and this is explicitly noted in the treaty."[1]

The British indicate that the convention was initiated by the Chinese representative, but China refused to let him put his full signature on the treaty. Between 1911 and 1949 when the Communists took control of China, Tibet had not been controlled by China, although a Chinese mission had been there. Throughout all these years Tibet was a feudal state with almost everyone being held in serfdom. "The lamas and nobility owned nearly all the land, livestock and other wealth."[2]

In 1949, taking advantage of the revolution in China, the Tibetans expelled the Chinese mission. The Chinese Communists responded by asserting their right to Tibet. On October 7, 1950, China attacked Tibet. The reason presumably was the ancient Chinese claim to Tibet. Yet there were other factors that cannot be ignored, such as the Communist desire to end both feudalism and the religious superstition that made it possible.

More important perhaps was the fear of U.S. activity there. The United States was fighting in Korea, and China

[1] Chao Kuo-chün, "The Chinese-Indian Controversy," *Current History*, December 1959, pp. 358–9.
[2] Edgar Snow, *The Other Side of the River: Red China Today* (New York: Random House, Inc., 1961), p. 590.

was expecting an American drive to the Yalu river border. There was always the possibility of a beachhead in other places near China. Edgar Snow refers to "reports of CIA activity along the Tibetan border (including air drops of arms and money) [which] may or may not have been true but they were taken quite seriously in Peking."[3] There was also fear in China that the United States might encourage Chiang Kai-shek to "liberate" Tibet.[4]

India protested the Chinese invasion of Tibet on the grounds that she claimed the earlier British rights and duties in Tibet. The Chinese, however, insisted that Tibet was purely a domestic problem. The United States during the Second World War had discussed this very problem with the British and the Chinese Nationalists. Edgar Snow describes the result in these words:

> In an aide-memoir in 1943 the British Embassy in Washington conceded "formal Chinese suzerainty" but also wished to secure for the Lhasa government "the full enjoyment of local autonomy" and the right to "exchange diplomatic representatives with other powers." In reply the State Department unequivocally declined support of the latter aim when it declared: "The Government of the United States has borne in mind the fact that the Chinese Government has long claimed suzerainty over Tibet and that the Chinese constitution lists Tibet among areas constituting the territory of the Republic of China. This Government has at no time raised a question regarding either of those claims."[5]

Tibet raised the issue of China's attack in the United Nations, but on India's recommendation, the UN decided against intervention. In a May 1951 agreement between China and Tibet, China took military control of the country but permitted certain autonomy in local affairs. On April 29, 1954, India and China signed an agreement on Tibet which in effect left Tibet to China. China's premier, Chou En-lai, visited India in June 1954, and Nehru visited China in October. Some months later,

---

[3] Ibid., p. 591.
[4] Ibid.
[5] Ibid., p. 589. Also U.S. Dept. of State, *Foreign Relations of the U.S., 1943, China* (Washington, D.C., 1957), p. 630.

in April 1955, at the Bandung Conference, both leaders encouraged friendship between their nations, which was maintained until 1959.

In March 1959, the Tibetans revolted and their religious–political ruler, the Dalai Lama (Buddhist), fled to India where he was granted asylum. India, however, refused to permit a Tibetan government-in-exile because this would mean breaking relations with China. China nevertheless retaliated by restricting Indian trade and the movement of Indians in Tibet.

The second problem between India and China was the border controversy. Actually, one border controversy in the east involving the McMahon line is related to the Tibetan conflict. The other border to the west is one where the British did even less to mark the dividing line. The Chinese have for centuries had a caravan trail running from Tibet to the Chinese province of Sinkiang through the disputed territory of the Ladakh area of Kashmir. In 1956 and 1957 the Chinese built a hard surface road over the caravan trail. But the Indians paid so little attention to the area that it was about two years after the road was paved that an Indian patrol discovered it and notified New Delhi.

Prior to the Tibetan revolt, there had been, beginning in July 1954, a series of border disputes which led to twenty-five notes being exchanged between China and India. But these incidents were not made public by either nation. Only in August 1959 did Nehru reveal that Chinese troops had crossed into Indian territory in the east and fired on an Indian post at Longju. In October 1959, a Chinese armed group killed nine members of an Indian patrol and captured ten others. Under the impact of mounting popular resentment, Nehru indicated that if the situation got much worse, India would become "a nation in arms." Nehru also declared India responsible for the protection of the small border states of Bhutan and Sikkim.

On September 8, 1959, Chou En-lai had written Nehru, and on September 27 Nehru replied. Chou asserted that "Indian troops after the Tibetan rebellion . . . overstepped the so-called McMahon line. . . . Indian troops invaded and occupied Longju, intruded into Yasher and are still in occupation of Shatze, Khinzemane, and Tamaden. . . ." Nehru replied that "Yasher is a place not known to the Indian Government," that "Tamaden, which has been ascertained as situated somewhat north of the McMahon line, has been vacated by Indian forces" and the other two places are "on Indian territory."[6]

Chou En-lai proposed an overall settlement based on "friendly negotiation." In the meantime, "the two sides should maintain the long existing status quo of the border, and not seek to change it by unilateral action, even less by force." Nehru wrote in similar vein.[7]

On October 20, 1962, after a number of border clashes, more serious fighting began. The Chinese accused India of launching "massive armed attacks all along the line on the Chinese frontier guards on October 20, 1962" and asserted that the border conflict had "been going on for a month."[8] *Time* magazine reported that "without consulting any of his military, Nehru publicly ordered [General] Kaul to drive out the Chinese invaders" in the northeast. But, says *Time,* "before Kaul had a chance to try and 'clear out' the Chinese . . . the Chinese struck first on October 20."[9]

Premier Khrushchev on October 22 wrote Nehru and Chou En-lai suggesting an immediate cease-fire and top-level negotiations. The Chinese agreed to withdraw twelve and a half miles and hold talks, but Nehru refused on the ground that this would still leave some Communist troops south of the McMahon line. Nehru did, however, accept a Soviet suggestion that diplomatic relations with China should not be broken.[10]

On October 25 the Chinese began a drive into Indian territory, capturing a key town in the northeast, Towang, and

[6] Chao Kuo-chün, "The Chinese-Indian Controversy," *Current History,* December 1959, pp. 358–9.

[7] Ibid.

[8] *New York Times,* November 21, 1962.

[9] "India," *Time,* November 30, 1962.

[10] *New York Times,* October 26, 1962.

moving toward another strategic military area, Chushul, in the northwest.

After pushing deep into India's northeast frontier and having moved to the plains of Assam, the Chinese suddenly on November 21 announced a cease-fire on all fronts and indicated they would pull back to positions twelve and a half miles behind the lines they held on November 7. The Chinese asked for Indian agreement, but said the troop withdrawal would begin on December 1 even without Indian concurrence, provided that India did not attack the withdrawing troops or try to push beyond the Chinese line of November 7. Nehru avoided acceptance of Chinese terms, but Indian troops did observe the cease-fire and withdrawal began.

Before examining the reasons for the Chinese withdrawal, we shall take a look at the reasons for the warfare itself.

1. When Tibet ceased to be a buffer state in which both India and China had an interest, the border between India and Tibet was really a border between the two great Asian powers.

2. China has traditionally claimed areas south of the Tibetan border. Sun Yat-sen regarded Burma, Nepal, Bhutan, and Siam as having belonged to China. So Chinese imperialism may have been in the picture.

3. Nevertheless, China concluded on January 4, 1961 a border agreement with Burma in which Burma got some land in exchange for some given to China. In addition, China got a mountain pass and route into Tibet.[11] Nehru, however, was unwilling to yield any land in Kashmir, just as earlier he had refused to negotiate with Pakistan over Kashmir. The Chinese appeared willing to trade border claims in the northeast in order to retain the disputed territory in Kashmir, through which their road to Sinkiang had been built. Nehru's intransigence thus seems to be another cause of the conflict.

4. Undoubtedly there was genuine misunderstanding as to where the border actually was. Nehru admitted in his Septem-

[11] Frank N. Trager, "Communist China: The New Imperialism," *Current History*, September 1961, p. 136.

ber 27, 1959 letter to Chou that "the India–China frontier which extends over more than 2,500 kilometers has not been demarcated on the ground and disputes may therefore arise . . . ."[12]

5. From the Chinese side there may have been other or secondary reasons. These may have included forcing Russia to take a stand in behalf of her Communist ally instead of continuing to give military and other aid to India. Incidentally, Russia was forced to take a stand somewhat in favor of China —at least enough to make Nehru aware that Russia would not stand with him. Russia, for example, approved the October Chinese negotiation proposal, not the Indian. China thus also to some degree severed the close ties between Russia and India.

6. China may also have wanted to reorient Russia's thinking about war. China heartily dislikes the Soviet doctrines: (a) that war is no longer inevitable and (b) that coexistence is essential. The Chinese think Russia, in practice, engages in appeasement. So the Chinese may have hoped to line Russia up on the side of limited war.

7. From the Indian side, there were conservative forces who reacted to the growth of Communism in India (particularly in Kerala), the shutting off of trade with Tibet, etc., and whose pressures on Nehru were designed to create a deterioration in Chinese–Indian relations.

8. Finally, there was Indian fear that if China succeeded in maintaining her border position, additional claims could be maintained against Bhutan, Sikkim, etc., and Nepal would be infiltrated and taken over. That Nehru was sensitive to this is evident in the India–United States cooperation in strengthening Nepal. India was building the Nepalese army and, together with the United States, giving economic and technical aid to Nepal, including the building of roads, airfields, and health and education programs as early as 1959.[13] China began economic penetration of Nepal in 1956 with an

[12] Chao Kuo-chün, "The Chinese-Indian Controversy," *Current History*, December 1959, p. 358.
[13] *New York Times*, August 3, 1959.

aid agreement. Even Russia was concerned about China and perhaps the United States in Nepal. India has told both Nepal and China that she considers Nepal in her sphere of influence.

The reasons for the cease-fire and withdrawal are also numerous. Probably all play a part in the final decision, though it is difficult to assert which are most important.

1. Khrushchev listed one reason in his December 12, 1962 speech. "There are some who already say that apparently China desisted from hostilities because India started receiving support from American and British imperialists [and] that if the armed conflict were to continue to develop it might become a big war. . . . Yes, clearly the Chinese friends considered the situation." The Chinese put it in slightly different words: "Particularly serious is the prospect that if U.S. imperialism is allowed to become involved, the present conflict will grow into a war in which Asians are made to fight Asians, entirely contrary to the fundamental interests of the Indian people."[14]

2. A second military reason is that China was overextended.

> Supply lines from the developed areas of China to the Himalayan fronts run from 1,000 to 2,000 miles across the mountain-girt roof of the world, the 15,000 foot Tibetan plateau. This transport route would daunt even a major power and the drain must be enormous on Communist China with her fumbling depressed economy, attempting to support the estimated 100,000 soldiers now in forward position in the Himalayas.[15]

3. A third military reason was winter which, in the form of heavy snows and icy gales, was about to interfere with Chinese transport.

4. Another possibility which *Time* called the prevailing theory is that the Chinese never intended to push on into India. They simply wanted to secure the border areas in the west that they wanted and were quite ready to bargain with India for their heavy gains in the east if they could keep the territory through which their road to Sinkiang ran.

[14] "India," *Time*, November 30, 1962.
[15] *New York Times*, November 13, 1962.

5. An important reason undoubtedly is related to Chinese political hopes. China has been engaged in ideological dispute with Russia, the goal of which is Chinese leadership of Asian, African, and South American Communist parties. The Chinese invasion of India began to nullify these hopes. Anti-Communist feeling in India rose to such violent proportions that the Communist party's national council voted to back Nehru in the war against China. S. A. Dange, the party chairman, with Nehru's consent went to the Soviet Union and Eastern Europe to build support for the Indian party position. Dange apparently secured from Nehru, in return for this help, release of the jailed secretary of the party and permission for the party to continue to function. Only the Chinese faction in the party would be arrested, thus saving the Russian faction from the necessities and results of a purge.[16] Presumably Dange also helped the Soviet Union decide to make good on its earlier contract to provide India with Soviet jet fighters. India sought Russian planes in the first place because the United States gave a squadron of F-104 supersonic fighters to Pakistan to shoot Russian planes photographing American equipment in Pakistan.[17]

Not only did China ruin her wing in the Indian party, but she failed to win the North Vietnam party, controlled by Ho Chi Minh. He followed the Russian line of backing the original Chinese peace offer, but restrained Vietnamese press criticism of India throughout the war.[18]

The lesson from these Asian parties was not lost in Peking.

These are the four major incidents in Asia involving Chinese armed forces: the invasion of North Korea, the limited action against Quemoy and the Tachens, the conquest of Tibet, and the border controversy with India. Presumably, these constitute the basis for American accusations that China is aggressive, accusations which are at the heart of the containment theory.

[16] Donald Kirk, "The Tortuous Path of the Indian C.P.," *The Reporter*, January 3, 1963.

[17] *Parade*, August 19, 1962.

[18] Donald Kirk, "The Tortuous Path of the Indian C.P.," *Reporter*, January 3, 1963.

A careful examination of these incidents reveals that China in 1958 withdrew all her troops from North Korea in spite of the fact the United States continued to maintain a substantial armed force in South Korea. China, however reluctantly, has not persisted in armed attacks on Formosa, Quemoy, and the Tachens in spite of the American occupation of what she regards as her territory. In India, after having demonstrated her ability to defeat India's troops, China withdrew to the border she had claimed. Tibet has been generally conceded as Chinese.

Sometimes it is suggested that China has helped Vietnam go Communist. However, Vietnam was effectively under Ho Chi Minh's leadership and Communist control in 1945, whereas China did not go Communist until 1949.

This analysis is not to suggest that China is innocent of military or subversive activity. Nations, especially great powers, cannot be characterized as innocent. All of them act in what their rulers conceive to be the national interest. This analysis is intended rather to put in historical perspective the claims that Chinese aggression makes necessary the U.S. military presence in Asia.

The United States had in 1969 in Asia, around the rim of China, approximately fifty thousand troops in Korea, fifty thousand in Japan, fifty thousand in Taiwan, fifty thousand in Okinawa and Guam, more than five hundred thousand in Vietnam, and forty-seven thousand in Thailand, with other thousands on naval patrol.

China is more of an excuse for maintaining U.S. troops in Asia than it is a reason. Walter S. Roberston, testifying for the State Department in 1954, told a House Appropriations Subcommittee, "The United States is undertaking to maintain for an indefinite period of years American dominance in the Far East."

McGeorge Bundy, a key figure in the Johnson administration during its first few years, put it this way: "More than four-fifths of all the foreign investing in the world is now done by Americans. . . . We have extensive actions in Europe, in South America, in Asia, and in all oceans. . . . We must put troops where they are most needed."[19]

This picture of American garrisons in Asia can be interpreted as necessary to contain China or as necessary for American world hegemony—for the Pax Americana role which some say the United States has adopted in order to safeguard her extensive interests and maintain the military–industrial complex. In line with this theory, the Department of the Army placed the following item in the bulletin with which the Department of Commerce advertises what the government wants.

> Service and materials to perform a RESEARCH STUDY ENTITLED "PAX AMERICANA" consisting of a phased study of the following: (a) elements of National Power; (b) ability of selected nations to apply the elements of National Power; (c) a variety of world power configurations to be used as a basis for the U.S. to maintain world hegemony in the future. Quotations and applicable specifications will be available upon request at the Army Research Office, 3845 Columbia Pike, Arlington, Va., until May 1, 1965.

It can be argued either that the American military presence or that the fact of Communist power in Asia is the reason for the various crises there. There is some truth to both theses. But it is also the mutual interaction of these forces that has created problems. In any event, Communism in Asia provides a convenient excuse for those who want to extend American military power into Asia just as the external American military threat is convenient for those Chinese who want to woo neighboring nationalist movements that fear the recurrence of Western imperialism.

[19] McGeorge Bundy, "The End of Either/Or," *Foreign Affairs*, January 1967.

13

VIETNAM
INTERVENTION

THE POLICY OF THE UNITED STATES toward Vietnam after 1945 was that of qualified support of French colonialism. When World War II ended, Bao Dai, who had been the puppet king under both the French and the Japanese, abdicated in favor of the Vietminh government headed by Ho Chi Minh. The Republic of Vietnam was proclaimed, and the Vietminh was solidly in power in the south as well as in the north. President Truman, however, decided to back the French effort to reassert military control. The British who occupied Saigon were unable to turn it over to France without the aid of the Japanese troops whom they rearmed for this purpose. General Douglas MacArthur, in a statement from Tokyo, said, "If there is anything that makes my blood boil, it is to see our allies in Indo-China and Java deploying Japanese troops to reconquer these little people we promised to liberate. It is the most ignoble kind of betrayal."[1]

The French fought from 1945 to 1954 to regain control of their former colony. The Vietminh, although led by Ho Chi Minh, a Communist, was primarily a nationalist independence movement, intent on eliminating French control.

The French began the policy which we have continued— of regularly labeling as Communist all who resisted them or their puppet king, Bao Dai. As a result, wrote two Cornell University professors, Kahin and Lewis,

[1] Edgar Snow, *The Other Side of the River: Red China Today* (New York: Random House, Inc., 1962), p. 686.

For more and more Vietnamese, that word came to connote something good—a badge of honor, representing patriotic nationalism and courageous opposition to French rule. Thus did French intransigence in Vietnam further strengthen the ties between nationalism and communism there—a circumstance unique in Southeast Asia.[2]

The United States began actively to support French colonialism in 1949 after China passed under the control of the Communists. In 1950 the United States sent its first military advisory group and gave the French $150 million. Economic aid increased to $1 billion in 1954 when the United States was paying 80 percent of the cost of the war. The United States evidently was embarrassed at the simple support of the French and preferred to have the appearance of supporting indigenous Vietnamese. The French cooperated by setting up in 1950 a nominally independent government under the emperor Bao Dai. The March 23, 1954 *New York Times* reported that "U.S. military experts believe the important thing is to train the Vietnamese to replace Frenchmen." The day before, the *New York Times* had reported that "the United States is financing the organization of a large Vietnamese army. It is training Vietnamese pilots in the Philippines. . . . It is not only willing but eager to take on some of the responsibilities for training the Vietnamese armies."

After the Vietminh launched their first major attack against Dien Bien Phu, the French chief of staff, Paul Ely, came to the United States to ask for American bomber support so that the French would not be defeated prior to the conclusion of negotiations which would begin in Geneva in April 1954. Ely's request was rejected, but Secretary of State John Foster Dulles made it quite clear in a major address on March 29 that the United States would not permit Southeast Asia to go Communist. On April 3, President Eisenhower invited congressional leaders, such as Lyndon Johnson, Richard Russell, John McCormack, and Joseph Martin to meet with Dulles to see what action Congress might support. There was gen-

[2] George M. Kahin and John W. Lewis, *The U.S. in Vietnam* (New York: The Dial Press, Inc., 1967), p. 29.

eral agreement that a negotiated peace would leave the Viet-minh in control and that this was unacceptable to the United States. They agreed to support intervention by American troops provided that the British and some Asian nations would also intervene, that the French would continue their military action, and that the French would move quickly towards an independent group of states in Indochina.[3]

The British and the French, however, told the Eisenhower administration that they would not agree to the U.S. program for intervention until they had made every effort to negotiate a settlement at Geneva.[4] John Foster Dulles persisted in his attempts to persuade the British and the French and finally sent a note in late April to the French indicating that if the French would join in an allied coalition to carry on the war, the United States would bomb the Vietminh troops surrounding Dien Bien Phu. The British were angry, and the French again turned down Dulles' proposal.[5]

The Geneva conference convened April 29 to discuss the Korean settlement. John Foster Dulles, who was at the conference, outlined privately for Anthony Eden the American plan for saving Vietnam. This included "the training of Vietnamese forces to defend their own country," which would "take perhaps two years to finish." In the meantime, Dulles indicated that the Allies "would have to hold some sort of bridgehead."[6]

Dulles apparently was successful in persuading the British to cooperate in a long-range program, for the *New York Times* of May 5, 1954 reported that Britain and the United States had agreed to discuss the defense of Southeast Asia, leading to the formation of SEATO. James Reston two days later wrote in the *New York Times* that "the United States, Britain and France are now in substantial agreement on a com-

---

[3] Chalmer Roberts, "The Day We Didn't Go to War," *The Reporter*, September 14, 1954; Dwight D. Eisenhower, *Mandate for Change 1953–1956: The White House Years* (Garden City, N.Y.: Doubleday & Company, Inc., 1963), p. 347.

[4] Eisenhower, *Mandate for Change*, p. 354.

[5] Sir Anthony Eden, *Full Circle* (London: Cossell, 1960), pp. 103–6.

[6] Ibid., p. 127.

promise plan for a 'protected armistice' in Indochina." The French, he said, were "prepared to fight on in Indochina unless the Communists agree to evacuate Laos and Cambodia and withdraw to certain 'fixed areas' in the third independent state of Vietnam." Differences, however, continued to exist. The British and the French were intent on achieving the best possible settlement of the war, whereas Dulles was more interested in continuing the war to prevent any Communist foothold in Southeast Asia.

After May 7, when Dien Bien Phu was lost to the Vietminh, the Geneva conference turned from a discussion of the Korean truce to the Indochina problem. During this discussion, the U.S. delegation tried to prevent a settlement by one means or another. Dulles was working in Paris to try to get the arrangements accepted for American intervention. The American attitude was evidently known to others, for Sir Anthony Eden, on May 15, 1954 wrote to Prime Minister Churchill that "the Chinese and, to a lesser extent, the Russians have all along suspected that the Americans intend to intervene in Indo-China whatever arrangements we try to arrive at here."[7] Another illustration of Dulles' tactics was the American proposal on May 19 that the restricted sessions where the Indochinese negotiations were taking place should be ended. The French foreign minister, Bidault, insisted that assent to that "would immediately bring his government down." Accordingly, it was agreed that "the restricted sessions should continue."[8] By the middle of June, according to Anthony Eden, the conference seemed near to a breakdown when President Eisenhower cabled Bedell Smith, Dulles' deputy, to try to bring the conference quickly to an end.[9] Eden also reported that he believed both the Russians and Chinese wanted a settlement and that Chou En-lai had told him he hoped to persuade the Vietminh to pull out of Laos and Cambodia.[10]

[7] Ibid., p. 135.
[8] Ibid.
[9] Ibid., p. 144.
[10] Ibid., p. 145.

Prime Minister Churchill and Eden on June 24 flew to Washington "to persuade the United States Government at least to give the French a chance of reaching a settlement at Geneva within the next few weeks." During their visit they agreed on a joint statement of the minimum terms they would accept at Geneva.[11] These terms were contained in the following:

1. Preserve the integrity and independence of Laos and Cambodia and ensure the withdrawal of Vietminh forces therefrom.

2. Preserve at least the southern half of Vietnam. . . .

3. . . . not impose on Laos, Cambodia, or (southern) Vietnam any restrictions materially impairing their capacity to maintain stable non-Communist regimes; and especially restrictions impairing their right to maintain adequate forces for internal security, to import arms, and to employ foreign advisors.

4. . . . not contain political provisions which would risk loss of the retained area to Communist control.

5. . . . not exclude the possibility of the ultimate reunification of Vietnam by peaceful means.

6. Provide for the peaceful and humane transfer, under international supervision, of those people desiring to be moved from one zone to another of Vietnam; and

7. Provide effective machinery for international supervision of the agreement.

Secretary of State Dulles later "succeeded in obtaining agreement" by the French premier, Mendes-France, "to a position paper which was essentially the same as that agreed between the United Kingdom and the United States. . . ."[12]

On July 20, 1954, there was an "Agreement on the Cessation of Hostilities in Vietnam," and on July 21, the "Final Declaration of the Geneva Conference." A comparison of the text of these documents with the joint British–American memorandum of minimum terms reveals that the United States was only partially successful in its demands. Instead of a

[11] Ibid., pp. 147–9.
[12] Eisenhower, *Mandate for Change*, p. 370.

guaranteed southern half of Vietnam, "the military demarcation line is provisional and should not in any way be interpreted as constituting a political or territorial boundary." Instead of "no restrictions" on the right "to import arms and employ foreign advisors," there was a conference agreement "prohibiting the introduction into Vietnam of foreign troops and military personnel as well as of all kinds of arms and munitions." Instead of no "political provisions which would risk loss of the retained area to Communist control," the conference provided for "free general elections by secret ballot . . . in July 1956 under the supervision of an international commission [with] consultations [to be] held on this subject between the competent representative authorities of the two zones from July 20, 1955, onwards."

The United States did, however, secure the withdrawal of the Vietminh from territory they were holding in South Vietnam and from Cambodia and Laos. It also won the right for the Roman Catholics in the North to move south to provide a political base for the regime of Ngo Dinh Diem whom Bao Dai, at the instigation of John Foster Dulles, had appointed prime minister on June 19, 1954, while the Geneva conference was in progress.

The Vietminh lost even more by their withdrawal from territory that they had won and occupied, for they controlled half of South Vietnam. The *New York Times* of July 25 in a dispatch from Geneva stated:

> Vietminh leaders are not entirely happy about the peace settlement in Vietnam. A number of members of the Vietminh delegation have declared openly that pressure from Chinese Communist Premier Chou En-lai and Soviet Foreign Minister Vyacheslav M. Molotov forced their regime to accept less than it rightfully should have obtained here.

Apparently, the Chinese who had fought U.S. troops in Korea and whose island of Taiwan was being patrolled by the U.S. Seventh Fleet did not want additional American troops to the south in Indochina. The Russians wanted France to reject the European Defense Community, which would have included a rearmed Germany. The best chance for such rejection would be the Mendes-France government which could stay in power only if reasonable terms for ending the war were accepted at Geneva.

The Geneva agreements were signed by the French and the Vietminh. The United States, which did not sign, gave a written pledge that "it will refrain from the threat or the use of force to disturb them. . . ." On the same day, July 21, President Eisenhower announced that "the United States is actively pursuing discussions with other free nations with a view to the rapid organization of a collective defense in Southeast Asia in order to prevent further direct or indirect Communist aggression in that general area."[13]

Immediately following the Geneva conference and for the rest of the year, the United States thought of Vietnam as one country. Philippe Devillers pointed out: "In November, 1954, wishing to maintain their consulates in Hanoi, the Department of State and the British Foreign Office asserted that Vietnam, according to the Geneva Agreements, was *one* country and that they thus had the right to maintain consulates in the North since they had recognized the Saigon government."[14]

South Vietnam, however, was soon organized on much the same pattern as South Korea and West Germany and with the same anti-Communist motivations. On January 1, 1955, "the decisive step was taken when with the assistance of the Federal Reserve Bank the Vietnamese banking and currency system was reorganized to the exclusion of the North Vietnamese."[15]

Diem, who had become prime minister with the joint support of Roman Catholic officials in the United States, especially Cardinal Spellman, and anti-Communist liberals like Arthur Schlesinger, Max Lerner, and Leo Cherne, Senators John F. Kennedy and Mike Mansfield, faced strong opposition at home, especially from the South Vietnam army. But the army was informed that U.S. military aid would cease if

[13] U.S., Department of State Bulletin, Vol. 31, No. 788, August 2, 1954, pp. 162–3.
[14] Philippe Devillers, "Generals Sing an Old Song," *The Nation*, September 18, 1967.
[15] Ibid.

it staged a coup d'état and eliminated Diem. In January 1955, all U.S. aid was put directly under Diem's control.[16]

Diem moved rapidly to consolidate his power. He purged the army of elements hostile to himself, destroyed the militia of the various sect groups, deposed Bao Dai through a rigged election, and arrested the Vietminh leaders in the south who were openly forming committees to plan for the free elections provided in the Geneva agreements.

Diem's tactics were not without the consent of American leadership. It was the large secret police organization which had been trained and subsidized by the U.S. government that enabled him to destroy his opposition.[17]

Philippe Devillers described the police-state tactics the Diem government used in arresting and imprisoning, without trial, persons suspected of being unfriendly to the regime. "This repression was in theory aimed at the Communists. In fact it affected all those, and they were many—democrats, socialists, liberals, adherents of the sects—who were bold enough to express their disagreement with the line of policy adopted by the ruling oligarchy. . . ."[18]

In the rural areas, the Diem government used two methods to bring the population under control. In October 1956, the central government destroyed the traditional concept of local rule by appointing village chiefs and, within the villages, chiefs for each hamlet. Cells of about five families each were also organized by the central government with appointed chiefs who were responsible for the loyalty of those under them. John McDermott wrote that "an extensive mutual spying system was instituted. All were to be fingerprinted and identity cards were issued. Permission to leave the village had to be obtained in writing, and counter-signatures were required before a man could leave the province. In short a totalitarian regime was imposed upon the countryside."[19]

The second method used by Diem was the destruction of

[16] John McDermott, "Profile of Vietnamese History, Part II," *Viet Report*, August–September 1965.
[17] Ibid.
[18] *I. F. Stone's BiWeekly*, October 28, 1963.
[19] McDermott, "Profile of Vietnamese History."

villages and the building of refugee villages known as agro-villes. The base for this program was the Roman Catholic population who had fled from North Vietnam. The villagers who were deemed untrustworthy were put in one kind of agro-ville. Adjacent to it, the Roman Catholic refugees were settled in the hope that by the example of their anti-Communism, and by their participation in local militia, they could help the army control the countryside.[20]

Since this whole process involved the raiding, searching, and in some cases the destroying or bulldozing of the villages, as well as torture and arrests, the peasants began to fight back. This fighting was not inspired by North Vietnam, for in January 1957, the National Assembly of the Democratic Republic of Vietnam decided on a policy of "building socialism in one country" as the Russians had done under Stalin's leadership in the period between World Wars I and II. "This meant," wrote John McDermott, "that any form of aggressive foreign involvement was to be sacrificed in favor of internal consolidation. In this they were supported by the Soviet Union, which in the same year proposed that both Vietnams be admitted to the United Nations."[21]

The peasant rebellion in the South over Diem's agroville policy led to debate within the Communist party of North Vietnam (Lao Dang), and in late 1959, a decision was made to give minor support to that rebellion.

Philippe Devillers wrote:

> The insurrection against Diem existed before the Communists decided to take part and they were simply forced to join in. And among the Communists the initiative did not originate in Hanoi, but from the grassroots, where the people were literally driven to take up arms in self-defense.[22]

A former *Time* reporter in Southeast Asia, J. L. Schecter, writing of the years from 1955 to 1959 said: "In North Vietnam, the Communists were immersed in the problems of

[20] Ibid.
[21] Ibid.
[22] *China Quarterly*, January–March 1962.

consolidating power and solving serious agricultural setbacks; they had little time then for subversion in the South."[23]

The State Department itself is authority for the fact that the Communists in the post-Geneva period (1954–1959) did not intervene militarily. Secretary of State Dean Rusk in his November 8, 1963 news conference said that "we were very much concerned when in 1959 the Viet Cong with public support from Hanoi moved to interfere in South Vietnam." The Republican white paper on Vietnam, in apparent confirmation of this, stated: "Although the Government of South Vietnam never established unchallenged authority in the entire countryside, a period of relative peace and stability extended from 1955 to 1959."[24]

There had been ample provocation for North Vietnamese intervention earlier. The free elections which were to have been held pursuant to the Geneva agreements were never held. The talks scheduled to begin in July 1955, according to those agreements, in order that there might be adequate preparation for all-Vietnamese elections in July 1956 were not even held to see whether both sides could agree on election procedure. Instead, the Diem government, with the support of the United States, rejected the North Vietnamese government's invitation to discuss the elections. The North Vietnamese might have reasoned that the Geneva agreements, in providing for free elections, had transferred the conflict from the realm of war to the realm of politics and that Diem's repudiation of a political settlement justified a return to war. The record, however, reveals no resultant military response to the rejection of the elections.

There is, however, evidence that the South Vietnamese government, with the support of the United States, began aggression against North Vietnam. As early as 1957, according to

[23] J. L. Schecter, "Bitter Harvest in Vietnam," *The Progressive*, October 1963.
[24] "The United States and War in Vietnam," Republican Conference House of Representatives, p. 15. (Reprinted from *Congressional Record*, 89th Congress, 2nd Session, Vol. 112, Part 17, September 20, 1966, p. 23313.)

General Nguyen Cao Ky, American-trained South Vietnamese commandos were parachuted north of the seventeenth parallel by U.S. planes to conduct sabotage raids on the North.[25] The Diem government earlier, on July 16, 1955, when it announced its refusal to meet with representatives of North Vietnam to plan the elections, stated:

> . . . the mission falls to us the Nationalists, to accomplish the re-unification of our country. . . . To those who live above the 17th parallel, I ask them to have confidence. With the agreement and the backing of the free world, the National Government will bring you independence in freedom.[26]

In 1958, the Diem government created the Committee for the Liberation of North Vietnam as commando raids on the North continued.

The second major act of aggression was in the Gulf of Tonkin in the summer of 1964. Earlier, on March 9, 1964, *Newsweek* revealed a plan by Walt W. Rostow, head of the State Department's policy-planning staff to escalate the war. It quoted from a Rostow plan No. 6 for escalation by "PT boat raids on North Vietnamese coastal installations and then by strategic bombing raids flown by U.S. pilots under either the U.S. or South Vietnamese flags. . . ." Four months later, in July 1964, these coastal raids were begun by vessels the U.S. Navy had given to the South Vietnamese. Senator Wayne Morse, who discussed this incident in the Senate on August 5, 6, 7, and 21, 1964, stated:

> The United States was connected with . . . the sending of South Vietnamese naval boats, boats that we supplied, that we armed, and whose crews were trained by the United States, to conduct the bombardment against the two North Vietnamese islands some 3 to 5 miles off the coast of North Vietnam. We had American naval vessels in the vicinity . . . they were a

[25] *Le Monde*, July 29, August 1, 1964, quoted in Franz Schurmann, Peter Dale Scott, and Reginald Zelnik, *The Politics of Escalation* (Boston: Beacon Press, 1966), pp. 38–9.

[26] Marvin E. Gettleman, ed., *Vietnam: History, Documents and Opinions on a Major World Crisis* (Greenwich, Conn.: Fawcett Publications, Inc., 1965), p. 194.

provoking element. There is no question that one of them was within the 12-mile limit of North Vietnam at the beginning of the bombardment.[27]

North Vietnamese patrol boats opened fire on one of the destroyers, the *Maddox,* on August 2 about forty hours after the coastal bombardment and while the *Maddox* was engaged in an electronic espionage mission. On August 3, President Johnson warned the North Vietnamese of serious consequences if another attack occurred and then provocatively announced the sending of two destroyers, the *Maddox* and the *Turner Joy,* into the same vicinity. On the night of August 3, a second coastal bombardment took place. On the following night, August 4, there was an attack alleged against the *Maddox.* This is the attack which President Johnson used as the basis for the Gulf of Tonkin resolution which the administration claimed as congressional authorization for all the military action he ordered thereafter. The following facts are therefore a key to the Johnson administration's conduct of foreign policy.

Well before the Gulf of Tonkin incident, wrote Tom Wicker of the *New York Times,* President Johnson had been carrying the Gulf of Tonkin resolution in his pocket waiting for a suitable occasion on which to use it.[28] William P. Bundy, assistant secretary of state for Far Eastern and Pacific affairs, told the Senate Foreign Affairs Committee that the draft of the Tonkin resolution was prepared some months before the Tonkin incidents.[29]

The *Providence Journal* reported:

> The *Maddox* actually fired both warning shots and shots directed at the North Vietnamese craft before the PT boats launched their torpedoes or fired their guns. A Navy Department spokesman has confirmed this interpretation of the chron-

[27] *Congressional Record,* 88th Congress, 2nd Session, Vol. 110, Part 16, August 21, 1964, pp. 20935–6.

[28] Tom Wicker, "Lyndon Johnson vs The Ghost of Jack Kennedy," *Esquire,* November 1965.

[29] I. F. Stone's review of U.S. Senate, Foreign Relations Committee's *Hearings on the Gulf of Tonkin: the 1964 Incidents, The New York Review of Books,* March 28, 1963.

ology. . . . The U.S. warships opened fire while the craft "whose apparent intention was to conduct torpedo attack" were still at least 5,000 yards—nearly 3 miles—away.

Three miles is within torpedo range, we are told, but it's a long shot for a torpedo boat, especially for attack against something as maneuverable as a destroyer.

Even on the thesis that the *Maddox* was justified in initiating action it is still not correct to say she "returned" the fire of the PT boat. We started the shooting.[30]

The testimony of one of the naval officers in the vicinity, as well as other testimony, bears out the contention that no attack took place. In a letter to the editors of the *New Haven Register*, December 6, former Lieutenant (j.g.) John W. White of Cheshire, Connecticut wrote:

> I maintain that President Johnson, Secretary McNamara, and the Joint Chiefs of Staff gave false information to Congress in their report about U.S. destroyers being attacked in the Gulf of Tonkin.
>
> In August, 1964, I was serving as a commissioned naval officer aboard the "USS *Pine Island*" (AV-12) in the Pacific. *Pine Island* was the first U.S. ship to enter the war zone in response to the "attack" upon the destroyers "*Maddox*" and "*Turner Joy*." I recall clearly the confusing radio messages sent at that time by the destroyers—confusing because the destroyers themselves were not certain they were being attacked. Granted that some North Vietnamese motor torpedo boats were in the area and used harassing maneuvers, the question is this: did they actually fire shells or torpedoes at U.S. warships? The answer is no.
>
> I learned this by speaking with the chief sonarman of the *Maddox* who was in the sonar room during the "attack." He told me that his evaluation of the sonarscope picture was negative, meaning that no torpedoes were fired through the water, at the ship or otherwise. And he also said that he consistently reported this to the commanding officer during the "attack." My naval experience as an anti-submarine warfare officer makes it clear that a chief sonarman's judgment in such a situation is more reliable than that of anyone else on the ship including the commanding officer. No one is in a better position to know than the chief, and in this case his judgment was that there was no attack.

[30] *Congressional Record*, 88th Congress, 2nd Session, Vol. 110, Part 16, August 21, 1964, p. 20936.

Commander Herrick of the U.S. Naval Task Force was on the *Maddox*. He sent a message to the admiral in charge of the Pacific Fleet:

> Review of action makes many recorded contacts and torpedoes fired appear doubtful. Freak weather effects and overeager sonarmen may have accounted for many reports. No actual visual sightings by *Maddox*. Suggest complete evaluation before any further action.[31]

The navy's own records of interrogation of North Vietnamese prisoners and the North Vietnam white paper on the alleged attack also indicate that the attack did not take place. "Extensive interrogation of all potentially knowledgeable sources reveals that they have no info concerning a NVN attack on U.S. ships on 4 August 1964."[32] The navy also reported a cooperative source "who obviously has traveled in higher circles and has proved himself exceptionally knowledgeable on almost every naval subject and event of interest. Yet he specifically and strongly denied that any attack took place."[33]

In spite of such evidence and the fact that the U.S. warships were not damaged by North Vietnamese torpedoes, President Johnson offered reprisals in the form of sixty-four bombing sorties over four bases and an oil depot in North Vietnam, resulting in the reported demolition of as many as twenty-five PT boats.

There was virtually no protest within the United States about these bombing raids. Such aggression against another state could take place because the American people had been told again and again by U.S. military leaders that troops from North Vietnam had been infiltrating into the south. In actuality, there was no such infiltration. Senator Morse told the Senate:

> I have been briefed many times, as have the other members of the Foreign Relations Committee, and all this time witness

[31] U.S. Senate, Foreign Relations Committee, *Hearing on the Gulf of Tonkin: the 1964 Incidents*, February 20, 1968, p. 54.

[32] Ibid., p. 75.

[33] Ibid.

after witness from the State Department and from the Pentagon have admitted under examination that they had no evidence of any foreign troops in South Vietnam from North Vietnam, Red China, Cambodia or anywhere else.[34]

The Gulf of Tonkin incidents very conveniently torpedoed efforts to reconvene the Geneva conference and put an end to the war. A thesis advanced by three university professors in *The Politics of Escalation* is that the Gulf of Tonkin incident occurred conveniently and immediately after U Thant, the secretary general of the United Nations, France, the Soviet Union, the National Liberation Front of South Vietnam, the North Vietnamese government, and China had agreed to a Geneva-type conference, without any preconditions for ending the war. The very day after China gave its consent, President Johnson ordered the bombing raids over the North, thus indicating that the United States was not interested. Actually, after the French president, Charles de Gaulle, proposed reconvening the Geneva conference, President Johnson rejected it as a device "to ratify terror" and asserted that "our policy is unchanged."[35]

On the surface it would seem that President Johnson with the help of a few advisors made the decision to continue and expand the war. But the pressures from the armed forces were very great. According to Arthur Krock in the February 14, 1965 *New York Times*, the Joint Chiefs of Staff had wanted to send forty thousand additional troops to Vietnam as early as the fall of 1961. President Kennedy rejected their proposal on October 11, 1961, not because of any disposition towards antiimperialism, but because he believed that the "special forces," the army, the CIA, and the South Vietnamese forces themselves would be able to "pacify" or subdue the country. In 1961, General Maxwell Taylor proposed a plan which Secretary of Defense McNamara said would defeat the insurgents in eighteen months.

[34] *Congressional Record*, 88th Congress, 2nd Session, Vol. 110, Part 14, August 5, 1964, p. 18137.
[35] Franz Schurmann, Peter Dale Scott, and Reginald Zelnik, *The Politics of Escalation* (Boston: Beacon Press, 1966), chap. 3.

A member of the White House staff who was on the special staff of the National Security Council summarized the military pressures for involvement.

> The "special forces" and the army were the military forces under President Kennedy who were given responsibility for the war. After the apparent failure of these forces to pacify the country, the Air Force lobbied for involvement. Using the Gulf of Tonkin as the pretext, the Air Force sent planes to South Vietnam as a "deterrent." But "deterrents" are vulnerable and can easily be destroyed by guerrillas as these were at Bien Hoa. . . . The Air Force's pride was wounded and it decided to prove itself through greater involvement. Once this occurred the Marines and the Navy (but less so) lobbied successfully for an expanded role. Not to be outdone, the Army also wanted increased participation. This was also granted by the White House. Finally the Strategic Air Command (SAC), in a non-nuclear way also wanted in. . . . Because of such a massive military involvement in the war, in a political sense it became very hard to impress our opponents of peaceful intentions or to counter those groups in the American government and the public who want a "win" in the military sense.[36]

There were also economic reasons for greater U.S. involvement. The United States was in serious danger of a business recession prior to the escalation of the war. A New York dispatch in the December 23, 1965 *Kansas City Star* began, "It was a close call. Little by little it has become clear that the longest peacetime expansion in the nation's history was in danger of petering out until the escalation of the war in Vietnam gave it a new lease on life." The same paper also reported, "The Vietnamese escalation was timed perfectly. It permitted the administration to apply the necessary stimulation without confessing its fallibility. It not only kept the economy from faltering but also salvaged the Johnson administration's reputation." More than a month earlier the *Wall Street Journal*, on November 4, 1965, had stated, "Both the Army's spending plans and those of the other services promise added zip for the nation's peppy economy. The accelerated

---

[36] Marcus Raskin, "A View from Washington" in *Ramparts* "Special Report on Southeast Asia," July 1965.

Army purchasing alone may, if nothing more, tend to delay the day of any business letdown."

The escalation of the war was a boon not only to those interests that profit from a stimulated economy but also to the professional officers for whom war meant a greater opportunity for promotion. These groups helped President Johnson determine that escalation was in the national interest, for he had long been responsive to their analysis of events.

14

VIETNAM
ESCALATION

IT WAS THE AMERICAN military build-up in Vietnam and chiefly the decision to bomb North Vietnam that brought North Vietnamese army units into the war. The United States first bombed North Vietnam in August 1964, but the steady daily bombing did not begin until February 7, 1965. The first deployment of combat divisions was in May 1965, more than ten years after the United States, in January 1955, began to give direct assistance to South Vietnam.

Charles Mohr, writing from Saigon about the continuing "defensive" nature of United States forces in Vietnam, reported interviews with "important military authorities."

> These authorities suggest that the "first build-up" of American combat troops, decided upon by President Johnson last July, has not achieved the expected results because of some widely shared mistaken assumptions. "We had an assumption that North Vietnam was not going to reinforce the Vietcong forces in South Vietnam, as it has done," one officer said recently. He added that the introduction of at least nine North Vietnamese regiments into the South had brought "an entirely new dimension to the war."[1]

The invasion by North Vietnamese troops was a risk taken by the administration when it made the decision to bomb North Vietnam. Charles Roberts, *Newsweek's* White House correspondent, reports that President Johnson made the decision to bomb in October 1964, but did not announce it during his campaign for election to the presidency. The reason

[1] *New York Times*, December 13, 1965.

was: "The American public . . . was not prepared psychologically for a deliberate calculated step-up in the war effort." He added: "The new policy, when put into effect, involved an obvious awesome risk—that North Vietnam and Red China would respond by sending hundreds of thousands of ground troops into South Vietnam, confronting President Johnson with 'another Korea.' "[2]

Johnson miscalculated and, by his escalation, led the North Vietnamese to escalate in turn. The administration had referred to North Vietnamese assistance prior to 1965, but this was always assistance in the form of training South Vietnamese cadres or sending individual participants. "Official South Vietnamese estimates of the number of cadres and military personnel illegally introduced from North to South in 1959 put the figure at only 300. The same estimates indicate a combined total of 21,700 in 1961 and 1962."[3] Even this assistance occurred after the United States had sent troops to South Vietnam.

The U.S. escalation was a unilateral decision. The civilian government, led by Premier Phan Huy Quat, which had come to power in February 1965 with the support of the United States, apparently wanted to end the war. Quat began to oppose U.S. plans to introduce more troops because it "smacks of permanency, of occupation."[4] The *New York Times* of April 25, 1965, in reporting Quat's opposition to the build-up of American troops, said he felt that "the landing of a large number of infantrymen would raise unpleasant recollections of the French Colonial War."

Quat released pacifists and neutralists from jail, arrested Catholic nationalists, and jailed the heads of military intelligence in an effort to eliminate elements blocking his attempts to bring an end to the war. "Finally on June 8 came the kiss of death: The U.S. Embassy withdrew its support. Two

---

[2] Charles Wesley Roberts, *LBJ's Inner Circle*, (New York: Delacorte Press, 1965), pp. 20–2, as quoted in *I. F. Stone's Weekly*, December 6, 1965.

[3] Sanford Gottlieb, "The Road To Negotiations," *Saturday Review*, December 18, 1965.

[4] *Washington Post*, April 25, 1965.

days later Quat threw himself on the mercy of the generals, and in another day his government abdicated."⁵

The Quat government was one of a number of successor administrations put into power by the United States after the overthrow of Diem. This overthrow illustrates the way the Central Intelligence Agency and the State Department collaborate in forcing U.S. policy decisions on client states, as well as the way events modify foreign policy. The story begins with President Kennedy's support of Diem. When Kennedy came to power, he increased aid to Diem. The Diem–Kennedy alliance would probably have continued until either Diem or the American troops were driven out of Vietnam if it had not been for Diem's overt persecution of the Buddhists. Neither Kennedy nor other U.S. officials were disturbed over favoritism to the Roman Catholic church so long as it did not become a public issue. J. L. Schecter reported, for example, that Archbishop Thuc, Diem's brother, "has used his influence to obtain special concessions for the church, and it is a matter of public record that through his relationship to Diem he has amassed rich forest land and valuable Saigon properties and business enterprises for the church."⁶

The *New York Times* of August 3, 1963, in a dispatch from Saigon, stated: "Observers feel that there have been limitations on the freedom of Buddhist priests and that Catholic priests have enjoyed unusual benefits from the Government. Finally there is what some Buddhists feel is the idea that Catholicism often seems an unofficial state religion."

One result of this favoritism was Buddhist reaction in Vietnam. The subsequent open persecution of Buddhists led the American people to oppose Diem. Another result was the opportunity this offered to the Communists. An Associated Press dispatch from Colombo, Ceylon, reported Buddhist reaction in that country and concluded, "The whole situation has been just great for the Communists. Their line is that the United

⁵ Martin Nicolaus, "The Wheel Comes Full Circle," *War–Peace Report*, September 1965.

⁶ J. L. Schecter, "Bitter Harvest in Vietnam," *The Progressive*, October 1963.

States and President Kennedy, a Roman Catholic, are responsible for anti-Buddhist action in Vietnam because they are keeping President Ngo Dinh Diem, a Roman Catholic, in power there."[7]

A third result was the reaction in Vietnam itself to raids on Buddhist pagodas. The Diem regime's "special forces, trained and financed by the CIA, raided Buddhist pagodas and jailed Buddhist monks. . . . American trucks are used to haul students to prison or stockades. . . . [The special forces of the Diem regime,] numbering about 2,000 men, were created by the CIA as its own project, independent of regular U.S. military assistance. . . . This military elite, hated and feared by the great majority of Vietnamese, also serves as a palace guard for the family of Ngo Dinh Diem and as the military arm of the secret police commanded by Ngo Dinh Nhu, the brother of President Diem."[8]

In spite of some reports that American officials opposed religious persecution, the continued financing of those doing the religious violence spoke louder than American denials.

The combination of these factors made it politically impossible for the Kennedy administration to continue its unqualified support for Diem.

In addition to these factors, there was the danger that the Vietcong or Vietnamese Communist-led forces would win so much support that the U.S. forces would be driven out. Kennedy could not withstand such a defeat, particularly if it became apparent before the 1964 elections.

Persecution of Buddhists, which had been going on for months, erupted into the newspapers of the West as a result of the Hué massacre of May 8. From May 8 to June 16, during all the religious repression, the United States maintained a hands-off policy. Thereafter, the United States began giving Diem additional public support. "Ambassador Frederick Nolting returned hastily to Saigon and made a public statement to the effect that Diem was resolutely working toward

---

[7] *Kansas City Times*, August 6, 1963.

[8] J. L. Schecter, "Bitter Harvest in Vietnam," *The Progressive*, October 1963.

democratization and had the support of the people. . . . He added that in his two years as American ambassador to Vietnam he had not seen any sign of religious discrimination."[9]

On July 18, 1963, President Kennedy told a news conference that, in spite of the religious strife, the United States would not withdraw its support from Diem.

The July 19 *Time* said Ambassador Nolting had conveyed to Diem "a personal message of confidence for Diem from John Kennedy."

By the beginning of August, the administration was worried enough to try to silence Madame Nhu, who had been pressing for sterner measures against the Buddhists. Mme. Nhu charged that the U.S. embassy had "threatened and blackmailed" the government in Saigon in an effort to "shut her up."[10]

On August 21, Buddhist pagodas were stormed, and in one of them more than one hundred monks were arrested. Just prior to this, Nolting had warned Diem of rising opposition to his government within U.S. diplomatic circles.

On August 23, a new ambassador, Henry Cabot Lodge, arrived in Saigon. The next day an urgent cable was sent from the State Department to Lodge with the approval of the Pentagon and the White House. The cable "included the suggestion that Washington would support a military coup against the regime if President Ngo Dinh Diem and his brother . . . persisted in their repressive practices against dissident factions in Saigon." Lodge asked the CIA chief in Saigon, John Richardson, to check on the possibility of a military coup. Less than forty hours later, Richardson reported "what the CIA knew all along: Nothing had changed. The military was neither able nor willing to make a move against Diem. Moreover, they were well covered by Diem's operatives."[11]

There is some reason to believe that Richardson was be-

---

[9] Erich Wulff, "The Buddhist Revolt," *New Republic*, August 31, 1963.
[10] *Kansas City Times*, August 8, 1963.
[11] *Kansas City Star*, October 19, 1963.

lieved by Vietnamese military leaders to be close to Nhu, Diem's brother. In any event he was, at Lodge's request, recalled to Washington in early October.

On August 26, Lodge told President Diem he must get rid of his brother, Nhu, and Madame Nhu or face a sharp reduction in American aid.

While this was happening in Saigon, Tad Szulc of the *New York Times* was reporting from Washington: "Some officials now believe that the only plausible solution may be to remove Nhu or both brothers through a coup d'état by Vietnamese military commanders. The Administration's leaning toward such a solution has been hinted. . . . A major effort is under way in Saigon to assess the political positions of civilian and military leaders."[12]

The August 31 *New York Times* carried a Saigon dispatch which stated: "Americans are known to have been contacting key people in the military recently."

On September 2, President Kennedy said that the government of Vietnam had gotten out of touch with the people and lacked their popular support, without which it could not win the war against the Communists. He said that popular support could be regained only if there were "changes in policy and perhaps with personnel." In reporting this, the September 3 *New York Times* said: "There is certain to be speculation whether the President . . . was inviting army action against the Nhus and intimating that it would have support from Washington."

On September 12, President Kennedy told a news conference: "We are for those things and policies that help to win the war, [and] we oppose" what interferes with the war.

As talk about a military coup mounted, Denis Warner, an Australian in Saigon, speculated about who might replace the Diem–Nhu regime. He said: "Of many possible groups, those linked with the names of two senior generals, Duong Van Minh and Tran Van Don command the most respect. . . . Duong Van Minh . . . has the closest relations with U.S.

[12] *Kansas City Times*, August 28, 1963.

senior officers and is highly regarded."[13] Van Minh had also received some training at the army's General Staff College at Fort Leavenworth, Kansas. It was these two, with the assistance of others, who led the generals in planning for the coup.

In late September, Secretary of Defense McNamara and the chairman of the Joint Chiefs of Staff, General Maxwell Taylor, flew to Vietnam, ostensibly to make a survey of the political and military situation. It is known that Taylor was "an old tennis playing acquaintance" of General Duong Van Minh. Apparently, the Vietnam military leaders wanted certain assurances from the United States before undertaking the coup. Exactly what these were can only be surmised. But two important developments took place immediately after Taylor and McNamara returned to Washington. The first of these was the recall of the CIA chief in Saigon. In a description of the coup, the November 6 *New York Times* reiterated the statement about CIA chief Richardson being believed by the military to be close to Nhu.

The second development was the United States government's suspension of a $10 million-a-month commercial import program which helped businessmen in Saigon. This was a clear indication of Washington's position and an invitation to revolt.

On October 31, the day before the coup, Admiral Harry D. Felt, commander of U.S. forces in the Pacific, flew to Saigon for consultations with Lodge and General Paul Harkins, commander of the U.S. military forces in Vietnam. Admiral Felt also talked with General Tran Van Don, one of the leaders of the coup.[14] That evening the *New York Times* correspondent and another correspondent in Saigon received a slip of paper with a coded message saying that the long awaited coup was imminent.[15]

Long after the assassination of Diem and his brother, Nhu,

[13] Denis Warner, "Vietnam: A Dynasty in Disorder," *Reporter*, September 12, 1963.
[14] *New York Times*, November 1, 1963.
[15] "South Vietnam," *Time*, November 8, 1963.

Frederick Nolting, former U.S. ambassador to Saigon, asserted that "our own Department of State . . . played important supporting roles in that fateful tragedy."[16]

There may have been additional reasons for the coup, such as the lack of military success against the Vietcong and reported efforts of Diem and Nhu to negotiate a peace with Ho Chi Minh. The November 6, 1963 *Kansas City Times* reported that the generals had called on Diem several weeks before the coup. "The generals, it is learned, were disturbed by Diem's reported dickering with the Communists in the North and the steady erosion of the war effort."

Reports of Nhu's overtures toward the North Vietnamese began to circulate a few days after President de Gaulle on August 29 had proposed a neutral, unified Vietnam. The September 5 *New York Times* reported: "Nhu is said to believe he can work out a deal with North Vietnam connections he has maintained in its capital. Diplomats and others who have talked with the President's brother say he thinks he can become the ruling figure over a united Vietnam." As a result of this belief, Nhu and the government stopped the previous policy of ostracism of the Polish member of the International Control Commission.

The same *New York Times* report indicated that the French embassy, the diplomatic representative of the Vatican, and the embassies of Italy and West Germany had constituted "an informal committee to bring pressure on Mr. Lodge for a more conciliatory U.S. approach to Mr. Ngo Dinh Nhu."

No discussion of American policy with respect to Vietnam would be complete without a discussion of the attitude of American leaders toward peace negotiations. Throughout the war, administration spokesmen maintained to the public that they had done all they could to get peace talks started. President Johnson, on July 28, 1965, said: "Fifteen efforts have been made to start these discussions with the help of 40 nations throughout the world but there has been no answer."[17] Secretary of State Dean Rusk also said, "We would be glad to

[16] *Kansas City Star*, July 9, 1967.
[17] *New York Times*, July 29, 1965.

go to the conference table but thus far Hanoi and Peking say no."[18] These statements and others like them were exposed as false when enterprising reporters revealed that North Vietnam had been willing to talk, but the United States had refused. U Thant, the secretary general of the United Nations, had gotten the consent of the North Vietnamese government to have talks with an American emissary in Rangoon. Eric Sevareid reported in the November 15, 1965 *Look* a conversation with Adlai Stevenson, U.S. representative to the United Nations, as follows: "Someone in Washington insisted that this attempt be postponed until after the presidential election. When the election was over, U Thant again pursued the matter. Hanoi was still willing to send its man. But Defense Secretary Robert McNamara, Adlai went on, flatly opposed the attempt." The State Department then confirmed the report in *Look* of Washington's refusal. The State Department spokesman, according to the November 16, 1965 *Washington Evening Star*, "said the United States had received many offers of talks from third parties who had spoken with Hanoi. Thant, he said, was only one of them. 'On the basis of the total evidence available to us, we did not believe at any time that North Vietnam was prepared for serious peace talks,' McCloskey said."

In November 1965, the president of the UN General Assembly, Fanfani of Italy, reported to President Johnson that on November 11 in Hanoi President Ho Chi Minh and Premier Phan Van Dong "expressed to two persons (known to me) the strong desire to find a peaceful solution to the conflict in Vietnam [and offered] to negotiate for peace."[19]

"The Fanfani letter," wrote Arthur Krock in the December 21, 1965, *New York Times*, "was turned over to Secretary of State Dean Rusk who with his advisers pondered it for two weeks before making a formal response of any kind including an acknowledgment of its receipt." Rusk subsequently asked Fanfani for clarification, but on December 15 before clarification could be made, U.S. bombers made

[18] *New York Times*, August 4, 1965.
[19] *Kansas City Star*, December 19, 1965.

the first air strike on a major industrial target in North Vietnam which the Air Force officially estimated knocked out 25 percent of the power and light facilities of Hanoi. The subsequent "release for publication of the Fanfani-Rusk correspondence, which was still unknown to press and public, and exploded any immediate step toward peace might have been pending, was a decision of the Administration," wrote Arthur Krock in the December 21, 1965, *New York Times.*

A widely publicized "peace effort" by President Johnson began in December, 1965, with a cessation of U.S. bombing of North Vietnam. The publicized purpose was mutual de-escalation. A report in the January 6, 1966, *New York Times* indicated that U.S. "envoys have told neutralist leaders that Washington is ready to extend indefinitely the pause in the bombings of North Vietnam if Hanoi will respond with a gesture of peace. . . ." President Johnson's envoy, Averell Harriman, was reported "as having said that the most important gesture would be for Hanoi to stop the infiltration of troops into South Vietnam." In his State of the Union address on January 12 President Johnson said, "We'll respond if others reduce their use of force."

In response to the bombing pause, North Vietnam began to de-escalate. On February 1 Roger Hilsman, former Chief of State for Far Eastern Affairs, told the House of Representatives subcommittee on Far Eastern Affairs that "there is evidence they (North Vietnam regular troops) pulled back at least into the mountains during the bombing pause—which may be a signal."

The February 3, 1966 *New York Herald Tribune* reported: "The South Vietnamese High Command said in Saigon yesterday that the Vietcong's main force still has launched no offensive operations since the Christmas ceasefire." Another report in the same paper revealed, "A U.S. military spokesman also confirmed an earlier South Vietnamese report that regular North Vietnamese units believed to have been infiltrated into the South last year have not initiated any battle since November."

A Saigon dispatch of January 29 to the *New York Herald*

Tribune stated: "A high military source in Saigon said there were indications that some units of the North Vietnamese Army had pulled back across the South Vietnamese border into Laos and Cambodia. The source also told United Press International that the Reds have been ordered to scale down their activities and avoid large battles with Americans."

In spite of all the evidence of de-escalation, President Johnson ordered a resumption of bombing. James Reston of the *New York Times* asked, "Why did the President choose to start bombing again now when no organized units of the regular North Vietnamese Army have been engaged or seen since mid-December?"[20]

There was public criticism of President Johnson, not only for failure to hold peace talks, but also for failure to abide by the United Nations Charter. Article 33 requires "the parties to any dispute, the continuance of which is likely to endanger the maintenance of international peace and security [to] seek a solution by negotiation . . . or other peaceful means of their own choice." Article 37 states that if the parties to the dispute "fail to settle it by the means indicated [in Article 33,] they shall refer it to the Security Council."

The United States raised the issue in the Security Council on January 31, 1966, following the resumption of bombing of North Vietnam. At that time President Johnson said the United States would present to the council a resolution which can open the way to the conference table. But a report in the February 11, 1966 *New York Times* indicated that Arthur Goldberg, U.S. delegate to the UN, "suggested today that the United States . . . would not necessarily press for action by the Security Council." Other sources revealed that "the Administration was retreating from a plan of pressing for formal Security Council action."

James Reston pointed up Johnson's hypocrisy in taking the Vietnam issue nominally to the Security Council. "How," Reston asked, "can he explain to the UN that he wanted its

[20] *Kansas City Times*, February 2, 1966.

help to get peace but started the bombing before he presented his case?"[21]

The position of the Johnson administration throughout the war was that negotiations would be useful either as a propaganda device or to permit the North Vietnamese a face-saving method of acknowledging defeat. General Earle Wheeler, chairman of the Joint Chiefs of Staff, defined the administration's understanding of the term. In an address to the Economy Club of Detroit in December 1967, he said: "Negotiation is not a face-saving device for abandoning the objectives we have been fighting for. It is a method of achieving our objectives." He added that the Communists could acknowledge failure anytime they wanted to, and "if negotiations would make it easier for them to cease their aggression, we would be happy to oblige."[22]

The position of both the Saigon and the American governments was that the war could be ended anytime both North Vietnam and the National Liberation Front stopped fighting and agreed to accept the South Vietnamese government. A State Department spokesman, Robert J. McCloskey, said:

> We have repeatedly made clear that our objective is that the South Vietnamese people determine their own future without external interference. The imposition of any coalition government would be at variance with this principle. We would oppose any proposal which would turn the Government of South Vietnam over to the National Liberation Front.

Mr. McCloskey amplified this by stating that the people of South Vietnam should "work out their own future, acting through electoral processes." He noted that the Saigon regime had announced a policy of "national reconciliation that would grant full citizenship rights to individuals now associated with the Vietcong if they accept constitutional processes."[23]

After "peace talks" began in Paris in May 1968, in response to a proposal by President Johnson on March 31, 1968, the chief U.S. negotiator, Averill Harriman, reiterated this policy.

[21] *Kansas City Times*, February 2, 1966.
[22] *Kansas City Star*, December 20, 1967.
[23] *New York Times*, December 9, 1967.

This policy, however, meant that the National Liberation Front as a group would have no voice in any political decisions, even though it had neither been defeated nor forced to yield control over much of the land in South Vietnam. The reference to constitutional and electoral processes sounds reasonable to Western ears, but the elections held thus far by the South Vietnam government, with the public support and approval of the U.S. government, revealed fraud in voting, intimidation, censorship of the press, restrictions on campaigning, and other measures illegal in constitutional democracies. One of the most serious electoral offenses was the denial of the ballot to persons suspected of being pro-Communist or pacifist or neutralist. After the presidential election of 1968, one of the presidential candidates who was also a major opponent of the military government was arrested and imprisoned because of his opposition to the war during the electoral campaign.

When Richard Nixon was elected President of the United States in November 1968, there were many who believed that he would take steps to end the war. His position, however, has not deviated from the Pentagon's policy during the Eisenhower–Nixon administration. That policy in 1954 was to train the South Vietnamese army to replace Frenchmen. Johnson's secretary of state, Dean Rusk, foretold Nixon's attitude when he said on October 6, 1968: "We are not going to abandon Southeast Asia whoever is elected in November and Hanoi should understand that." He meant, of course, that the basic decision about Vietnam had already been made at other levels of government and by other elements in the U.S. power structure.

In 1969, the Nixon administration announced the beginning of withdrawal of very small contingents of troops on the assumption that the training and supplying of South Vietnamese troops would permit some withdrawal of U.S. soldiers. Nixon and the military–industrial power structure remained committed to the position they held during the Geneva negotiations, that the southern half of Vietnam must remain in the Western sphere of influence.

Some Americans who have opposed the war have believed that the president has not always been adequately informed of peace overtures from North Vietnam or that peace efforts have been sabotaged by elements within the military. Both of these points, which have been advanced by Norman Cousins,[24] are undoubtedly true. But they do not explain either President Johnson's or President Nixon's failure to dismiss subordinates responsible for not following presidential policy. Nor do they deal with the more basic issue that neither president has been willing to see South Vietnam leave the U.S. sphere of influence on any basis whatever, including neutralization. Such a policy offered the National Liberation Front and North Vietnam nothing to negotiate except how they would submit to U.S. goals.

The White House, State Department, and Pentagon continued the war for essentially the same reasons that they became involved in the first place. The reasons for American military and diplomatic action in Vietnam can be summarized in three ways. The first and most important, as has already been noted, is the desire to have Southeast Asia in the American sphere of influence. The second reason was stated by Secretary of Defense Robert McNamara:

> Southeast Asia has great strategic significance in the forward defense of the United States. Its location across east–west air and sea lanes flanks the Indian sub-continent on one side and Australia, New Zealand and the Philippines on the other, and dominates the gateway between the Pacific and Indian Oceans. In Communist hands, this area would pose a most serious threat to the security of the United States. . . .[25]

"And third," wrote McNamara, "South Vietnam is a test case for the new Communist strategy." By this is meant the decision made by Premier Khrushchev in January 1961 to rule out world wars and local wars in the nuclear age and instead resort to "liberation wars." McNamara indicated that

[24] Norman Cousins, "Vietnam: The Spurned Peace," *Saturday Review*, July 26, 1969.

[25] "United States Policy in Vietnam," *This Changing World*, U.S., Department of Defense, Armed Forces Information and Education for Commanders, Vol. 3, No. 20, April 15, 1964.

our aim is "to prove in the Vietnamese test case that the free world can cope with Communist 'wars of liberation' as we have coped successfully with Communist" action of other types.[26]

This three-fold American strategy or rationale for military action in Vietnam must be judged in the light of the following:

The United States is not only opposing social and political change by adopting a counterrevolutionary role, but is also opposing the nationalist aspirations of people who have for more than a century been under Western domination.

There is no monolithic world Communist authority determining Communist strategy. Russia, China, Yugoslavia, Cuba, and some other "socialist" countries have independent foreign policies. The North Vietnamese government has shown every evidence of wanting to remain independent of China. American policy could have encouraged this independence as it successfully did with Yugoslavia. Instead, the American military action in Vietnam has forced North Vietnam, Russia, and China into a working relationship that otherwise might not have been possible.

Instead of strengthening international or United Nations authority in order to set a different pattern for the settlement of disputes or for promoting freedom of the seas and the air, the United States has taken extralegal, unilateral action to dominate the very sea and air lanes that it asserts the Communists want to control.

The lessons learned in fighting guerrillas in Vietnam have led, not only to more brutal methods of warfare within Vietnam, but also to the training at U.S. bases in Panama of Latin American armies in counterrevolutionary warfare. The effort by successive administrations to continue an unpopular war and to oppose revolution elsewhere by military methods rather than by ending imperialism has resulted in disillusioning many Americans with their own government.

26 Ibid.

The concealment from the American people of the government's real war aims and the various efforts to prevent serious peace negotiations have led to what the press called a credibility gap, or a doubting of the integrity of national leaders. The Vietnam war has been clearly evil. But it has had its good side in the awakening of millions of Americans, including many Christian and political realists, to the dangers inherent in the military–industrial complex.

In short, the war in Vietnam has demonstrated, for all the world to see, the American imperialist goals and the harsh brutality of the American military–industrial complex which seeks those goals.

CONCLUSION

A REVIEW OF THE VARIOUS CRISES in United States foreign policy since 1939 reveals that the direction of American policy has been to thwart political or social change that interferes with a narrowly conceived national interest. It has been in the interest of military and financial circles to make war and to garrison other lands, quite as much for the expansion of American control as for the destruction of Fascism and the containment of Communism. Where the United States or its allies have control, the realist emphasis of maintaining the status quo by armed power has been bolstered by the pseudo-morality of opposing aggression in the interest of peace. Where the United States or its allies were not in control, the policy of military aid and steady pressure was maintained. And in other cases, notably Vietnam, Guatemala, and countries, not discussed herein, where the CIA has been active, the U.S. policy has been aggressively to seek dominance by war or by subversion. The CIA, for example, has bragged about its role in overthrowing the Mossadegh regime in Iran that was pursuing a policy of nationalizing U.S. oil companies.

Unless the sole basis for determining ethics is the national interest, it is difficult to find any ethical rationale for the consistent use of American military and economic power to gain world hegemony. It can be argued with respect to a given crisis such as World War II that the United States had additional aims, such as opposing Nazism or dictatorship, but it is difficult to maintain such an interpretation in the light of American economic support of dictators in Fascist Spain, Por-

tugal, Asia, and Latin America and in the light of the resultant American, rather than German or British–French, domination of Western Europe.

If ethics is to make a contribution to foreign policy, as was
suggested in Chapters 2 and 3, the national interest must not
be so narrowly conceived as to be primarily concerned with
activity of economic and strategic advantage to a few powerful Americans. Rather, it must be concerned with a broaden-
ing of the national interest on the assumption that a responsibility for the welfare of enemies and neutrals, as well as
current friends, will contribute to America's security and
prosperity. In these terms, the primary aims of U.S. foreign
policy ought to be the prevention of war, the promotion
of world-wide economic health, and the development of
a genuine world community. All three are interrelated since
there can be no peace if some nations are poor and others
privileged. Neither can there be peace or justice on the basis
of paternalism, for both peace and justice require participation by all nations in the decision-making process, which necessarily means genuine world organization.

The prevention of war involves a wide popular recognition
that war can no longer serve any genuine community interest. The creation of nuclear and thermonuclear weapons has
changed the nature of war; a war fought with such weapons
cannot protect the people war is designed to defend. A top
military officer was quoted in the October 1960 *Armed
Forces Management* as saying:

> Concurrently the advent of nuclear weapons as a primary
> means of defense in war has many people questioning whether
> "security" will in fact be provided by the military if they are
> called upon to perform. If "security" will henceforth involve
> the destruction of the people being protected, along with those
> of the aggressor, the cure becomes as painful as the disease.

As early as April 1957, the British Government stated in its
Defense White Paper, "It must be frankly recognized that
there is at present no means of providing adequate protection
for the people of this country against the consequences of an
attack with nuclear weapons."

If nuclear war is obsolete as a method of security, so also is conventional war between nuclear powers. Any conventional war worth fighting would have to involve some vital national interest; by the same token neither side could accept defeat or loss of a vital interest without an effort to change the outcome by nuclear weapons. There will most certainly never be another conventional war in Europe like World Wars I or II. Neither the United States nor the Soviet Union could afford to let the other conquer Europe. This suggests that any future wars involving the United States will be confrontation between major nuclear powers or imperialist wars wherein a nuclear power seeks to conquer a small, probably underdeveloped nation. In recognition of this, Communist strategists have emphasized coexistence between major powers and wars of national liberation involving guerrilla tactics when small or underdeveloped nations oppose the rule or invasion by a major power.

The war in Vietnam has demonstrated that guerrilla warfare may also invite such wide destruction by a major power as to render the word *security* meaningless. The women and children in even the remotest villages could not be protected from bombing and napalming. Neither could the United States protect the civilians of Saigon and other cities from destruction by guerrilla attacks. Modern war, in either its nuclear or guerrilla form, involves whole populations in the fighting and therefore necessarily involves the destruction of the people it was designed to protect. Nevertheless, an imperialist war, in which a nuclear power is prepared to crush an underdeveloped nation in order to control it, is still possible. So also is guerrilla warfare capable of success, especially where an underdeveloped nation is prepared to accept devastation and destruction instead of capitulation. By being able to outlast a major power in a long and expensive or unpopular war, it may still be possible to speak of victory. But such victory for either side inevitably raises questions. Is the expense in lives and property of such a war worth it? Could the goal implicit in victory have been achieved by nonmilitary means?

The United States has demonstrated in Yugoslavia that a

willingness economically to help a Communist country has produced results that could not have been won by war. India, Zambia, Ghana, and other former colonies have demonstrated an ability by nonmilitary methods to achieve independence. Yet no one can say with certainty that the use of nonmilitary means can always or generally accomplish a purpose any more than one can say the same about war. It can, however, be said that there are always nonmilitary methods of defense and of penetration of another nation's culture or economy if a nation has the unity, will, and patience to use them.

War between small nations, the outcome of which does not seriously affect the vital interests of a nuclear power, is of course always possible. But the pressures of the nuclear powers and others in the United Nations have often been able to bring the actual fighting to a speedy conclusion, as was evident in the British–French–Israeli invasion of the Suez Area in 1956. The sporadic warfare in the Middle East in 1969 and 1970, involving Palestinian or Arab commandos and Israel, is less susceptible to quick solution because of the lack of unity of the great powers, rivalry of the United States and the USSR in trying to secure or maintain economic and military hegemony in the area, and the American preoccupation with the war in Vietnam. The Near East conflict may continue until the United States and the USSR find that it is too dangerous and too costly or until the nations directly involved decide they cannot indefinitely stand the economic and other costs to their own people. Either side, however, by unilateral action could have changed the psychological climate and contributed to an ending of the war. If Israel had taken concrete steps toward settlement of Arab refugees—including making a major diplomatic effort with other countries in need of immigrants and/or giving sustained economic assistance to refugees for resettlement in Palestine or neighboring areas—and had shown a willingness to negotiate other outstanding issues, the war could have been ended. Similarly, if the Arab nations had indicated a willingness to guarantee Israel's security in return for Israeli geographical concessions, peace would be more possible. The United States, which made a special effort to receive middle- and upper-class refugees from Castro's Cuba, has never expressed the same interest in assisting politically and economically the resettlement of Arab refugees. Nor has it shown any interest in sharing the petroleum resources of the area with the Soviet Union. Neither has it indicated an interest in internationalizing all strategic waterways, including the Suez and Panama Canals. In other words, the United States has been willing for the conflict to continue if the alternative involves any significant sacrifice on the part of American interests or any recognition that the United States has contributed to the maintenance of an unjust status quo.

The kind of imperialist war the United States waged in Vietnam is possible only because Vietnam was not vital to the national interest of another nuclear power, such as Russia. If China, for example, had been a well-developed nuclear power, the United States would no more have been able to invade Vietnam without a nuclear confrontation than it could have invaded Hungary during the Hungarian revolution.

It is the failure to grasp the new dimensions of the war problem which has led some churchmen to talk of "just wars" as if a theory developed in medieval Europe could be applied to wars where nuclear missiles, saturation bombing, napalm, antipersonnel bombs, and chemical warfare are the technological methods. The just-war tradition is really the idea that war and violence are needed, or are an outgrowth of the nature of man, but should be limited in the interest of justice and love. Only an optimist whose doctrine of man is thoroughgoing liberalism could believe that, in the heat of a crucial modern war, leaders of government would for Christian reasons restrain their armies or air forces within some degree of proportionality if this meant possible defeat. Any government leader who would risk the defeat of the United States in the interest of the Christian rationale behind the just war would probably have withstood the pressure to enter the war in the first place.

It is possible to assert that the United States might go to war to preserve the independence of a smaller power and therefore serve an ethical purpose; but such reasoning is naive. Great powers do not go to war for ethical reasons but only to defend or enhance their own national interests. The United States, for example, did not try to maintain the independence of either Czechoslovakia when Russia invaded her in 1968 or of Biafra during her war with Nigeria.

If war fails the fundamental pragmatic test of being able to provide security for the people, if its chief practical use is in the invasion of smaller countries, and if it fails the test of being "restrained within the limits of justice and love" as just-war theory provides, then it is difficult to believe that it serves any ethical purpose.

It is possible to say categorically that the United States will not be invaded by a smaller nation, such as Mexico or Costa Rica, or by any nonnuclear power. The United States could be physically endangered only by another nuclear power. But the actual fighting of a nuclear war by two nations would involve such destruction of both as to remove any basis for claiming such a war could be in the national interest. The whole doctrine of deterrence is a tacit acknowledgment by the military that wars between nuclear powers are too dangerous and must be prevented by threats or psychological means.

If warfare as such is not in the public interest, are there not occasions when armed force is necessary to patrol borders, maintain order, or police a given tension area? One answer to this is that such policing is the business of the world community or of a neutral nation acting at the request of the world organization or of both parties to the dispute. If it is suggested that the United Nations Security Council or General Assembly will not act in dealing with certain threats to peace, it is possible that other nations do not agree with the U.S. or USSR interpretations as to what constitutes a threat. The use of police forces is necessarily very limited. None of the great powers, for example, could be policed by the

UN. Perhaps there is no adequate answer until the United Nations is reorganized and made fully inclusive of all nations in a disarmed world.

The prevention of some wars could, of course, be arranged if the influential business and political groups of the nation were to become convinced that war and preparation for war seriously jeopardized their interests. Most of the citizens of any country are persuaded by propaganda, conscription, or appeals to patriotism to support war. They do not initiate war. Unfortunately, it is precisely the influential business and political groups that profit from military preparations and who are involved in the military–industrial complex.

Some wars are caused by comparable interests in other countries; therefore, war as such is not likely to be eliminated by the decision of one nation or its power elite. Yet the world is sufficiently interdependent that the angry criticism of people around the world does influence regimes of every political hue. The task for those concerned about the ending of war is not the providing of blueprints for disarmament or world governments; these can easily be arranged by the intellectuals in the employ of governments. Those who want to end war must provide the incentive for governments and power elites to abandon war. Such incentives have been illustrated by the criticism of the war in Vietnam, the organized dissent, the overt resistance to conscription, and the revolt of those in urban ghettoes who have been deprived by military spending and the excessive profits of the military–industrial complex. Incentives could also be provided for the Soviet Union if Communist parties in the Western world would engage in serious dissent and noncooperation with the Russian party when an invasion of Czechoslovakia or some other country is threatened or carried out.

From the standpoint of the U.S. national interest in the contemporary world, there are two probable sources of trouble. One is from revolutions designed to eliminate American business or other influence or control. The other is from the spread of Communism.

The problem of revolution is not an insuperable one. The

first thing to recognize is that a revolution can be prevented by eliminating the injustice or problem that makes it possible. Without a very serious grievance that motivates a large number of people, it is impossible to organize enough support to sustain a revolutionary organization. The same is true of guerrilla warfare. James E. King of the army's operations research office wrote in the August 1957 *Army* magazine: "The fact is that the experiences of Korea, the Philippines and Malaya demonstrates that guerrilla warfare is possible only if the political regime within a country is so unstable or so disliked as to have alienated a large part of the population."

King went on to indicate that a political rather than a military approach is necessary if the alienated population is to be won away from the guerrillas or from those leading the revolution. His position is negatively confirmed by the course of events in Vietnam and positively by the ability of President Magsaysay to undercut the Huk rebellion in the Philippines by means of political and economic change.

If it is asserted that revolution in Latin American countries will eliminate economic control by certain U.S. business interests, it can be demonstrated that the nationalization of American oil companies by Mexico in 1938 did not wreck the American economy. Neither did the expropriation by Cuba of all U.S.-owned industry there. Mexico and the United States continue to trade with each other. The decision to end trade with Cuba was made by the United States, a further indication that American economic health is not dependent on business relations with Cuba. The economic health of the United States does not depend on the exploitation of underdeveloped countries for the benefit of a few American businessmen or their allied stockholders.

An underdeveloped nation with few roads and little industry can only trade its limited, raw materials for some of our industrial products. But if that same nation is industrialized, builds roads and modern cities, etc., then there is a market for American automobiles, oil, refrigerators, and other items that will help maintain overall employment in the United States as well as in that nation.

American industry has found it more profitable in under-developed nations to make investments in the mining, oil, and agricultural fields than in industry and has made its major industrial investments in developed nations. This means that the providing of capital to underdeveloped nations for their development will be undertaken chiefly by governments. The resulting trade from such development will not depend on American ownership of their industry but on their need for products made in the United States.

The total amount of income from the overseas investments of American business which was repatriated and pumped into the American economy in 1967 was $4.5 billion, or less than 2 percent of the gross national product.[1] It is the foreign trade and domestic business rather than overseas ownership that is at the root of U.S. prosperity.

The second probable source of trouble, the spread of Communism, is likely only if American policy remains static and counterrevolutionary. The only modern industrial nation to go Communist is Czechoslovakia, and this was a direct result of U.S. leaders' agreement with Stalin that it should be within the Soviet sphere of influence. The major attraction of Communism is to underdeveloped countries that want to industrialize quickly. If the United States should decide not to try to subordinate the national interest of those nations to a few American industries but should assist those nations to develop in conformity with their own interests and potentials, there would be little reason for the spread of Communism.

The United States' national interest is not inconsistent with a servant or colleague role in helping underdeveloped nations achieve economic health. The long-range advantages to the American economy, as well as the prevention of the spread of Communism, would be in the national interest of the United States. The paradox of the American position is that the surest way to prevent the spread of Communism and provide long-range advantage to the U.S. economy is by ending the present foreign policy of anti-Communism based on

[1] U.S., Department of Commerce, *Survey of Current Business*, July 1968, p. 23; February 1968, p. 3.

American military and business control of other countries. American foreign policy today is controlled by those who want, as Omar Khayyám once said, "to take the cash and let the credit go, nor heed the rumble of the distant drums."

Just as it is in the interest of most Americans to assist other countries in achieving economic health, so it is in the American interest to encourage the development of a genuine world community of nations. The United States, as was true of ancient China, Greece, Rome, Babylon, and modern Britain, will not forever be the world's strongest economic and military power. Its power is limited and fully capable of being eroded or destroyed. If the United States for a time dominates a large part of the world and in order to maintain such control has to fight, garrison, or otherwise manipulate other nations, the time will come when this becomes too burdensome. But, in the effort to dominate, the United States will have perpetuated a pattern for another great power or powers to follow. It would be in the interest of most Americans to develop another pattern, that of self-determination of nations and of joint decision-making by those nations on a world level. The details of such organization are less important at this point than the orientation of American foreign policy in the direction of a world in which control is shared by all nations and all peoples. The reality of internal American politics is control by power groups, with the facade of democratic control, since no one can run successfully for the presidency or other key offices without the financial and political support of the economically powerful. Likewise, the reality of world politics is a United Nations in which the votes of a substantial number of countries are determined by the economic, political, or military pressures of one or two great powers.

Realism demands the acceptance of such power realities and functioning within them. Idealism offers blueprints for structural substitutes; but the need is to change the internal and external power relationships so that policy is determined by a broader group than the privileged few and for a larger purpose than their economic or political gain. A foreign

policy geared to the meeting of human needs—chiefly, the prevention of war, world economic health, and world-wide political participation—is dependent on a changed conception of
the national interest and on greater popular participation in
determining it. This will be recognized immediately as requiring a very radical or fundamental change in the American
political system.

At the very least this involves the elimination of the power
of the military–industrial complex by putting the Pentagon
under strict civilian control with drastically reduced budgets
and manpower. The bureaucracy in the Pentagon must be
forced to yield its present economic and political decision-
making to Congress. But since the most militaristic group of
civilians in the United States sit on the House and Senate
Armed Services Committee where they are steadily cultivated
by the military, those committees in turn need unofficial or
citizen committees to examine and publicly criticize every decision and move they make. This taking of power away from
the Pentagon is not a utopian, but only a partial, approach
to the prevention of war. Such curbing of the now largely
unbridled military power requires a quite different public
opinion from that which permitted the rise of a huge military establishment.

Public opinion permitted the growth of military power because it was convinced that Communism posed the ultimate
danger or threat to all that is good in life. If the United States,
as we were told, was the only power capable of containing or
restraining Communism, then Americans had to sacrifice and
be willing to suffer. This notion that Communism is the ultimate evil or that men will accept it forever is the product of
unbelief in God or in the fact of a constantly changing world.
The irony of modern life is that at the moment when men
have rejected the concept of a cosmic devil who causes evil
in the world, they have accepted human devils in the form of
Communists or Communist nations. The perspective of history will change such a polarized conception of devil nations
and messianic nations if history is permitted to continue. Certainly fifty years of coexistence have revealed that much of

the evil in the world is caused by American anti-Communists, which is what the Hebrew–Christian doctrine of sin should have forewarned us.

In turn the idea that Communism is the ultimate enemy for which we must be willing to sacrifice the last American and the last Russian or Chinese or even half of our respective populations is a concept that we have been sold by the military–industrial elite. We must reinterpret the national interest so that, instead of accepting the idea of calculated death, we can think in terms of enhancing the life of even the poorest people in this and other lands.

The people must decide that the national interest requires a cessation of the arms rivalry with the USSR and a cessation of military protection of U.S. private business investments or expansion overseas. There are steps that can be taken to curb or eliminate the arms race and to defuse the potential of the CIA and the military for starting wars. None of these new thought patterns or political changes will take place unless the American people or a vanguard of them point the way to social change by their own involvement in it.

Nations which do not undergo social revolutions periodically tend to let ruling elites determine domestic and foreign policy in terms of what is best for the elite. They therefore lose their power of attraction for other people and tend to become objects of fear or hatred.

The United States for many decades after its founding had a moral foundation or emphasis on freedom which was widely recognized throughout the world. It did not always exemplify its professed aims. But there was freedom from military conscription, the bane of nineteenth-century Europe; freedom of religion, which was not true in most of Europe; freedom of the press; freedom of association; free enterprise; and the right of privacy. Freedom was more often associated with the name of America than was equality or justice, in view of U.S. attitudes toward racial minorities and lower economic classes. In those days the United States, unlike many European countries, was not a major colonial power. It did not have the reputation of wanting to dominate other countries. Its own economy offered the opportunity others wanted. For much of its existence the United States had a power of attraction for many other peoples. Even Ho Chi Minh, in drafting the Vietnamese constitution, used parts of the U.S. Constitution.

What is often not recognized is that the moral, and therefore the political, influence of a nation may be far greater because of its demonstration of qualities others can see and desire for themselves than because of its ability to dictate to or dominate others. A superior way of life produces emulation, whereas the attempt to coerce produces resistance.

The Soviet Union also had a power of attraction at one time, when many intellectuals and workers thought she would establish economic democracy and a better way of life for working people. The early Soviet Union renounced the Russian territorial claims, opposed imperialism, and urged complete world disarmament. The rise of the Communist party in other countries, and groups prepared to cooperate with it, was evidence of the power of attraction the Soviet Union had for millions of people. The ruthless dictatorship of Stalin, the crushing of the Hungarian Revolution, and the interference in the internal affairs of Czechoslovakia, Poland, and other countries eroded the Soviet moral position.

The U.S. moral position was chiefly damaged by its internal violence, its failure to provide dignity, equality, and justice for minorities, and by the war in Vietnam. This loss of American moral authority was illustrated in the silence of the U.S. Government when the Soviet Union moved to stifle the democratization and liberalization of Czechoslovakia in the summer of 1968 after years of Stalin-like rule in that country. James Reston wrote in the July 24, 1968 *New York Times*:

> For part of the tragedy of Vietnam is that it has clearly weakened the moral authority of the United States in world affairs. What could Lyndon Johnson say today that would rally the community of nations against Soviet interference in Prague? Who would listen to complaints from Washington about using

pressure on a client state in defense of national interests—at a time when Mr. Johnson had just summoned President Thieu of South Vietnam to Honolulu?

Reston also pointed out that "in the eyes of much of the world American intervention in Vietnam seems much more brutal than Soviet intervention in Czechoslovakia and it is hard to escape the unpleasant conclusion that the Russians are freer to be beastly to the Czechs partly because our moral position has been compromised. . . ."

It would be a mistake either to assume that a nation could be so moral in its foreign policy as to prevent injustice everywhere or to assume that a moral position has no influence. A nation's power of attraction for other peoples can greatly influence the conduct of nations. A nation's power of attraction can be as powerful a method of national defense as any other method. A clue to the possibilities in such power is seen in the events surrounding the Allied invasion of Russia in 1919 and 1920. While this invasion was in process, and during the occupation of parts of Russia, the supporters of the Russian revolution were active in France and England telling of their hopes for a new and more abundant life as well as for peace if the revolution succeeded. The Russian revolution captured the imagination of many in organized labor who simply wanted to give the Russians a fighting chance to make good on their hopes and promises.

When the French government dispatched five cruisers to the Baltic as a part of its anti-Soviet effort, "the sailors on their ships struck against war. They were brought home in disgrace but they had spiked the guns of the French navy so far as the crusade was concerned."[2]

> Of immeasurably greater import was the prevention of a British war against Russia in 1920. The Cabinet fire-eaters were determined on joining openly in the warfare which they had been carrying on covertly by the aid of the subsidized White Armies in new Russia. There was a conscription bill up in

[2] Devere Allen, *The Fight for Peace* (New York: The Macmillan Company, 1938), p. 633.

Parliament at the time, and this added fuel to the mounting flames of Labor revolt. The Triple Alliance, made up of the Railwaymen, the Miners, and the Transport workers, served notice on the government that it demanded the recall of the conscription project, the withdrawal of all British troops in Russia, the release of all conscientous objectors still imprisoned, and the raising of the infamous blockade, which had brought useless and untold agony to a war-destitute people. A joint conference of the Labor Party, the Parliamentary Labor Party, and the Trades Union Congress explicitly warned the authorities that "the whole industrial power of the organized workers will be used to defeat this war." The war was defeated; the prestige of the Labor groups was enhanced rather than diminished. . . .[3]

The assumption held by many that a nation without arms or with relatively little strength is defenseless is not necessarily true. Nations with a strong sense of purpose derived from a faith that they are solving such basic problems as poverty, inequality, injustice, and war are seldom defenseless. Paradoxically, a nation with great military power may be seen as a threat or may be so hated as to have very little real influence in the affairs of other nations; a relatively weak military power, by its power of attraction and skillful diplomacy, may have much greater influence on the internal and foreign policy of others.

Unfortunately, neither the United States nor the Soviet Union today offers real hope to the world for peace or freedom or justice. The power of attraction that will move men down these roads must therefore come from the minorities in both nations, and in other nations, who will not be seduced by the call to war or by the rewards of political conformity, but who will lead in social criticism and social change. It is the thesis of this book that a foreign policy which disregards ethics, which regards persons as expendable, and which believes that the status quo must be defended against change, carries within it the seeds of destruction for that nation it was designed to serve. Conversely, a person-centered foreign policy, designed to meet creatively the changing needs of people, is the nation's greatest security.

[3] Ibid.

Index